TALLAHASSEE
LIBRARY
COMMUNITY COLLEGE

D1591678

DINGO MAKES US HUMAN

Life and Land in an Australian Aboriginal Culture

This original ethnography brings indigenous people's stories into conversations around troubling questions of social justice and environmental care. Deborah Bird Rose lived for two years with the Yarralin community in the Northern Territory's remote Victoria River Valley. Her engagement with the people's stories and their action in the world leads her to this analysis of a multi-centred poetics of life and land. The book speaks to issues that are of immediate and broad concern today: traditional ecological knowledge, kinship between humans and other living things, colonising history, environmental history, and sacred geography. Now in paper-back, this award-winning exploration of the Yarralin people is available to a whole new readership. The boldly direct and personal approach will be illuminating and accessible to general readers, while also of great value to experienced anthropologists.

Deborah Bird Rose is a Senior Research Fellow at the Australian National University. She is the author of *Nourishing Terrains: Australian Aboriginal Views of Landscape and Wilderness* (1996), and *Hidden Histories* (winner of the 1991 Jessie Litchfield Award). She has worked with Aboriginal claimants on land claims and in land disputes, and has worked with the Aboriginal Land Commissioner as his consulting anthropologist. Writing in the fields of anthropology, history, religious studies and environmental studies, she publishes widely in scholarly journals and edited books in Australia, America and the UK. Her work in both scholarly and practical arenas is focused on social and ecological justice.

DINGO MAKES US HUMAN

Life and Land in an Australian Aboriginal Culture

DEBORAH BIRD ROSE

Australian National University

PUBLISHED BY THE PRESS SYNDICATE OF THE UNIVERSITY OF CAMBRIDGE
The Pitt Building, Trumpington Street, Cambridge, United Kingdom

CAMBRIDGE UNIVERSITY PRESS
The Edinburgh Building, Cambridge CB2 2RU, UK
40 West 20th Street, New York, NY 10011–4211, USA
10 Stamford Road, Oakleigh, VIC 3166, Australia
Ruiz de Alarcón, 13, 28014 Madrid, Spain
Dock House, The Waterfront, Cape Town 8001, South Africa

http://www.cambridge.org

First published 1992
First paperback edition 2000

Printed in China by Colorcraft Ltd

Typeface New Baskerville (*Adobe*) 10/12 pt

A catalogue record for this book is available from the British Library

National Library of Australia Cataloguing in Publication data
Rose, Deborah Bird.
Dingo makes us human: Life and land in an Australian Aboriginal culture
2nd ed.
Bibliography.
Includes index.
ISBN 0 521 79484 6
1. Aborigines, Australian – Northern Territory – Yarralin – Social conditions.
2. Aborigines, Australian – Northern Territory – Yarralin – Religion.
3. Aborigines, Australian – Northern Territory – Yarralin – Land tenure. I. Title
306.089991509429

ISBN 0 521 79484 6 paperback

Contents

Illustrations

(Photographs are by the author except where noted otherwise.)

Figures

Maps

Hobbles Danayarri: master story teller and political analyst, October 1981.

Old Tim Yilngayarri: former clever man, November 1980.

Big Mick Kankinang: the old man who knows everything, October 1982. (D. Lewis)

Daly Pulkara: the son of warriors and a man of strong memory, October 1982. (D. Lewis)

Allan Young Najukpayi: always seeking to understand more fully, September 1989. (D. Lewis)

Riley Young Winpilin: an intense and sensitive man, January 1982. (D. Lewis)

Jessie Wirrpa: taking exquisite notice and care, March 1986.

1 *Remembrance*

The conquest of Australia was born in the oppression of the poor and dispossessed in England, Scotland, Wales, and Ireland. Those in power assigned the cause of social problems to those who suffered most, and sought to alleviate problems by getting rid of people: transportation to the Antipodes. The aim was not only to displace people, but also massively to control them. Power and terror were key values; in actualising them in a new society the powerful re-created much of the system which had led them to seek penal colonies in the first place.

In the new land convicts, itinerant rural workers, and bushrangers (outlaws) developed their own values for survival and resistance. 'Mateship' and a 'fair go', the social and cultural representations of equality, became essential features of Australian identity (Ward 1958 offers an eloquent analysis). Subsequently, these values came to inform those social movements, particularly trade unionism, aimed at resisting oppression. The poet Henry Lawson wrote in 1894: 'When the ideal of "mateship" is realised, the monopolists will not be able to hold the land from us' (in Wilkes 1978:215).

The colony was meant to be self-sufficient. Exploration, settlement, and development were officially the key processes by which land was to be 'discovered', occupied, and made to be productive. Less officially, it was a matter of forcibly wresting control of the land from the people who already lived there. This continent-wide undeclared war of conquest was based on a single intent: winning.

Aboriginal people in the Victoria River valley of the Northern Territory of Australia first encountered European settlers in 1883 when Victoria River Downs, then the largest cattle station in the world, was established. At that time there were four or five thousand Aboriginal people living in the area. Fifty-five years later only 187 remained.

Most of this conquest has happened within living memory, and Aborigines tell the stories. Hobbles Danayari, a master story teller and political analyst, located the origins of conquest unmistakably in the past, and clearly stated the brutality of the process: 'We have been shot. Captain Cook came knocking [killing] people for land and for gold.' Many white Australians will find these words quaint. They know that Captain Cook did not venture anywhere near the Northern Territory of Australia, as Aboriginal story tellers assert. Nor was he conspicuous in his brutality; compared to subsequent events, his actions were humane. Aboriginal historians locate the facts of many portions of their recent history in the person of Captain Cook. In Hobbles' account, Captain Cook, and Europeans generally, had an insatiable desire for land and minerals. When other people got in the way, they were killed. Equally importantly, in Hobbles' view, European invaders killed Aboriginal people because they did not want survivors who could tell the truth about what had happened.

Many Aboriginal people who discuss Captain Cook express a mixture of revulsion and disbelief: that Europeans preferred to shoot rather than to converse, and that they held the lives of human beings to be of less value than those of cattle. Stated so baldly, this is not the stuff of proud legends.

Invasion is a sustained process with no end in sight. In 1988, Australia's bicentennial year, it was clear that Australian history is not so much a set of events or social relations as an arena of self-definition, and that the strategy of denial is not confined to the past. The indigenous people are the official losers, but when we step away from the fanfare of ideologies, we hear another story. The invaders focussed their options along the barrel of a gun, and their denial of the past constantly distorts their assertions of their own identity, and of their relationships to others.

Europeans most frequently construct Aborigines as emblems: persons are envisaged as signs which signify European-defined Aboriginality. Their art, their archaeological remains, their concepts of the sacred, and their physical presence are appropriated to fuel images of national identity. Shadowy but essential figures in Australian mythology, Aborigines have been represented as intrinsic to Australia's past and largely irrelevant to its future. In a society which takes progress as a self-evident marker of success, images of Aborigines most frequently serve to contrast the past and the present. They rarely figure at all in images of times to come.

This book tells of some of the Aboriginal survivors of the great Australian holocaust known as colonisation. What forms of remembrance, what understandings of humanity, of living systems, and of the future sustain these people and inspire them to reach out to others?

* * *

I went to the Victoria River valley for the first time in September 1980 as an aspiring anthropologist. It was the end of the dry season; the earth was red and grasses were yellow, gold, orange and brown. On the plains the scattered gum trees had strikingly white trunks and dusky green leaves. River and mesas provided a contrast of colour and form: sudden dark hills moved snakelike toward the horizon, and a dense tree-green marked the path of the Wickham River. The sky was big, and immensely blue. It was the most beautiful country I had ever seen.

The small Aboriginal settlement known as Yarralin had a different appeal. In a broad but superficial view it looked like the setting for a documentary movie on fourth-world misery, featuring poverty, neglect, abuse, and disease. On looking closer, I found aspects of Yarralin that seemed inexpressibly sweet to me because they reminded me so clearly of the shanty town near which I had lived when I was a child in Wyoming. Here were the same remains of broken down cars with smashed out windows, car seats with springs poking through serving as outdoor couches, discarded clothing, and a seeming proliferation of children and animals. Here, too, were the signs of care which transfigure images and illuminate people: a tiny plant carefully surrounded by wire, babies in lacy pastel dresses.

There were times when being in Yarralin was hard for me; when I was bewildered, confused, and exhausted. But no matter how utterly strange, exasperated, or heartbroken I felt, I could look to the country to lift my spirits. And the small reminders of my childhood brought me back to my essential sense of our shared humanity which underlies the search to understand each other.

In the two years during which I lived in Yarralin, and during many subsequent visits, people gave me a great deal: instruction, friendship, happiness, skills, and understanding. I arrived at a time when Yarralin people were optimistic. They had come through great hardships and had acquired, through their own actions, an area of land excised from Victoria River Downs station. They knew that there was still much to be achieved, and they hoped that making themselves known to other people around the world would help them in their efforts.

In order to appreciate why and how Yarralin people chose to teach others about their world, we need briefly to consider what has happened during the hundred years of invasion.

The Victoria River valley

The great Victoria River of the Northern Territory rises in the sand plains of the desert fringe and winds north through increasingly well-watered savanna grasslands and range country. Mesas and flat-topped ranges of broken sandstone and limestone border much of the Victoria catchment or cut haphazardly across the valley floor through a mosaic of basalt and limestone plains. On the basis of natural vegetation, influenced by rainfall patterns, the region can be divided into three zones: woodlands and tall grasslands in the northern high rainfall areas, sparse low woodlands in the intermediate rainfall areas, and in the arid south, shrublands (Perry 1970).

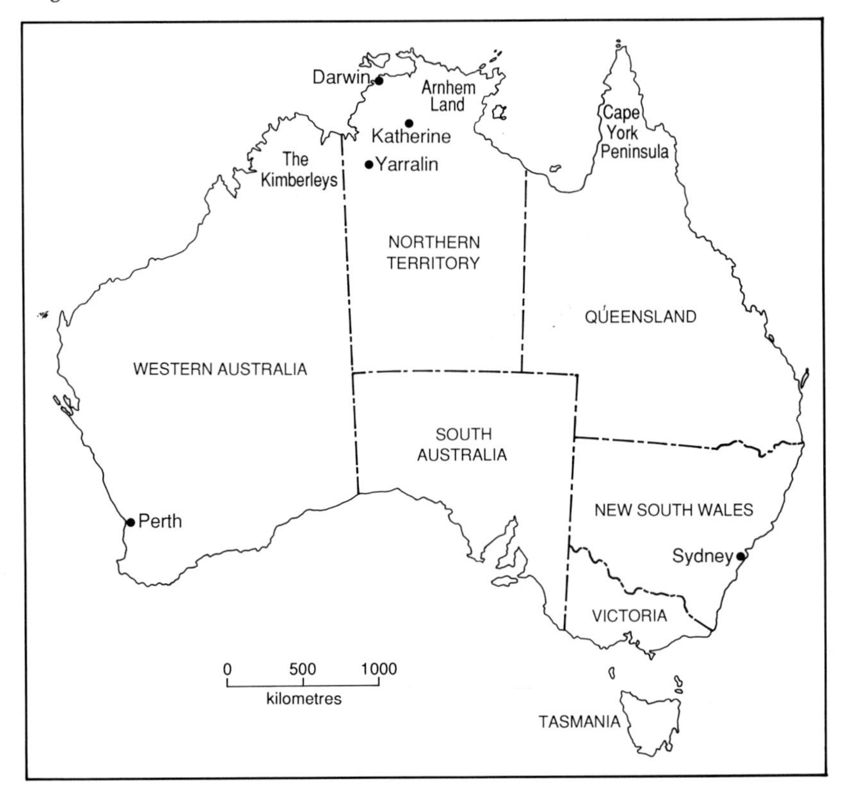

Map 1 Australia

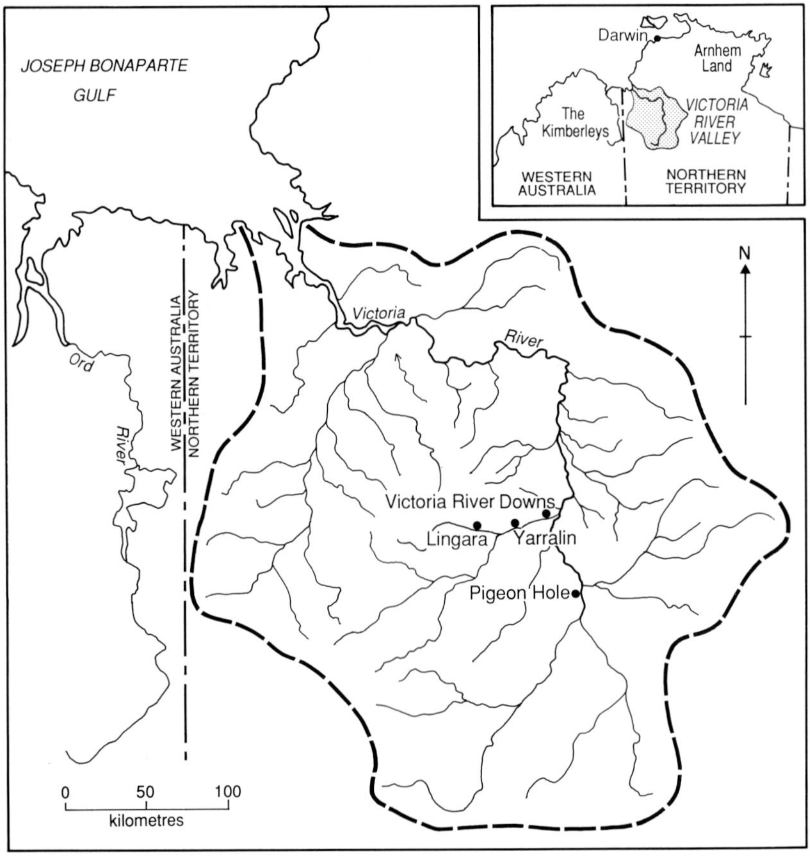

Map 2 Victoria River valley

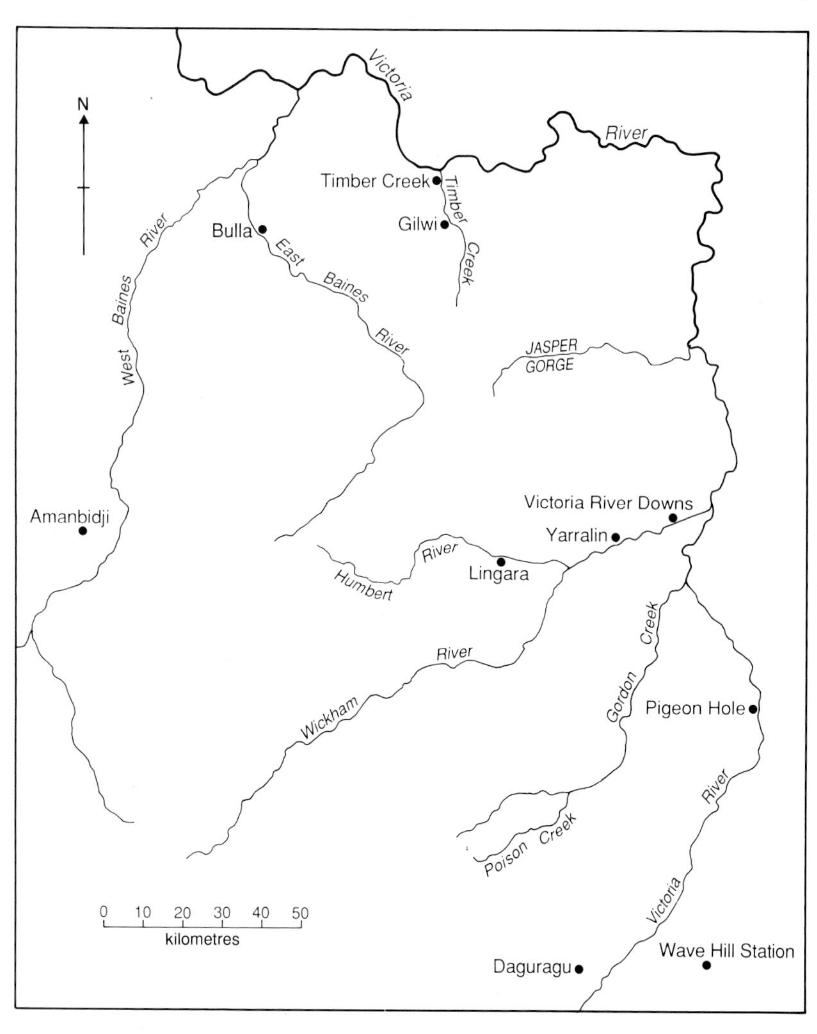

Map 3 Research area: community locations

The climatic regime is a wet-dry cycle with rains, which come during the summer months, preceded by a period of intense heat and humidity. Seasonal conditions may be extremely harsh. July, the coldest month, has average temperatures ranging from a minimum of about ten degrees celsius to a maximum of about twenty-seven. From October to February continuous high humidity is accompanied by daily temperatures of up to forty-five degrees and average overnight lows of about thirty degrees. Average rainfall figures vary, but are usually stated to be between 600 and 700 mm (Slatyer 1970:63; Hassall and Associates 1986:6). These average figures do not show the extreme fluctuations. Both rainfall and temperatures vary significantly from year to year.

There has been no archaeological work done in the Victoria River catchment to provide dates for human occupation. Prehistorians estimate that the Australian continent has been inhabited for at least 50,000 years and there is no reason to suppose that the Victoria River valley is anomalous. Work carried out to the west (Dortch 1977) and to the east (Davidson 1935; Mulvaney 1975) offers circumstantial evidence for the supposition that Victoria River Aborigines' adaptation was much the same as that of other Aboriginal people throughout the continent.

Prior to invasion, Aboriginal people in the Victoria River valley lived a life that was similar, as far as can be determined, to that described elsewhere in Australia (Meggitt 1962; Myers 1986; Tonkinson 1978; and Warner 1937 are some of the 'classic' ethnographies). Living for part of the year in family groups, they hunted and fished, collected, propagated and stored vegetable foods, moving through the country as resources reached peak conditions. During the dry season they were restricted by the necessity of staying close to water, a requirement that does not appear to have posed difficulties in this well-watered environment. During the wet season they retreated to the high country, living in rock shelters. Following the wet season the country was particularly rich in foods, and at this time people congregated in large numbers to perform ceremonies, carry on trade, arrange marriages, and resolve disputes. There was a basic, but not rigid, division of labour: men provided meat and women provided plant-derived foods; younger people provided for old people.

Broad estimates derived from hunting and gathering people elsewhere in Australia suggest that about two to four hours per adult per day were spent in producing a livelihood (see Sahlins 1974 for a discussion of 'original affluence'). Working with a relatively simple tool kit, the basic element to subsistence was neither technology nor labour, but knowledge. Freely available to all adults within their own country, knowledge consisted minimally of resource locations, water sources, ecological processes, types of landforms, seasonable variability, animal behaviour, cycles of growth, and types of plants and animals suitable as technical items, foods, medicines and 'tobacco'. Much of the knowledge was coded in song and story–not so much as maps to places unknown, but as condensed ecological history, and as guides to understanding variation and stability.

The Victoria River valley was affected late in the processes by which the continent was brought under the control of European settlers. Europeans had briefly explored the lower Victoria River in 1839 (Stokes 1846). However, the first major European account of the area is that of Gregory (1884) whose expedition traced the entire length of the valley in 1855–56. Gregory's explorations revealed to Europeans the tremendous extent and richness of country suitable for pastoralism, although the first settlers did not arrive until nearly thirty years had passed.

Gregory's expedition also revealed something of Europeans to the thousands of Aborigines whose country he traversed. Unlike those Europeans who were to arrive, en masse, thirty years later, Gregory and his party did not set out to shoot or otherwise molest Aboriginal people. In the country that would later become Victoria River Downs station, he established a temporary camp where his men were harassed by Aborigines who, as near as they could ascertain, were telling them to leave the area. Gregory's men fired, and one Aboriginal man may have been wounded. The party did leave, but only after they had completed their explorations.

But like the settlers who were to come later, the explorers went where they chose, making no acknowledgement of Aborigines' rights of ownership. Nor did they seek advice on routes, terrain, waterholes, or dangerous places. With the benefit of hindsight it seems bizarre that he and other explorers chose to treat as unknown wilderness a country that was known intimately to the people for whom it was home. Gregory, like other explorers and settlers, must be seen as a man who exemplified the practices which have generated the 'great Australian loneliness' (Hill 1940). Surrounded by people with whom he could have communicated, who might have offered him assistance, and who would certainly have set him straight on basic facts, he ignored them and made his own hard and isolating way.

Gregory's reports led to European settlement of the Victoria River district; one of the major costs of that settlement was Aboriginal people's lives. It is only possible to estimate the Aboriginal population of the Victoria River district prior to invasion. Birdsell (1953) suggested that a language-identified group (often referred to as a 'tribe') tended toward a mean of 500 persons. He based his assessment on estimates which place the total pre-European population of Australia at about 300,000. Recently, however, these estimates have been revised upwards and it is now thought reasonable to suggest that the total population was of the order of one million (Butlin 1983). White and Mulvaney suggest the figure of 750,000 as a conservative compromise (White and Mulvaney 1987:117).

When Victoria River Downs station (hereafter referred to as VRD) was first demarcated on a map it comprised some 13,060 square miles (SAPP 1910). Included in this area were the homelands of two language-identified groups–Karangpurru and Bilinara. There were also portions of the territories of four others–Ngarinman, Ngaliwurru, Mudbura, and Wardaman (Map 3). The most conservative estimate, based on a figure of 500 persons per language group, suggests that the area which was to become VRD encompassed a population of about 1,400 Aborigines. Bearing in mind the current revisions, a more reliable, and in my opinion still quite conservative, estimate would triple this figure: 4,200 people.

The first census available to me was prepared by VRD station in 1939. The Aboriginal population on VRD was given as 187 people. The population loss between 1880 and 1939 can be calculated to give varying, but equally horrendous, figures depending upon which estimates we take as a base line. Over the years, somewhere between 86.5 per cent and 95.6 per cent of the Aboriginal population of the VRD area was lost. These figures are comparable to others in the north. Ian Keen (1980:171), for example, estimates population loss in the Alligator

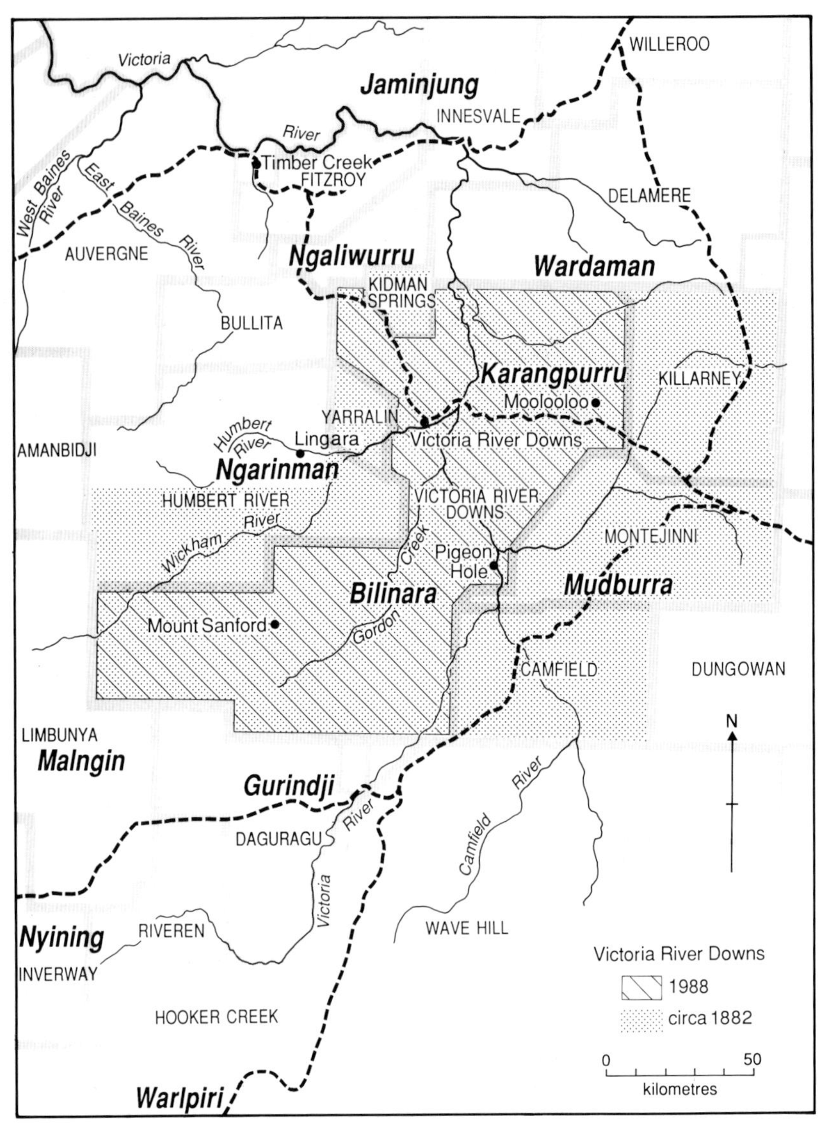

Map 4 Pastoral boundaries and language areas

River region at 97 per cent. With such estimates in mind, we can begin to ask: what happened to all these people?

In 1883 Wave Hill station and Victoria River Downs station, which together comprised the greater part of the Victoria River valley, were permanently stocked with cattle. Officially, there was no war; certainly there were no treaties. Persons wishing to take up pastoral leases in the Northern Territory (then administered by the Colony of South Australia) applied to the Colonial Secretary. VRD was taken up by the wealthy financiers and pastoralists Fisher and Lyons (Makin 1983:52–7).

In addition to pastoralists, other Europeans also came to, or travelled through, the Victoria River District. Within three years of settlement, payable gold was discovered in the Kimberley region west of the Victoria River. Many aspiring millionaires came across the east-west road which passed through Victoria River Downs. Police, too, were soon in the area. In response to a decade of European complaints about Aborigines, the first police station in the Victoria River District was established in 1894 (*Gordon Creek Police Journal*, 14 May 1894). The sole policeman, Constable W. H. Willshire, had earlier been tried on charges of murdering Aborigines in the Alice Springs District (*ADB*), and was acquitted, as were most people charged with that offence. It is possible that he was posted to the Victoria River frontier precisely because of his reputation.

From the beginning the Victoria River District was primarily cattle country, and the process of establishing cattle stations was the one which had the most profound impact on Aboriginal people. Most of the managers and workers came to the Northern Territory from Queensland where they had apparently developed strategies through which the country could efficiently be made safe for their purposes. It seems that the initial tactic was to kill; after this period of ruthless extermination, the second tactic was to incorporate the survivors into the station work force.

There were thus two major directions to the conquest strategy: killing and control. Of necessity, Aboriginal people responded differently to each. Initial European violence was met with violent resistance, while later European attempts to acquire and control a labour force were met with various forms of coerced co-operation, as well as non-violent resistance. The two strategies overlapped for about forty years between 1900 and 1940.

Violence and resistance

In the early years of settlement, cattle men and police were engaged in the serious business of conquering the country by decimating its people. They were equally engaged in assuring that word of their actions not be made public, for by the 1880s there had developed behind the frontier, in the southern colonies, a society of settled citizens who protested against the gross ill-treatment of blacks.

G. W. Broughton went to the Kimberley as a young man in 1908, seeking the romance of the outback. Much later he wrote a book of reminiscences in which he stated:

> Native life was held cheap, and a freemasonry of silence among the white men, including often the bush police, helped keep it that way. In far-off Perth, clerics and various "protection" societies tried to get at the truth of stories of native killings . . . but up in the north men kept their mouths shut. The basic philosophy . . . was that the cattlemen had battled their way into this empty land with great hardship and high cost in lives and money; that they were there to stay, and if the wild blacks got in the way, or in other words speared men and killed and harassed cattle, they would be relentlessly shot down. It was as simple and as brutal as that. (1965:53)

When Aboriginal people in Yarralin first started telling me about the hidden history of the north, they did so out of a particular set of concerns, one of which was their awareness of the silence which has surrounded their history, and the ideologies of conquest (see Reynolds 1974) in which it has been masked. The story of their dispossession has often been treated as if it were inevitable, or as if, somehow, it did not really happen. Broughton's statement that cattlemen battled their way into 'empty country', and then killed its occupants in order to establish their own control, epitomises the central contradiction in Australian ideologies of what is euphemistically termed 'contact'.

To be sure, European sources are not completely silent; particularly in the early years it was accepted that killing was essential. To quote Ernestine Hill, a journalist who interviewed many of the early settlers:

> The business of establishing a cattle empire depended upon killing. To the new station you brought working blacks from some far country–no conspiracies, they were terrified of the "bush niggers" . . . There was "quiet nigger" country and "bad nigger" country, but on most of the far-out stations cattle-killers were a grievous trouble for thirty or forty years. (Hill 1970:175)

The Europeans who made their way there often described themselves as 'practical' men (cf Rowley 1974:286–7). They were cattle men, duffers (rustlers), miners, fugitives from southern justice, bagmen (itinerant workers)–a mixed mob of frontier opportunists. Many were recognised for their brutality, and some were rewarded. Matt Savage, a drover during the early decades of this century, recounted his life story to Keith Willey. He stated that 'a reputation for being "hard on blacks" was worth a dollar a week extra to a stockman–and that was big money on the wages of those days' (Willey 1971:52). Jack (John) Watson, the second manager of VRD, illustrates the point. He had previously worked at a station in Queensland, and the story is that once, when the owner complained that the blacks were giving him a hard time and that his men were so lazy he had to do all the 'dirty work' himself, 'Watson reached into his pocket and pulled out three sets of blackfellows' ears. He slapped them down on the table and snarled: "Take a good look at those, and then say I haven't been doing my job!" ' (ibid: 26).

Constable Willshire was stationed at Gordon Creek while Watson was managing VRD. Although they appear to have been hostile toward each other, there were some matters on which they could co-operate. Willshire's response to a letter requesting information about a certain Aboriginal named Pompey described two men of that name whose deaths he had witnessed as a participant. He concluded by discussing a third man named Pompey and his companion Jimmy, both of whom were killed by Aboriginal warriors:

> I went out and brought both their sculls (sic) in and buried them in my

> garden at Gordon Creek, as the late John Watson manager for Goldsbrough Mort . . . [then owners of VRD], stated that he wanted Pompeys scull for a spittoon. (In Mulvaney 1989:128)

European accounts, whether sombre or flamboyant, give us a sense of what was happening, but provide only a gross outline of how their actions affected the lives of others. Aboriginal accounts tell a more detailed and personal story. According to Yarralin people, there were isolated incidents in which Aboriginal individuals were shot, beaten to death, poisoned. There were also large-scale massacres.

In the first three or four decades, which Aboriginal accounts identify as the time of most intense killing, two language-identified groups–Karangpurru and Bilinara–were virtually annihilated. This was a loss of somewhere between 1,000 and 3,000 people. In addition, other language-identified groups were severely diminished and were forced into refuge areas. It is not possible to calculate the loss to the latter groups, but it must have been of the order of hundreds, if not thousands of people. Not all of these people were deliberately killed by Europeans. Introduced diseases certainly took a large toll, and intensified Aboriginal warfare also affected the numbers and locations of people.

Karangpurru country lay mostly in the open downs which were ideal for grazing, and which offered limited areas from which to resist or take refuge. In addition, the western road passed through their country. The Kimberley gold rush preceded the period which Aboriginal memories document thoroughly. However, there is a statement cited in the South Australian Parliamentary Papers that during the gold rush of 1886, when Europeans were pouring across to the west, Aborigines were 'shot like crows' (Dashwood 1899:23).

We can be certain that there were at least 500 Karangpurru people in 1880; it is far more likely that there would have been about 1500. In 1980 there were fifteen adults and about twice that number of children and young adults. Most of them trace their ancestry back to one man who survived the annihilation to ally himself to the whites at the VRD homestead. There he fathered four sons (no daughters) who were the fathers of eleven of the fifteen adults whom I met in 1980. The near-total destruction of Karangpurru people occurred virtually without European documentation, and prior to the period in which Aboriginal remembrance takes up the story in detail. The fact that the police journals, beginning in 1894, make no mention of Karangpurru people or country indicates that these people had been virtually obliterated within the first decade of settlement. The name Karangpurru does not even appear on Tindale's (1974) comprehensive 'Tribal Boundaries Map'.

The story of the Bilinara and Ngarinman is more complex. Both groups had refuge areas, although that of the Ngarinman people was far more extensive. The first VRD homestead was set up in Bilinara country close to where Ngarinman, Bilinara, and Karangpurru countries come together. The permanent VRD homestead, established a few years later, was in Karangpurru country, again close to Ngarinman and Bilinara. Willshire's police station was also located in Bilinara country. The Ngarinman people along the lower reaches of the Wickham River were close to these establishments, and their country was also crossed by the east-west road which was so well used during the gold rush period. One segment of Ngarinman people appears to have been among the early casualties.

Further upstream, in the rough ranges and gorges, Aborigines from the open, unprotected plains sought refuge. From the sandstone they carried out warfare against Europeans and, later, against other Aborigines who also sought refuge. By about 1896 Ngarinman people from the west and north were well established in the sandstone, when Bilinara people sought to join them. According to a Ngarinman man, Bilinara people sought refuge there for a while because their own country was 'too dangerous'.

Dangerous indeed. Although Bilinara people had their own sandstone fortress, Willshire was relentless in shooting them whenever they ventured out into the open, and in pursuing them back into the sandstone. One account will suffice:

> Next morning [June 1894] we went on, picked up another set of tracks on Black Gin Creek, followed them up, and at 3 p.m. came upon a large mob of natives camped amongst rocks of enormous magnitude and long dry grass, growing like a thick crop of wheat on the side of a mountain. They scattered in all directions, setting fire to the grass on each side of us, throwing occasional spears, and yelling at us. It's no use mincing matters–the Martini-Henry carbines at this critical moment were talking English in the silent majesty of those great eternal rocks. (Willshire 1896:40–41)

Ngarinman people agreed to allow the Bilinara in, but disagreements arose among them and warfare broke out. Lives were lost on both sides, but the Bilinara seem to have suffered the most. In addition to the direct deaths among warriors, it appears that once the Bilinara fighting force was decimated, other men took the opportunity to steal Bilinara women.

What Europeans called 'bad nigger' country was country in which Aboriginal people were able to resist invasion. The descendants of Aboriginal warriors note their forebears' resistance with respect and compassion. Daly Pulkara, the son of warriors and a man of strong memory, says that the old people were ignorant at first of the power of European weapons. In Daly's view, they quickly realised that Martini-Henrys and Winchesters had certain advantages over spears and spearthrowers. Nonetheless, they decided to carry on their resistance, even though they expected that they would not survive. With their lands encroached upon, their food, water supplies, and other resources monopolised or eliminated, and their chances of long-term resistance diminishing rapidly, they had few options. In Daly's words:

> And some *kartiya* [whitefellows] reckon this place too cheeky [fierce, defiant], them *ngumpin* [blackfellow] Ngarinman. Well, *ngumpin* Ngarinman been here. They didn't know that fight been on through [because of] *kartiya*. Didn't know. And *ngumpin* didn't know that bullet turnout [didn't understand bullets and rifles]. Well, they been see that. Yeah, *ngumpin* been fall down from that bullet. They been think about [it] now: '*Kartiya* got a rifle'. They didn't know, first time. Just hearem that banging, banging, banging. Some believe: 'Oh! Killing *ngumpin!* All right. We turn and fight. We might beat someone'. That means he's going to fight him [whitefellows] longa [by means of a] spear. . .. 'Ah,' they sing out, 'oh, here now. We buggered up for hunting, and all this country round here all around [buggered up for us]. They trying to kill us. I'll kill that alabad [them].'

Their efforts were not entirely fruitless; a few Europeans were killed on or near VRD station. Most attacks, however, were not fatal, and European retaliation was invariably fierce and indiscriminate. European death tolls loom large in the European Australian imagination. Aboriginal deaths are rarely counted; black deaths, like black lives, are most frequently acknowledged only to be consigned to the backdrop of historical pageantry. While European settlers, police, and travellers shot or poisoned nameless and countless blacks, Aboriginal people experienced the traumatic loss of fathers, mothers, spouses, and children, as well as lands and livelihoods. The silence with which whites have surrounded their actions, and their depictions of Aborigines as anonymous victims, has facilitated the outback myth of an empty, lonely, heartless country. Constable Willshire's testimony is invaluable. So, too, are the scattered statements, the very brevity of which creates a kind of poignance. For example, the first manager of VRD, Lindsay Crawford, wrote in 1895 that:

> during the last ten years, in fact since the first white man settled here, we have held no communication with the natives at all, except with the rifle. They have never been allowed near this station or the outstations, being too treacherous and warlike. (Crawford 1895:180).

Lindsay Crawford was buried 160 miles east of VRD near the Overland Telegraph line he had helped to construct. His grave is unusual in that part of the world: there is a marble tombstone topped with a cross and surrounded by a metal picket fence. The epitaph reads (in part):

LORD WHEN THY KINGDOM
COMES REMEMBER ME.

Control and covert resistance

Initially, European settlement of Australia had depended on unpaid convict labour. By the time Europeans directed their attentions to the north, convict labour was no longer available. Aboriginal labour appeared to be a reasonable substitute, as experience in Queensland and elsewhere had shown. By the turn of the century Europeans had begun to use local Aborigines as well as to kill them. By this time the initial hard-hitting violence had assured that in setting up working relationships with local Aborigines, Europeans were dealing with people who were already weakened. It seems that Europeans brought 'working boys' with them when they invaded, and that they initially relied most heavily on local Aboriginal women rather than men.

If warfare was one requirement of conquest, the other, according to the men involved, was sex. There were very few European women on the frontier; men satisfied their desires with Aboriginal women. According to Constable Willshire, 'men would not remain so many years in a country like this if there were no women, and perhaps the Almighty meant them for use as He has placed them wherever the pioneers go' (1896:18).

But there was more to the relationship between European men and Aboriginal women than casual sexual contact (see McGrath 1987). During the early years women worked as trackers and guides, and as stockmen, riding, mustering, cooking. Often they were described as being more reliable than men. Black women were also used as a commodity: they were captured, as placenames like 'Kitty's Capture' attest, and were distributed to Aboriginal men as part of the reward for working with Europeans and against other blacks.

There were certainly people who joined the workforce seeking European patronage as a means of survival. For example, while Townsend was manager of VRD (1904–1919) a large group of Ngarinman and Ngaliwurru people had congregated in a valley near the VRD homestead in order to perform ceremonies. They were attacked before dawn, and most or all of them were killed. It was after this massacre that a number of Ngarinman and Ngaliwurru people sought refuge at VRD or other stations. Better to work with the station than wait to be picked off in the bush.

It is also possible that some young men and young women may have seen in station life an opportunity to escape from the constraints of their own society. Then, as now, the practice of promising young women as wives to older men would have resulted in dissatisfaction among the young. This area of constraint appears to have been recognised and put to advantage by 1900, and possibly earlier. Jim Ronan, VRD manager from 1900–1903, has the reputation among Aborigines of being a man who brought people in to work. In a biography written by his son, Ronan is said to have had two 'splendid local boys' whom he found particularly trustworthy. The younger Ronan states that 'the white men had enabled them to escape the tyranny of the old men,' and cites an alleged statement by one of the 'boys' to the effect that old men and women made inordinate demands on young men (Ronan 1962:178;187). Both Ronans have their own interests to represent in such accounts. The only certain points are that both men and women did become involved in station life, and that not all of them did so under overt duress.

To both men and women, the option of working on the station may have appeared to offer enhanced freedom. Aboriginal accounts make it clear that men working under Europeans had the protection which allowed them to prey on the bush people, stealing women with relative impunity. Once they had worked for Europeans, however, many Aboriginal people were caught in a trap. Men, in particular, were required to kill other Aborigines. Hobbles says that the policemen and station people (often not clearly distinguished in the earliest stories) told these men–'trackers'–to tell them everything they heard from their countrymen, and to shoot people as required: 'That tracker really . . .frightened. He couldn't do anything. Because people been really feeling too much sorry, and this lot been shooting their own colour [people].'

One of Daly's father's brothers was killed by his own son, a police tracker acting on European orders. According to Daly:

> His son called Kurlu. And he was shot him again. [He shot] His own father . . .. Gordon [the father] run away down there, and he [the son] shot him two legs. You know that big bullet with the Martini. He knock him in the two legs, right off. Bullet too big with leg. He's levelled the lot, two of them. And he roll back, and they shot him, after, right in the head. Ah, they cut the hand off, both hands, left hand and right hand, take them down and show them down to the policeman. Policeman took it back, and after that, right up to Sergeant. 'Here's that man, murderer.'

There was a cycle involved here. Once a man had become a police 'boy' and had shot people, his own people could no longer trust him. Should he seek to rejoin them, he might not find a ready welcome. When Constable Willshire's 'boy', Jim, escaped, along with three 'boys' from VRD, they were armed with guns. Willshire was terrified that there might be a general uprising among the blacks, as were his trackers who remained. His journal entries for the period show a man careening wildly between bravado and fear:

> I must go out tomorrow and look them up & promise you [the Police Commissioner] I will do my duty to the very last out in the open, I am not afraid of any blackfellows with firearms but their treachery lurks beneath so many guises such as long grass, behind rocks, in creeks, and up high in gorges. (*Gordon Creek Police Journal*, 20 March 1895)

He need not have worried himself. Two of the men became frightened and returned quickly to the security of the police station, while the other two, Jimmy and Pompey, were killed in the bush. Big Mick Kankinang, a man with a most prodigious memory, recounted the story of one of the men who was killed. He said that when the man joined up with people in the bush, he was flattered into demonstrating the workings of a rifle by unloading it. Once disarmed, he was killed. The stated purpose of killing him was revenge because while working with the policeman he had killed men in order to obtain their wives.

Daly Pulkara, Riley Young Winpilin, and Darrell Lewis at the bottle tree which commemorates the death of Gordon Jangala in June of 1910. A faint inscription reads: 'GORDON J SHOT → 18 10'.

Big Mick's account is less compassionate than Hobbles'. It illustrates a further point. For a very few men, European invasion provided a new opportunity to achieve power. An example is an ancestor of many Ngaliwurru people: Luwurtmawu. The road connecting VRD to its source of supplies at Timber Creek went through a narrow gorge over which towered sandstone cliffs. Luwurtmawu moved into, and established Aboriginal control over, this strategic position. He was employed by Europeans to help maintain the road, and was paid with food, tobacco, and protection. His strategy was to employ men and women to do the work, promising them food, tobacco, protection, and wives (for the men) in return. It is not clear how he obtained access to the numbers of women he appears to have attached to his retinue. Food, tobacco, and protection were undoubtedly factors. However, in a story reminiscent of King David, he sent one old man down to VRD and apparently arranged to have him killed. Luwurtmawu then took over his wives.

There were few such positions of brokerage. In spite of the isolation forced upon those who took up these positions, and in spite of their increasing dependence on Europeans, there was here a new and powerful opportunity for political manoeuvring. A great many Yarralin people trace their ancestry to such men, for in spite of their unenviable position, their chances of surviving and founding families were relatively high. It can hardly be an accident that the warrior Gordon has no direct living descendants and that at least eighteen adults in the Victoria River District trace their ancestry to Luwurtmawu.

By about 1930 a majority of the Aboriginal people in the VRD area were living on cattle stations regularly, if not permanently. Those who stayed away lived in the ranges where they were visited by family and friends on 'holiday' or seeking temporary refuge from station life. Many reasons as to why Aboriginal people chose to live on stations have been suggested–the desire for relative safety, the desire for what was initially perceived as freedom, and the opportunities for power. Other combinations of necessity and contingency were likely to have been operative, as Read and Japaljarri (1978) demonstrate with reference to Wave Hill station (see also Rowse 1987).

Many of the young people who had joined the station work force over the years since 1900 had, by the thirties, borne and raised children. There was a generation of station Aborigines who were related to bush people, had no quarrel with them, and relied on them for refuge when station life got too hard. And there were people in the bush whose numbers were diminishing, and who needed social relationships with station people. There appears to have been considerable movement between station and bush which Europeans tolerated because it was convenient and non-threatening.

Cattle station economies

Throughout the dark decades between 1900 and 1965, life for Aborigines on cattle stations was a set of cruel hardships. The essence of the cattle station economies was that as Aboriginal labour was virtually free, labour-intensive production was profitable. Unwilling to cut into profits by investing in capital intensive production, station owners maintained a strong interest in keeping the cost of Aboriginal labour as low as possible. Initially, Aboriginal people's welfare was the responsibility of the Commissioner of Police who was designated, apparently without irony, the Chief Protector of Aborigines. In 1927 this position was transferred, the Government Health Officer becoming Chief Protector (Rowley 1974:259). After the Second World War, Aboriginal welfare became the responsibility of the Director of Welfare. At no time, however, was there sufficient political support to allow Aboriginal people's welfare seriously to be protected (Rowley 1981:96–7).

Until 1967 Aborigines were not counted in official censuses, were not allowed to vote or to travel away from the stations without permission, and unless they obtained official exemptions, were, for the whole of their lives, wards of the state. Not allowed to marry Europeans without official permission, to manage their own money (if they had any), to raise their own children if those children were part-

Aboriginal, to purchase alcohol, and subject to numerous other onerous restrictions (Rowley 1974), Aboriginal people's lives until 1967 were massively controlled.

Hobbles described the conditions under which he grew up and lived for much of his adult life (1930s–1960s):

> Right. And my people been start to work around, old people. And really frighten for the white people coming from big England. They didn't ask. And they been really, really sad, poor buggers . . .
>
> Captain Cook's orders: 'Don't give him medicine. Don't give him medicine. When they getting crook [sick], old people, you killem him first. When they on the job, that's right, you can have them on the job. But don't pay him. Let him work for free. While we run that station. . . . If you put them on a job, make them prisoner. Make them work for you. . . . And no pay, just maybe the beef. Whatever dead bullock, him dead longa road, sick one bullock on the road, they'll have it. . . . Whatever they cutting posts right round, make a yard, they cart them on shoulder. If him sick and tired, he don't lift that thing, kill him right there.'.
>
> And lotta people been work round, my people. That means we're prisoner.

There is sufficient European documentation to corroborate Hobbles' assertions of lack of wages, minimal health care, appalling living conditions, violence, back-breaking work for men and women, and insufficient and unhealthy food. However, from the time of invasion through to the mid-sixties, VRD Aborigines, and cattle station Aborigines throughout the north, were largely isolated from Europeans who might wish to ameliorate the conditions of their lives. Arndt, himself a concerned outsider, states the case for VRD:

> Missions were not established and ethnologists were not welcome. The 'soft touch' of the anthropologist was regarded as a threat to the maintenance of discipline and there were . . . dark deeds to hide from the prying eyes of outsiders. This ban was effective because one man, viz. the manager of Victoria River Downs . . . controlled 18,000 square miles. (Arndt 1965:243)

The 1939 census was taken at a time when station life was having a terrible impact on Aboriginal population dynamics. The figures demonstrate the cumulative results of both European strategies: killing and controlling. Of the 187 people listed, only twelve were children. This was a population that was not on a survival trajectory. Yarralin people who grew up during these disastrous years recognise a number of factors which account for the terrible rates of infant mortality and the high chances of being killed or wounded during the course of a working life. Generally, like Hobbles, they lump these factors together under the common theme of European indifference.

Ronald and Catherine Berndt (1987) have provided excellent detailed documentation of the living conditions on neighbouring stations for the period 1944–5. Nothing of what they say would be out of place in a discussion of VRD. Lack of uncontaminated water to drink or bathe in, thoroughly inadequate shelter and hygiene facilities, and deliberate underfeeding leading to socially-induced starvation are prominent (see also Rowley 1974:262–3). A variety of diseases–influenza, malaria, tuberculosis, sexually transmitted diseases, leprosy, trachoma, respiratory and gastro-intestinal infections–were rife (see also Beck 1985; Mathews 1986). Infant mortality rates were appallingly high and many women died in childbirth (Berndt and Berndt ibid:76). In addition, some women chose not to bear children, but I have no evidence that this was so among VRD women. Berndt and Berndt (ibid:90–3) state that at the stations they visited they encountered deep concerns among women about their own and their children's future, as well as a sense that there was not much point to bearing children whose lives would only be taken over and used up by whites.

Between about 1916 and 1953, the government had the right to remove part-Aboriginal children from their families and place them in institutions where they were raised as wards of the state (Rowley 1974:280; 1981:121). Unfortunately, there are no figures available to me to indicate how many children were forcibly removed from VRD. As European men continued to demand sexual access to Aboriginal women, part-Aboriginal children were a fact of life. Equally a fact of life was that Aboriginal women were not in a position to refuse European men, both because of the latter's greater power and because starvation 'forced the women into prostitution' (Rowley 1974:262; see also Berndt and Berndt ibid:102–3; 117–8).

The labour which Aboriginal people performed for the stations consisted of skilled cattle work–mustering, droving, breaking in horses, branding, castrating, and spaying; skilled domestic work–cooking, cleaning, ironing, child minding; and various types of unskilled hard labour–making roads and airstrips (in later years), carting water in buckets attached to yokes, and carrying posts. In the early years both women and men worked with horses and cattle. By about 1930 women were largely confined to domestic work which included the job of carting water from the river up the bank to the homesteads. Education in basic literacy and numeracy was simply not on the agenda.

An itinerant European worker named Matthew Thomas, in a letter to the editor of the Darwin newspaper, described road building at Wave Hill station in 1937. He describes women and men performing hard physical labour: felling trees and clearing bushes, and repairing the road using picks, shovels and bars. His descriptions are unusual for that time in that he notes that men received more food, clothing, and tobacco than did women (*Northern Standard*, 20 August, 1937).

Given the fact that Europeans depended on Aboriginal labour for the success of their business, one might suppose that they would have shown some consideration for the well-being of their workers. There are some indications that family-owned enterprises, such as Humbert River station, did provide more adequate living conditions. The big stations were owned by powerful and remote companies: VRD was owned by Bovril for much of the time and Wave Hill was owned by Vestey. On such stations indifference was the prevailing attitude (Berndt and Berndt 1987).

Aboriginal resistance under these circumstances took the covert forms of remembering, learning, teaching. The one saving grace, for cattle station people, was that work could be effectively carried out only during the dry season. Aborigines were turned off from the stations during the wet, largely because from the station point of view it would have been wasteful to provide them with food at that time. They were given small amounts of supplies and told to 'go bush'. The result was that for part of every year Aborigines in this region were living in their own country, and were using and maintaining the ecological, technological, social, and religious knowledge required for the continued care both of the country and of the relationships between people and country.

During the worst years, people saw most of their children die, or had them wrenched from their arms to be taken to institutions. Sick people were taken away, and those with leprosy were permanently consigned to quarantine islands. In terrible pre-dawn raids their private parts were inspected for signs of venereal disease, their children and sick people grabbed, their dogs shot. Through it all, they sought to maintain the knowledge of self, society, and cosmos in which their essential identity was based. They held on in the hopes that at some future day they would be free. And they maintained a covert resistance so that when that day came there would be Aboriginal people who knew who they were, what traumas they had survived, where they belonged, and what was incumbent upon them.

Strike time

Between the 1930s and the mid-1960s, European Australian society underwent a series of massive social changes, but for Victoria River Aborigines it was a time of stagnation. The issue of wages and improved living conditions for Aboriginal workers in the Northern Territory pastoral industry was raised a number of times (see Franklin 1976 for a critical assessment of Aborigines and trade unions). By the end of the First World War, the Australian Workers' Union was pressing for equal pay; a form of modified payment was introduced in Queensland but not in the Northern Territory. A report on the Northern Territory by the Queenslander Bleakley in 1929 outlined the appalling living conditions and recommended a very modest system of wage and improvements. These recommendations were not taken up (Rowley 1974:259–278). Rowley's caustic summation tells the story:

> the pastoralists' assumption [was] that Aborigines and even part-Aborigines born on the station property would live out their lives there as dependants of the mangement–a beautiful arrangement not to be spoilt by sordid issues of money. (Ibid:277)

Only after the Second World War were wages introduced for Aboriginal workers; in spite of Unionists' arguments for equality they were well below the minimum, or award wage, and did not keep pace with the inflation of the 1950s (Rowley 1981:96–7). Evidence offered by the Director of Welfare (then responsible for Aboriginal people's welfare) in 1965 indicated that:

> . . . only twenty of about two hundred stations in the Northern Territory had 'made a real attempt' to meet minimum housing requirements; that his patrol officers could only 'persuade' (since in a colonial situation the white man's business had a direct channel of communication to the colonising government); that all but a few managements had resisted attempts to establish government schools and even health services on the pastoral leases. (Rowley 1981:97)

The significant break was made in 1966 when the Aboriginal people at Wave Hill station (Gurindji country) went on strike demanding wages, decent living conditions, and a return of some of their land. Jack Doolan, a Welfare Officer at the time of the strikes, and one of the few who actively supported the Aboriginal people for whose welfare he was meant to be responsible, describes the strike period as that in which:

> Aboriginal people of the area have probably done more through their own efforts to secure for themselves a better way of life, as they see it, than during any other period since occupation by whites in the early 1880s. (Doolan 1977:106)

The strike received wide publicity through the efforts of European Australians such as author and activist Frank Hardy (1968). It became a national issue, receiving strong support from trade unions, southern Aboriginal organisations, and from several support groups, at least one of which was university-based. As the strike spread from station to station many owners and managers became willing to agree to the demands in order to salvage their profits by regaining their labour force.

There are a number of theories about why and how the strike began (for example, Hardy 1968; Franklin 1976; Middleton 1977; Briscoe 1986); many accounts suggest that initially people were demanding wages and only later decided to ask for land. Such accounts are accurate descriptions of the events, but differ significantly from Yarralin people's statements of the intent behind the strike. While Yarralin people recount the same series of events, they do so from the point of view of participants. Their accounts place these events within a much broader context which includes the unvanquished desire to regain control over their land and lives, the perception of unbalanced reciprocity through which their land and labour had been used by others, the demand that Europeans reciprocate immediately in cash (the one medium local whites clearly did control), and the underlying assertion that only by regaining their land could they regain the control over their lives which would allow them, in future, to engage equitably with Europeans.

Aboriginal people working for Victoria River Downs and Humbert River stations walked off in March 1972. VRD was then owned by an Australian conglomerate, L. J. Hooker Investment Corporation Ltd. Over the years, government regulations had required that the original 13,060 sq. mi. (33, 825 sq. km.) be reduced, so that by 1972 it consisted of 12,359 sq. km. Still a vast area, it was and continues to be operated through a head station at VRD homestead which loosely administers outstations at Moolooloo, Pigeon Hole, and Mt Sanford. In contrast, Humbert River station was much smaller (5,631 sq. km.), and had been owned and managed by Charlie Schultz for a period of about fifty years. He had maintained relationships of consideration and some respect with his workers, and Daly Pulkara, one of his head stockmen, described him as a hard but fair man: 'a good old bloke'.

The people who went on strike had had differing experiences of station life, although these differences were at most surface variations on a basic structure. There were, accordingly, some differing motivations for striking. Their aspirations, however, were identical: to obtain equal treatment under Australian law, and to obtain the return of portions of their land so that they could become economically independent of European Australian control.

In 1973 negotiations began between Gurindji and Vestey representatives, Department of Aboriginal Affairs officials, and pastoral consultants for an agreement by which Wave Hill station would relinquish a 2,500 sq. km. block of land to the striking Aborigines. In that same year VRD and Humbert River Aborigines and the Department of Aboriginal Affairs began negotiations with the Hooker Company. The final agreement was to excise some 504 sq. km., significantly less than the Aborigines had originally hoped for. The new community, located at the site of an old outstation on the banks of the Wickham River, was called Yarralin. Eighty-three people moved there in October 1973; at about the same time Aboriginal workers returned to Pigeon Hole and to the VRD head station where they continued to live in their own countries, awaiting the excisions which they believed had been promised to them.

In 1975 the agreement concerning the Yarralin block was to have been given specific legal status by being presented to the Interim Land Commissioner, Justice Ward. After 1975, Yarralin was treated as if it were an independent community occupying its own land. People stocked the block with cattle and horses; the Department of Aboriginal Affairs funded housing; the Department of Education funded a one-room school and two qualified teachers. Legally, however, the title was not handed over until 1985, and until that time major improvements such as electricity and a reliable water supply were withheld.

The Yarralin block is located within Ngarinman country near the

Eastern section of Yarralin, May 1982. (D. Lewis)

boundaries of Bilinara, Karangpurru and Ngaliwurru country. European Australians apparently expected that one excision would satisfy the demands of all VRD people, and perhaps those of all Humbert River people as well. In fact, people whose own country is some distance from Yarralin do not find their needs satisfied, nor do they believe they have been recompensed for the years of work they and their forebears put into the stations. In March 1980, a group of people left Yarralin to start a new community, called Lingara. Located on Humbert River station, thirty-five kilometres from Yarralin by rough dirt road with four major creek crossings, Lingara is a small family-oriented community.

Lingara is frequently referred to as an outstation–a satellite community dependent on a central source of goods and services. In many parts of the north, to be living on an outstation may imply the choice of getting away from white society, 'white' problems such as alcohol, and the stress of having to deal with a tense, and often racist, environment. The Lingara mob was not leaving a European-controlled settlement; rather, their perception of Yarralin was that there was not enough 'space' for them there.

Their statement may have referred in part to the lack of housing at Yarralin, but was more specifically directed to the fact that there had not been enough space for this group in the political life of Yarralin. The move satisfied a deep longing to be back in the country for which they were responsible, in which their parents and grandparents had died, and where they wanted to maintain continuity between past and future. In addition, Lingara people believe that as they and their forebears are owners (in the Aboriginal sense) of the land controlled by Humbert River station, and as they had worked for that station all their lives, so that station owed them a return.

The pastoral strikes had a national impact in two areas, becoming an effective part of a general shift in popular white Australian opinion toward Aboriginal aspirations for justice and equality in Australia. They probably influenced the 1967 referendum which granted Aborigines citizenship, and was passed by a 93 per cent majority. They were also influential in the move toward a national system of Aboriginal land rights. While the Commonwealth Government has very limited powers to make laws relating to land which are binding on the States, it has far more scope with respect to the Territories. The legislation implemented for the Northern Territory has allowed many Aboriginal people to regain direct control of portions of their land. Other States have since formulated their own versions of Aboriginal land rights laws, some progressive, some not.

The distinctive identity of cattle station Aborigines was developed in cattle station work and bush life. In some areas people now look back on the hard working days with some nostalgia (Morphy and Morphy 1984; McGrath 1987), but people who worked for VRD and Wave Hill, for the most part regard the decades of work for others as a time of horrendous hardship, deprivation, and oppression. They hang on to the memory of these times because invasion still controls their lives, and because remembrance still encompasses the longing for freedom. And they hang on because they believe that it matters. Unlike many European Australians, Victoria River Aborigines believe that the lives of all Australian people are inextricably bound together, as are the soils, water systems, and the lives of plants and animals. In refusing to deny or forget the past, they assert the value of their own understanding for Australian life, in particular, and for the future of life on earth.

2 *Expectations*

For slightly over two centuries now, images of Australian Aborigines have had a peculiar hold over the European imagination. Cast in uplifting or in denigrating moulds, most images have been harnessed to the purposes of others. Within Australia, images are selectively appropriated as emblems of national identity. Beyond Australia, Aboriginal societies and cultures have been of greatest interest to anthropologists. Kenelm Burridge (1973) has analysed the encounter between anthropologists and Australian Aborigines and concluded that Aboriginal life has become a field in which many of the intellectual structures of the west have been reflected, examined, tested, and evaluated, and in which many a personal and intellectual battle has been fought. Throughout the history of this encounter, Aboriginal life has remained elusive. From the European viewpoint, according to Burridge, Aboriginal life constitutes a paradox: it is both 'primitive' and at the same time 'perhaps the most complicated representative of human life' (ibid: 238).

The story of anthropological interest in Aborigines is one I know well. It was during my last year of post-graduate studies in anthropology at Bryn Mawr College (1978) that I took a course on the ethnography of Australian Aborigines. My professor, Jane Goodale, had worked with the Tiwi of North Australia and her study (1971) was one of the few to represent Aboriginal people as living and feeling human beings. Jane well understood my interest in contemporary social theory and my concern for social justice. When other students were allowed to select an ethnography of their choice, I was required to read *The Unlucky Australians.* Written by the novelist and social critic Frank Hardy (1968), it is a first-hand account of the Gurindji pastoral strikes between 1966 and 1968.

Anthropology, defined differently by different people, is at its best a search to encounter with others the fullness of our shared humanity (cf Diamond 1974). Frank Hardy's study is journalistic rather than anthropological; he introduces readers to the compelling humanity and individuality of Aboriginal people in a way that very few ethnographers ever do. His superbly honest reporting had me hooked.

By 1980, I had been awarded grants by the National Science Foundation and the Australian Institute of Aboriginal Studies which would allow me to carry out anthropological research oriented to issues of cultural identity. At that time Jack Doolan was the Australian Labor Party member of the Legislative Assembly of the Northern Territory, having been elected to represent the Victoria River District. It was he who approached Yarralin people on my behalf, receiving their permission for an anthropologist to come and live with them.

Coming to Yarralin took me out of the indirect world of books, and brought me straight to one of the most basic of all human questions: who are you? This is not a question that can be answered with a name, nor can it be answered satisfactorily in words. Rather, the question requires qualitative demonstrations. Answers emerge in the lived experience of relationships developed in shared time and place. Ultimately, answers are a sharing of perceptions, attitudes, experience, and, I think, compassion. The engagement changes those who are involved, so that, like approaching the speed of light, one gets closer, but one never arrives. I am not the same person I was when I first went to Yarralin. And although my voice is richer for the experience, it is still mine.

Yarralin people rightly regard themselves as the experts on their culture. Daly Pulkara explained, in 1986, that old people with strong knowledge are like trees whose roots are firmly in the ground, while a person like myself, like leaves or annuals, is still new, ungrounded, and possibly ephemeral: 'Cause we know everything. Because you won't be, you won't get up there. You only been learn. [You, Debbie] Just been grow up today.'

Old people, having a lifetime of experience to draw on, are well aware of the gulf which separates Western and Aboriginal cultures and are most desirous of bridging it. As I became increasingly sensitive to the breadth of this gulf and the intense effort required to construct a bridge which would endure, my sense of the purpose and value of the research deepened. At the same time, this process deepened many of my friendships. Mutual affinity became transformed to strong affection based on recognition of our achievements in understanding each other.

I lived at Yarralin for two years between 1980 and 1982. In subsequent years I have returned regularly to work on land claims and to document sacred sites for registration. I have also carried on further research into religious identity and, more recently, into ecological knowledge and practice. Letters, phone calls, and taped messages help to sustain the communicative bridges that we have built. Initially, we developed a relationship based primarily on learning: Yarralin and Lingara people were my teachers and I was their student. This relationship persists but has been augmented by others: friendship, shared concerns and responsibilities, and alliance in the interests of community projects and land claims. Further work has also allowed me to have greater involvement with the people at Pigeon Hole, and many of their views are represented here.

In much of this work I refer to Lingara and Yarralin people collectively as Yarralin people unless it is important to distinguish between them. I do not intend to undermine the independence of people in either community; I conflate the two as a matter of convenience, and in recognition of the fact that there is constant movement between the two communities. Much of what I say about Yarralin and Lingara people is also true for Pigeon Hole people but because I have spent far less time with them, I do not group them with the others. In addition, their own sense of themselves precludes such grouping.

There are probably as many styles of field research as there are anthropologists. Except when employed as a consultant to carry out a specific task, my own is quite unassertive. In the 1980s and early 1990s Yarralin people lived their lives out of doors. The government-funded houses, locally known as dog boxes, were corrugated iron sheds with a veranda set in a concrete slab. The windows were frames covered with metal louvers. Running water was available from outdoor taps; pit toilets and showers were shared among several households. Kitchens were outdoor fires, usually covered with a scrap metal structure to deflect rain in the wet season. People slept outdoors except during storms and very cold weather. Family and community life was all outside, open to others. People cooked, ate, washed clothes, raised children, played cards, fought and chatted in the open. Socialising in Yarralin meant wandering through the various camps, joining in whatever was happening at the moment. Many of my days have been spent visiting and chatting, often without directing the conversation or taking extensive notes.

I had made it clear from the outset that I wanted to write a book about Yarralin people's culture. Almost every person of middle age and older took a keen interest in my progress, and actively involved themselves in teaching me what they felt I needed to know. They have been patient with my often fumbling questions, delighted when I have demonstrated that I have understood and remembered, and extremely thorough in going over information with me to make sure that I have understood correctly. At times I have become so intensely interested in things that I forget to take notes, and usually someone nudges me and reminds me to write it all down. Other times people have been bemused by the fact that I think commonplace things worth the trouble of recording. On a few occasions I have been told not to write things in my book because, as secret knowledge, they should not be 'mixed up' with other information and are best kept only in my head.

Old people (55 and over) are regarded, by themselves and others, as most competent to teach me, and it is they who have been most willing to assume the responsibility of teaching. Within the category of middle-aged and old people, I divided my time fairly evenly between men and women. In Yarralin, in contrast to some Aboriginal communities (see for example Bell 1983), men and women spend most of their time in each other's company. There are places where men can meet away from women (the single men's camp and men's area) and vice versa (the river and the women's area), but most of the people spend most of every day in the presence of the other sex. Yarralin women do not exclude men, so I do not either.

Like Aboriginal people throughout much of Australia, Yarralin men and women control separate and secret domains of knowledge and action, usually referred to as 'business'. Many anthropolgists have sought to determine the relative status of men and women in Aboriginal society (cf Kaberry 1939; Goodale 1971; Gale 1970, 1984; White et al 1985; Merlan 1988 provides an excellent overview of gender issues). Access to domains of secret knowledge is frequently seen to be a critical marker of hierarchy (cf Bern 1979; Hamilton 1981; Bell 1983; Langton 1985). I have taken women's and men's statements about the value of each other as human beings, about the necessity and vitality of each other's business, and their overt actions toward each other as kinds of information. Invariably I find that while men promote the value of their own knowledge and ritual, they do not do so by denigrating women's knowledge, and the reverse is equally true. The division of labour in daily life is clearly complementary and non-hierarchical; so too, in my experience, is the organisation of gender-specific domains.

More importantly, the organising matrix of identity, knowledge, and action is country; it is the responsibility of both men and women. I will be suggesting that an inflexible and hierarchical organisation of access to knowledge, resources, or information is deeply inimical to life as Yarralin people live and understand it (chapter 13).

I have found that in general men and women teach me different kinds of things, and teach me in different ways. Men concentrate on verbal explanations, telling me history, myths, rules and Law, and answering my many questions about social, cultural, and ecological systems. Women, in contrast, initially socialised me to being a woman in their terms. I believe that for both men and women learning takes place primarily through example. Men, of course, could not socialise me to being a man; they have concentrated on those aspects of knowledge which could be communicated verbally. In contrast, women have most consistently taught me by allowing me to observe their actions and to learn by doing, although they have, of course, explained many things to me.

The result is that much of what I have learned from men can be stated verbally with a sense of confidence about verifiability. In contrast, much of what women have taught me I have had to translate from actions, events, and experience into words. I have developed my ideas using these different learning experiences dialectically. Hypotheses which I constructed to account for my behavioural learning have been tested verbally with both men and women, while verbal explanations have been tested with other men and women and with events. In spite of all my testing, it remains the case that that which I feel I know best through personal experience is sometimes the most difficult to communicate in words.

Jessie Wirrpa is acknowledged locally to be 'the leader' in relation to use and care of country. She became my good friend and teacher. Much of what I came to understand about living systems, particularly the more abstract propositions, was first brought to my attention by Jessie. We spent many happy days in the bush and it was she who taught me to take notice of country, to see it as a living system which would keep me healthy and allow me to nurture others. Never a voluble person, her words are not the best expression of her being. In sharing her life with me she taught me, with great eloquence, about the value, purpose, and ineffable wonder of life.

Verbal learning, although it may seem straightforward, is often opaque to the newcomer. On my third day in Yarralin, Old Tim Yilngayarri told me a story: 'There was a man who shot dogs and he's dead now.' As I subsequently came to understand, for a Yarralin audience at that time this story spoke volumes. To me, however, it said nothing. Realising that I was incapable of making sense of it, Old Tim went on to give me a fuller account of how a European stockman had been mustering in an area that is important to dingo life, how he had been warned not to shoot dingos, and had ignored the advice Aboriginal people gave him. His shots were followed by a loud booming noise which signalled something out of the ordinary, and he later died.

Old Tim told me this story just three days after the manager of VRD had arranged for dingo bait to be dropped by plane throughout the area. The plane flew low over Yarralin, dropping poison there as well. Old Tim is an owner of country rich with Dingo Dreamings; he is a 'dog man' *par excellence*, with an intimate concern for, and understanding of, dingos and dogs. His life is connected to dingo life and he has assumed a special responsibility for canines. European use of poison was specifically intended to be detrimental to dingos, and Old Tim took it upon himself to show a continuity between past and present. His story demonstrated that arrogant European actions are not confined to the past, and hinted at retribution. For people whose lived experience is marked by so many injustices, including having had their dogs shot by police and by station personnel, the briefest story, told in the right context, resonates with memory and understanding.

A few days later Hobbles Danayarri explained to me how he believed the poison event fitted into broader social processes, and what it had to say about the future. He told me a story which began with Captain Cook and European invasion, and continued through the pastoral strikes and the move to Yarralin. He said that he had been telling this story around Yarralin over the previous few days because he wanted people to understand that they ought not to feel secure in their tenure of land until they could prevent violations such as had just occurred. He thus broadened the context of the event, linking it to European invasion and Aboriginal land rights, and issuing the directive that as long as such invasive acts can be performed with impunity, land rights have not been achieved.

I went to Yarralin with questions. Frequently I was told stories. Although I was initially unable to perceive many of the subtleties, it became clear that Yarralin people's stories bring past and present, specific and general, individual and collective into a shared matrix. Stories are told by people who have particular interests with respect to the issues involved; they draw on shared memories and construct continuities between past, present, and future, and between the specific and general. There is no collective Yarralin position articulated by a single spokesperson. There are stories: many voices joining together. Often the voices are in agreement, but consensus is by no means a necessary condition to a story.

The other major way in which my questions were answered was through physical demonstrations. If I asked about food distribution, I was taken fishing. When it became apparent that I did not know how to fish, I was shown. My best teacher, Jessie, was also a stern one. When I caught my first turtle, and hollered for help in the sudden realisation that I had no idea what to do with it, she came over and said: 'I'll show you this one time, and after that you do it yourself!' When I asked about young men's intitation ceremonies, I was told to wait and see. The time came, and I was told to dance. When I asked that someone teach me, I was told to do what the others were doing. My attempts were greeted with howls of laughter; after I had gained some competence the young and lively girls told me that it had been more fun before when I had looked 'just like a frog'.

Having been shown, I was expected to know. Subsequent questions which I hoped would help me understand have often been answered with the statement: 'You know that. You've been there.' Pressing for more understanding, further questions have elicited a final assertion: 'Dreaming Law.' Beyond that statement, questions have rarely been welcomed and answers rarely provided.

Of the approximately one hundred and fifty people who have chosen to live at Yarralin and Lingara, most are affiliated to nearby language-identified areas–Ngarinman, Ngaliwurru, Karangpurru, Bilinara, Wardaman, Mudbura, Gurindji, Malngin, and Nyining. Among my teachers are people who identify with each of these languages. Marriage also brings people to Yarralin from as far away as Arnhem Land and Western Australia.

Kriol is the language most frequently spoken in everyday life, and it is the mother tongue of the children. Adults all speak Aboriginal English–'varieties of English-related Aboriginal speech on a continuum between Standard Australian English' and Kriol (Sandefur 1986:25). Most older people are fluent in several traditional languages as well.

Kriol is spoken by approximately 20,000 people in the northern parts of Australia, particularly in the Northern Territory and Western Australia (Harris 1986:9). The language is English-based; its syntax is simplified in comparison both to English and to indigenous languages (Steffensen 1977); it has developed from a pidgin, drawing on English and original vernacular languages. Kriol often functions as a continuum along which utterances can be formulated to suit particular contexts. While the grammar and verbs may remain fairly stable, lexical items from any language can be accommodated. When Yarralin people make tapes in which they address native English speakers, they use Aboriginal English. Most of the time people use Kriol and include Ngarinman, Ngaliwurru, Mudbura, or Gurindji lexical items. Old people, in the context of addressing country, dead persons, or performing other formal speech acts, usually use a traditional language exclusively.

My primary working language is Kriol. As Yarralin is in Ngarinman country, I learned far more Ngarinman than any of the other traditional languages. My grasp of traditional grammar and verbs is very sketchy, but Yarralin and Lingara people have said to others that I speak Ngarinman and that other people should speak Ngarinman to me to make me understand. I have gained a working comprehension of Ngarinman, although I have never become fluent in that language, and I take people's statements to indicate their assessment of my identity rather than of my language proficiency.

Most of the transcriptions presented in this work are taken directly from tapes Yarralin people made to address non-Aboriginal audiences. Following Yarralin people's intention to make their words as accessible as possible, I have retained an English-based orthography even where a Kriol orthography might be a more accurate rendering of the words. Quotations taken from dictation do not flow as easily as the transcriptions because of my inability to write as fast as people speak. Rather than guess, in retrospect, at what was probably said, I have kept to my original notes.

Throughout Aboriginal Australia each group of people regards its own country as the best and finest. Each country is the centre of the world for the people who live there (cf. Michaels 1986). In the following chapters I will be exploring this idea as it is expressed by Yarralin people. Here I want briefly to examine some of the sociological issues that arise when the 'centre of the world' is inhabited by historically deprived people and is located in an isolated backwater of a nation state.

Yarralin people expected that with control over their own land they were entering a new phase of life in which dependence relationships and servitude to others would be broken for ever. According to Hobbles and others who discussed these matters with me, their understanding of the 1967 Referendum was that they would finally be treated as equals. Jack Doolan describes several changes in people's attitudes between 1971 and 1973:

> I saw them in late 1971 before they left Victoria River Downs, and they were a most apathetic and dejected group. When I visited them again in April 1972, following the walk-off, they were quite elated over the direct action which they had taken. Between then and October 1973, the mood of elation had left them and they were once again beginning to look and act in a dejected way. Now that they are back again and full of hope for the future, they are again a happy people, making all sorts of plans for the cattle station which they hope one day soon to be operating by themselves. (Doolan 1977:112)

During most of my initial two years at Yarralin I agreed with Jack's assessment that people were, by and large, optimistic. Since then, however, this understanding has had to give way to more sombre assessments; the optimism has largely evaporated.

Marc Gumbert (1984) argues persuasively that the Land Rights Act fails to achieve reasonable justice (see also Macintyre 1985:118–137). The Yarralin story demonstrates the point. Under the *Aboriginal Land Rights (Northern Territory) Act 1976* only 'unalienated crown land'–land that has not been leased–can be claimed. In the Victoria River District there is very little unalienated land indeed, but several Aboriginal claims have been heard and freehold title given over to Aboriginal owners (see McConvell and Palmer 1979; McConvell and Hagen 1981; and Bauman, Akerman and Palmer 1984). One of these was the Gurindji claim to the land which they had been formally granted as a lease in 1975, as a direct result of the strike at Wave Hill.

'Aboriginal Freehold' land is held by an Aboriginal land trust, the members of which are traditional owners of the land. This title is inalienable and allows the trustees a great deal of control, including the right to accept or veto mining exploration and exploitation.

For years Yarralin people argued that they would only accept Aboriginal Freehold title for their land, for it is the only truly secure form of title, and they believed that if the Gurindji mob could get it, they could too. After more than a decade of unsuccesful negotiations, they agreed to accept an alternative. The Yarralin block of 504 sq. km. is legally divided into two portions, the larger of which is held in trust by the Northern Territory Development Land Corporation (a Northern Territory government agency) and can be resumed at any time.

The majority of people who lived and worked on VRD and Humbert River stations have not found that land rights legislation has recompensed them for their years of hard labour. Karangpurru and Ngaliwurru people waited for twelve years to put forward their claim to a small block of unalienated crown land north of Yarralin and for several sections of mile wide stock route (Rose and Lewis 1986). Their claim was heard in August 1988 and the Land Commissioner found that the claimants were traditional owners within the meaning of the Act to most of the area they had claimed. His recommendation has gone to the Minister for Aboriginal Affairs. If the Minister agrees to turn the land over to the traditional owners, they will gain title to some of the stock route sections and to a block of land which, while technically unalienated, is being used. Section 14 of the Land Rights Act ensures that the users and occupiers have the right to remain for as long as they wish to continue to use and occupy the land. Efforts to negotiate a more reasonable allocation of land have so far been unsuccessful, although the issue is being discussed. Unless some agreement can be reached, the claimants' dream of becoming economically independent will be impossible to achieve.

Bilinara people at Pigeon Hole (VRD) have also presented a land claim to a portion of unalienated stock route (Rose and Lewis 1989). Here again, the Aboriginal Land Commissioner has recommended that title to a portion of stock route be granted to the Aboriginal traditional owners, and here again negotiations toward a more reasonable settlement are stalled [as of March 1991].

Riley Young, one of the Lingara bosses, expressed his desire for land and his belief in the justice of his demands this way:

> Old people been get shot. Why? By [because of] land. Just stealing the land. The white man been coming here stealing the land from blackfellows. Wasting blackfellows, shooting blackfellows from land.
>
> 'Don't worry about blackfellow, [we] want to be finish off for this country.' That's what they, that's what the Captain Cook been talk for olden times . . .
>
> Why don't you think about that law? You been enough wasting, shooting people from this country . . . My father been born la [at] that place. My *kaku* [father's father] been born la that place. He been there longa that country forever and ever, till my father been die, till my *kaku* been die. And Riley Young [the speaker] taking over that place now. [You] Should be realise for that place. How long I been here? My father been working [here] very young. No money. He been working [just] for bread and beef. Just for bread and beef. Just for blanket and trousers, shirt, that all he been working for. Why don't you think about that?. . . Why don't you realise that thing, and give us the land back today. How many times I been asking?

The answer to his last question is: too many to count. The Lingara mob has been offered a four square kilometre block of land to serve as their homeland.

It is common knowledge throughout the north that Aboriginal communities are particularly defenceless against outsiders who, from a position of trust, engage in unsound or unscrupulous financial practices. Very few unscrupulous persons are brought to law, and this factor undoubtedly increases the incidence of such practices. Australian libel laws make it difficult to write about known incidents. Suffice it to say that already in the community's short period of existence, Yarralin people have found it owing at least $139,000 and have faced the possibility of losing at least one of their titles to land. The experience has been a brutal demonstration of vulnerability.

The problems associated with running a cattle station have proved to be a further demonstration of dependence. The 504 sq. km. Yarralin block may not be large enough to run a profitable cattle enterprise, although it is certainly adequate for subsistence needs. In

Bardi Jalukarri, Yarralin stockman, April 1982.

addition, most of the men who have the age, skills, and respect required required for leadership do not have the accounting skills necessary for financial management. Consequently, they have been dependent on over-worked European advisers whose advice may not always have been sound. They have also been dependent on government grants, most of them channelled through the Department of Aboriginal Affairs (DAA). In recent years, despite the fact that at the time of the strikes the clear intention was to run a cattle business and achieve economic independence, DAA staff and other government personnel have stated that grants to assist a cattle enterprise will no longer be forthcoming because Yarralin was never intended to be a cattle station.

In spite of restrictive legislation, pastoralists' intransigence, official Northern Territory government opposition, bureaucratic indifference, and diminishing commitment among the wider Australian public, Aboriginal people in this area still contend that recognition of their rights to land, coupled with a fair return of portions of land, is the only basis on which just relationships between white and black can be established. If there is to be a future in which all Australians are assured a fair go, land reform to benefit both Aborigines and Europeans must be the first priority.

One major positive change during the period 1939–1973 was a reversal of the decline in population. Population pyramids developed from 1939, 1946, and 1972–3 censuses indicate that while the population did not grow significantly, the structure changed dramatically.

These changes are attributable to three factors: government intervention in health care delivery; the 1953 decision to stop removing children of mixed descent from their families; greater government involvement in cattle station people's conditions of life. What these diagrams do not show is the fact that many Aboriginal people in Australia, Yarralin included, continue to suffer high infant mortality rates, high rates of incidence of communicable diseases such as hepatitis and sexually transmitted diseases, and high rates of middle-aged death.

Taking the Australian population as a whole, the average life expectancy at birth is 72.1 years for men and for 78.7 years for women. Aboriginal men in Western Australia have an average life expectancy (at birth) of 56.1 years, while that for women is 62.7 years. In country New South Wales the life expectancies are 49 and 55 years for Aboriginal men and women respectively.

These statistics can also be expressed as a standard mortality ratio. In the Northern Territory an Aboriginal person is 3.39 more times likely to die, on average, at any given age when compared with the national averages (Thomson 1986:6–7). A breakdown by age of the standard mortality ratio is only possible at this time using information from country New South Wales. In that area the ratio peaks around early middle age. Aboriginal men between the ages of 35 and 44 are 12 times more likely to die than would be expected from statistics from

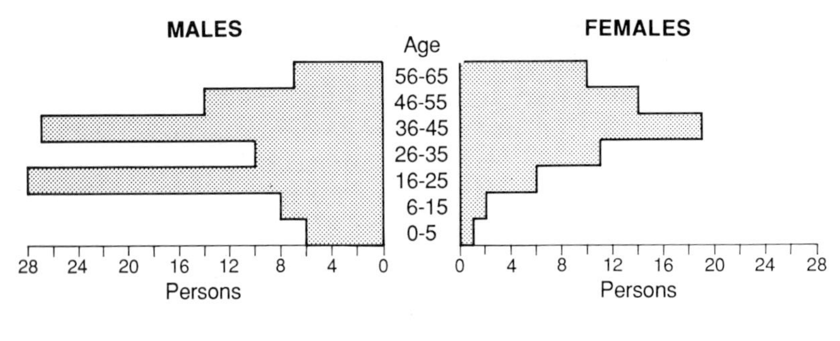

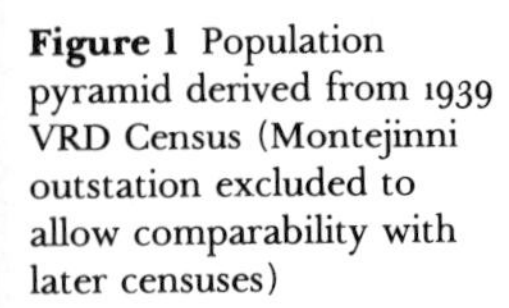
Figure 1 Population pyramid derived from 1939 VRD Census (Montejinni outstation excluded to allow comparability with later censuses)

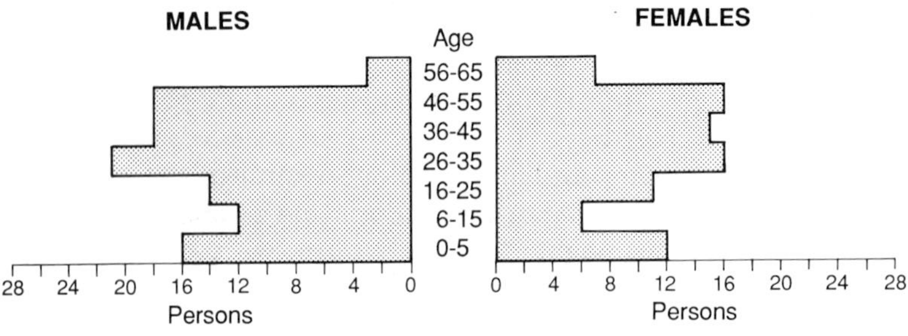

Figure 2 Population pyramid derived from 1946 VRD Census

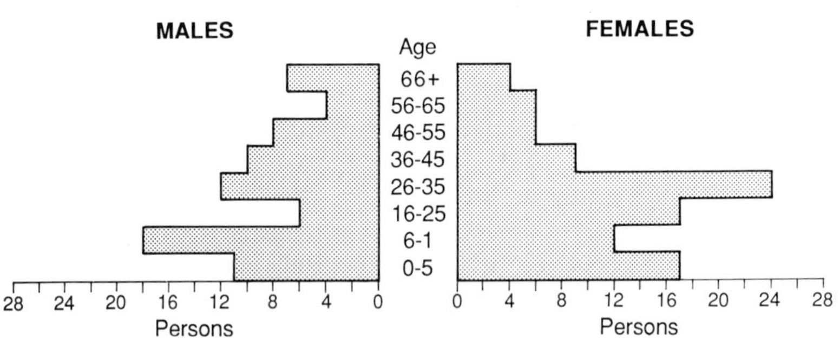

Figure 3 Population pyramid derived from 1972–3 Welfare Census

the total New South Wales population. Women between the same ages are 11 times more likely to die (Thomson and Smith 1985:51).

Diseases of the circulatory system, including heart disease and particular types of diabetes, are implicated most significantly in these figures for middle-aged death. Mortality rates attributable to these diseases are about 20 times those of the total population. Of those Aboriginal deaths recorded with the Aboriginal Health Unit, alcohol is implicated in 34 per cent of the male deaths and 15 per cent of the female deaths, and is almost certainly under-reported. While the causes of this phenomenon (middle-aged death) are not well understood, factors which are referred to under the generic term 'lifestyle' are strongly indicated (Thomson 1986:6–7). There are no comparable figures for Aboriginal people in the Northern Territory, but it is safe to conclude that an equivalent assessment would be unlikely to show a significantly more favourable set of statistics.

Physical impairments such as blindness (from trachoma) and deafness (from ear infections) are rife. Beck's brief description of

Aboriginal children's low standard of health in Alice Springs is equally applicable to Yarralin:

> The pattern observed is one of a high level of under-nutrition associated with a high level of morbidity, especially gastrointestinal and respiratory tract infections. The prevalence of eye, ear, skin and dental disease is also high. ... Of all children, 35 per cent have signs of chronic under-nutrition (i.e. they are stunted) and 39 per cent display signs of acute under-nutrition (i.e. they are wasted). Of the latter group, 19 per cent have signs of both protein and caloric deficiency and 20 per cent display mainly protein deficiency. (Beck 1985:109)

In sum, although the population in this area is showing healthy changes in overall numbers and proportions, the physical well-being of the people is still far below national averages. As much as possible, people continue to provide themselves with foods and medicines from the bush. Aborigines are legally entitled to hunt, gather, and make use of natural water throughout the area, irrespective of European land tenure (Rowley 1981:75). A number of Yarralin people who are unemployed spend at least half of their time in subsistence activities. Hunting, fishing and gathering fruits and vegetables are important activities; the resources improve the quality of life, and the activities provide opportunities for teaching younger people skills and country, and for sustaining ideals of independence. However, Yarralin people's insistence that their own foods and medicines will provide for them is severely threatened by the daily evidence of ill health.

The adoption and enforcement of a policy of award wages made it uneconomic for the pastoral industry to rely on its former labour intensive production. Since 1970, and rapidly increasing since 1978, VRD and other stations have relied ever more extensively on helicopter mustering (Makin 1983:160). Some job opportunities do exist on cattle stations, but it is no longer possible for more than a small fraction of the Yarralin population to be employed locally. The other side of this issue is that many Yarralin people have resisted the option of working for Europeans, arguing that they went on strike in order to break their dependence.

In the 1980s and early 1990s, most people spent most of their time socialising, playing cards, and hunting and fishing. The majority of Yarralin people relied on government welfare for their cash income, and unemployment benefits, child endowment, invalid and old age pensions, and supporting parent benefits were the mainstay of the cash economy, supplemented by wages and sale of artifacts. Some men continued to work on neighbouring stations for part of the year, and within Yarralin and Lingara a few government jobs existed–teaching assistants, health workers, and the like. A recently established National Park also offered Aborigines a few jobs as rangers.

Another of Yarralin people's expectations was directed toward education. The Yarralin school teaches children through to grade six (approximately). Children learn in a foreign language–English–and their progress is relatively slow, in part because of physical difficulties, in part because many of the teachers have had little training or assistance in bi-lingual, bi-cultural education. Young people who want to pursue their education further must attend boarding school in Darwin. There has been considerable resistance to this arrangement. Parents believe that their children become wild and unmanageable in Darwin, while many of the young people find the school environment to be so uncongenial that they run away. As there is very little local employment for young educated people, the incentives to continue are not great.

Although missionaries were not welcomed in the Victoria River District during the decades when the pastoralists were in control, some Christian ideas were brought to Aboriginal people. Yarralin people have had no difficulty in granting God and Jesus space in their own cosmology, and a message of personal love and assistance has occasionally given people added strength in times of crisis. Most recently Pentecostal missionaries (some associated with the Assemblies of God church) have been active in the area. Their activities can also be understood as a demonstration of vulnerability, for their message consists primarily in the assertion that Aboriginal culture is the work of the devil, and that non-converts will go to hell. Yarralin people's response to the missionaries has been varied. A few (as of 1988) have converted and remained as converts. Many people have dismissed the missionary message as 'lies' or 'bullshit' (Rose 1985; 1988).

The effect of recent missionary activity, more evident in other communities but ramifying throughout the region, has been to undermine the authority of older people, to disrupt those practices through which Aboriginality is sustained, and to offer a cosmology which is set in absolute opposition to the beliefs and practices through which Yarralin people have survived (chapter 13). On the other hand, missionaries also teach that alcohol is the work of the devil, and some people in the region have improved significantly the quality of their lives through converting to Christianity and renouncing the use of alcohol (cf Brady and Palmer 1988).

The 1967 Referendum gave Aboriginal people citizenship rights, including the right to purchase and consume alcohol ('grog'). Alcohol consumption is a significant part of many Australians' lives and is often construed as a marker of mateship. Drinking together, as songs and poems testify, solidifies and sustains relationships of equality ('mateship'–usually among males). Many Aborigines thought that citizenship would mean equality with whites and that equality and grog were reflexive; many of these same people now find themselves disillusioned.

In 1980, Yarralin people were well aware that alcohol abuse constituted a major social problem for many communities. The legal apparatus existed for them formally to declare the Yarralin block a 'dry' area, and in 1981 they did so. Laws are not necessarily obeyed

Big Mick Kankinang, Laddie Papitawurru, Little Mick Yinyuwinma, Barry Young Kurangala, and David Gordon Jangi have just put up the sign announcing that Yarralin is a 'dry area', September 1981. (D. Lewis)

simply because they exist, of course, and one of the problems for remote communities is that of enforcing laws. Yarralin people defended their status as a dry community quite vigorously for several years, but this defence appears to be in decline. There is also the broader problem of the many ways in which people can destroy themselves and each other through alcohol related accidents and violence in all the places where access to alcohol is not restricted.

At a time when alcohol-related violence was a major concern at Yarralin, Hobbles exploded with anger. His words were addressed primarily to other Yarralin people:

> We never been walk off for grog. No, we don't want him. We just want this land back. We only got one Law. Government make a lot of people mad [crazy], tell them lotta lies. They forget about rown [their own] culture, rown people . . . Citizenship just for grog, and grog been fuck the lot of them. We never been strike for grog. We been strike for land. Government never been like [care for] we. Why don't you think about that?

In sum, people's expectations have been flattened against a wall of circumscribed opportunities and continuing inequalities. Optimistic plans for independence have been swamped in a pervasive dependence at least equal to what was experienced before. Servitude to others has been replaced with a lassitude that is difficult to comprehend unless one has experienced it. The small blocks of land, such as

Kitty Lariyari and Debbie Rose at Lingara, August 1982. (D. Lewis)

the proposed Lingara block, which the Northern Territory government offers as a gesture to 'land rights', trivialise people, culture, and ideals.

Living in small, remote pockets of poverty, disease and increasing hopelessness, Hobbles' assertion that the government was telling lies makes perfect, if desperate, sense. VRD Aborigines broke through the barrier of invisibility with their strikes, greatly assisted by white Australians, such as Frank Hardy, who helped them gain publicity. But since that time their lives have moved in a direction they never anticipated. With their labour power marginalised, and their culture frequently ignored or denigrated, only their dependence, poverty, and appalling 'standard of living' statistics gain national attention. That attention focuses on Aborigines as a collective national problem which no one seems certain how to address.

Yarralin people have put considerable effort into teaching me because they hope that the written word will become a vehicle for their oral testimony. I do not think that this is a book that any Yarralin person, or group of people, would have written. I have chosen to examine many of the cultural premises in which overt statements and actions are embedded because without that understanding much of the communication makes only a shockingly narrow kind of sense. In the following chapters I will explore concepts of choice, interdependence, systems, and boundaries which connect rather than divide.

My primary purpose is to bring clarity to a set of issues which I understand to be those which most concern Yarralin people, particularly older people. There is no hierarchy to these points, but they include the following:

- understanding that behind the poverty of cattle station Aborigines there is a sense of responsibility that keeps people in their own country, attempting, against all odds, to take care of it;
- understanding that Yarralin people have not died out, lost their culture, or forsaken their beliefs;
- understanding that in spite of current attempts to structure Aboriginal society and culture according to European designs, Yarralin people want to be independent self-defining people;
- understanding that life is a gift, and that respect for life's manifestations is the only form of reciprocity worthy of such a gift.

3 *Earthborn Law*

Salt water covered all the earth in the beginning, according to Yarralin people; then the tide pulled back and the earth appeared. A few hills and ridges were in existence, but mostly the earth was relatively featureless, a damp, sandy and malleable ground. According to Yarralin people, the earth is female. In her moist and pliable state she gave birth to all the original creative beings. Holes or caves are analogous to wombs–the places of origin for all life. Earth is the initial mother and, by virtue of being original, is now and forever the mother of everything. All the different kinds of living beings, and all knowledge, are ultimately born of earth.

Walking, running, slithering across the earth, the creative beings have imprinted their passage on the body of the mother. Plants grew directly from the earth, often originating in particular places and spreading out across the earth as their seeds were scattered or as they were carried by mobile creative beings. Mobile life forms include all animals, many things which Western cosmology defines as inanimate: sun and moon, for example. Footprints of the moon and the dingo have hardened into rock and can still be seen. The track made by the great snake, Walujapi (black-headed python; *Aspidites melanocephalus*) is a sinuous cliff face, and Jasper Gorge was carved out of the earth by her motion. Likewise, the Nanganarri women who danced in the Victoria River bed at Pigeon Hole left tracks which are identical in shape, but not size, to those now made by women when they dance. All of these marks are visible and vital parts of the land on which we walk.

Walujapi travelled from the salt water in the west to the salt water in the east–thousands of kilometres. In Jasper Gorge she decided to make camp, sitting down on a hill called Kaljaki. The outline of her buttocks is clearly visible there now. There is now a rock painting of her at that place. Yarralin people often use the term 'photo' to identify rock art; but the term is misleading for native speakers of English, as is the term 'rock art', for Yarralin people say that most of these images

Kaljaki; Walujapi Dreaming hill. (D. Lewis)

are the Dreaming (see Lewis and Rose 1987 for a more thorough discussion of rock art). The image of Walujapi at Kaljaki **is** Walujapi, and when we have visited there people who are responsible for that hill have gone up first to tell her that we were coming.

Men say that if they look too long and intently at this 'photo' they will go blind, perhaps even die. In addition, there is much secret knowledge attached to the site. It is allowable to say publicly that in their shapes the Walujapi 'photo' and the hill are reciprocals. The hill is the impression–a negative image. The 'photo' is the positive–the shape of the black-headed python woman that was impressed on the earth when the ground was still pliable.

The earth as she is now–covered with vegetation, marked by different land forms, home to a great variety of living things–is the visible and consultable record of origins. Those who know how to look can see in the earth the story of our beginnings. Those who have the knowledge to understand can find in this visible story the meaning and purpose of life.

Dreaming

Aboriginal people use the term 'Dreaming' to refer to a wide range of concepts and entities which are not all covered by the same term in

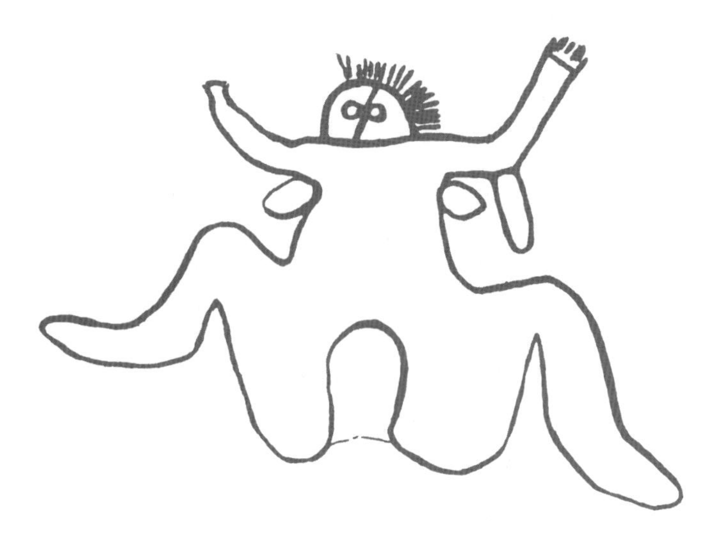

Figure 4 Line drawing of Walujapi

their own languages. In Yarralin usage, Dreaming is a Kriol word and minimally refers to the following:

- the creative beings who were born of earth and who walked first, creating geographical features, different species, and the Laws of existence;
- the creative acts of these beings;
- the period in which these things happen;
- many of the relationships between humans and other species.

Dreaming is both a model for, and a celebration of, life as it is lived in the present. As a model, Dreaming can be understood as a particular kind of map. Stanner's proposition (1979b:24) that the Dreaming constitutes 'a kind of logos or principle of order' best expresses the abstract and enduring qualities of Dreaming as map. As a source of celebration, Dreaming maps are used with reference to past, present, and future. Stanner's definition (ibid:29) of Dreaming as 'a poetic key to Reality' hints at the dynamism of Dreaming in the present. Models and practices all emanate from this life. Neither map nor inspiration to action, Dreaming is the source which makes possible all maps and celebrations–life in its variety, particularity, and fecundity.

Dreaming beings generated the Law by which life is sustained. Law is about relationships; but Law does not talk about itself. I suggest that the relationships established by Dreaming conform to a set of what may best be termed meta-rules: rules about relationships. The first is balance. A system cannot be life-enhancing if it is out of kilter, and each part shares in the responsibility of sustaining itself and balancing others. The second is response; communication is reciprocal. There is here a moral obligation: to learn to understand, to pay attention, and to respond. Third: symmetry. In opposing and balancing each other, parts must be equivalent because the purpose is not to 'win' or to dominate, but to block, thereby producing further balance. The fourth is that parts are autonomous. This is established as fact through Dreaming Law: no species, group, or country is 'boss' for another; each adheres to its own Law. Authority and dependence are necessary within parts, but not between parts.

Relationships only exist where there is difference. Abstractly we would say that the relationship between A and B depends in the first instance on there being a distinction between A and B. Dreamings created the variety by which difference is marked; their creativity thus underlies all further discussion.

In Dreaming most life forms had a basic human shape, although they were able to change shape at will. Just as people are now shaped–two arms, two legs, and so on–just this shape did Dreamings have before. Dreamings walked like people, bringing language, rituals, songs and dances, special objects, and knowledge of tools, hunting, and cooking. Some fought, some were mates, some ran away or became angry, some were killed and others grieved.

Boundaries between species, expressed as shape, colour, behaviour, and habitat are an example of conditions determined in Dreaming. Although creative beings were not bound by these conditions, and could change size and shape, their actions determined the present. Many animals now have characteristics they acquired when they were Dreaming. During a war between the flying foxes ('fruit bats', family: *Pteropodidae*) and the little bats (genus: *Taphozous*), for example, bat hid under a rock and flying fox poked a spear into his anus. He squealed in a way that is characteristic of him now, and his tail appears to pierce the tail membrane. When flying foxes started their travels a couple of them forgot their axes and had to go back and fetch them; now when we see a troop of flying foxes take off there are always a few who turn around and go back.

Westerners have engaged in seemingly endless speculation about what distinguishes us from animals, be it the gift of language, of consciousness, of foreknowledge of death, of the ability to speculate, imagine, plan and execute plans. For Yarralin people shape is the key. All animals have language. That ordinary people cannot understand the language of birds is not surprising–we cannot even understand the language of other people if they come from far away. Likewise, all animals have ceremony. Brolgas (*Grus rubicundus*) are an example. With their grey bodies and bright red heads they look painted for ceremony and in their elaborate and mesmerising courting rituals they dance, moving their bodies and stamping their feet as people do.

To be the same, minimally, is to share a shape and hence the potential to share a culture. To be different is, initially, to have a different shape, a different physical being. Out of that shape emerge other differences–animals of one shape, one species, share a language, a set of ceremonies, certain kinds of food, a way of life. In Kriol this specific way of life is termed 'culture'. This usage is similar to that of many anthropologists; it differs primarily in identifying culture as a necessary part of all life. We are not different from other species by having a culture which they lack; we are different in that our culture, like our shape, is different from theirs.

Most Dreamings finished by changing to become as they now are. No longer walking in human form, flying fox Dreamings, for example, 'changed over' into the flying foxes we now know. Most Dreaming beings are no longer with us in their original Dreaming form. Rather, Dreaming power exists in the sites where the Dreamings were before, and all the living species of earth derive their life from those sites. Individuals of every species live their lives according to the conditions of existence which were determined for them in Dreaming. Yarralin people assume, usually on the basis of specifiable evidence, that all species (some plants may be an exception) are made up of conscious and thinking individuals who speak, fight, plan, joke, perform rituals (men's and women's), according to their own Law. The disjunction involved in changing over can be drawn along a number of lines, but consciousness and responsibility have not been altered.

When Dreamings 'changed over' they became immobile, and at the same time they lost their range of options. The power of each was focused in a particular direction, becoming the on-going life of species (including humans) who now live according to Dreaming Law. Compared to the species alive now, Dreamings had a vast range of options. They changed in size, becoming small or huge in different places. They changed shape; the Nanganari women, for example, changed into possums and then changed back to humans again. And, because the earth was still moist, they imprinted their tracks in the landscape in the forms of hills, valleys, rivers. They carried seeds and tubers, establishing plant communities that persist.

Among the living beings with whom Yarralin people share their world are some whose presence can be dangerous to humans. Death adders, for example, are deadly. One of their origin sites is regarded as dangerous because any disturbance to it will stimulate the death adder population; their life must be contained in the interests of all living things. Daly Pulkara and others requested that this site, a large stony hill close to a station road, be registered as an 'Aboriginal Sacred Site' under the *Aboriginal Sacred Sites Protection Act, Northern Territory* (1979). Their concern was that station personnel might decide to cut the road closer to the hill, disturbing the stones and releasing death adders. In discussing this site, neither Daly nor any of the others suggested that death adders do not have a right to exist, only that they must be contained for the good of all.

Dreamings are spatially immobilised, but they are not dead. That which is Dreaming endures forever (chapter 12), barring diasaster, and in this ordinary time of change, of birth and death, gain and loss, Yarralin people care for and respect that which endures.

Mother and father dingo

In Dreaming, only the dingo (wild dog, *Canis familiaris dingo*) walked then as he does now. He was shaped like a dog, he behaved like a dog, and dingo and human were one. It was the dingo who gave us our characteristic shape with respect to head and genitals, and our upright stance. Ancestors and contemporaries, dingos are thought still to be very close to humans: they are what we would be if we were not what we are.

Old Tim Yilngayari told about the dingo origins of humans on a number of occasions. The stories are told in an elliptical style because some of the knowledge and ritual relating to dingos belong to a domain that is exclusively controlled by men. Old Tim told this story for a mixed audience:

> In beginning, when we come out of that hole [in the earth] we had long nose like a dog. Dreaming been walk, catch that sugarbag [native honey and wax] and make a head [round one]. That's we. Beginning Dreaming been working. Dreaming didn't like his head like a dog, he wanted it to be round. Dreaming [Dingo] called the little bat–that's the doctor–little one that flies at night. Lubra [women] one been just like dog. Bat says: 'You come to me.'
>
> And he fixed her up. Girls get cut and boys get tail pulled back [spoken with gestures indicating that genitals are being arranged to human form].
>
> Dingo dog come around and look: 'Hey, you been doing wrong! Long nose, big mouth, Dreaming been doing wrong.'
>
> Takem off head . . . [and made a round one out of] sugarbag [wax]. That's that beginning Dreaming been work. Same for women, same for boy. Now everything come good . . . White lady, Aboriginal boy, that Dreaming been work longa everybody. *Kalu:* him walk, him stand up, him finished longa dog now, him proper man, *janga* [women], *ngumpin* [men]. Mother and Father Dingo make Aboriginal. White children out of white dog; Dingo for Aboriginal. True God! God's a man: Lord Jesus.

We are like no other animals in the shape of our genitals, but in Australia human beings are closest to dogs and other placental mammals. This is easy to see when one looks at Australian marsupials: male kangaroos, for instance, have their testicles and penis back to front; female kangaroos have a pouch. Before, we had genitals like dogs. Women had a vulva that stuck out the back and men had a penis that was attached up the belly, and when they mated they became stuck together the way dogs do. Old Tim said, with characteristic emphasis, that people used to get stuck together for days, or even weeks. The dingo called in 'doctors' to fix us up. The bat cut a new vulva, and put a mussel there to keep it from closing up again. Bower bird (*Chlamydera nuchalis*) was the 'doctor' for the men. He put the penis at the

Maryanne Clipper and Chantal Jackson are observers as the boys torment dogs which have become stuck together, October 1981.

proper place and positioned the testicles correctly. Male operations of circumcision and subincision are performed in contexts which belong only to men, and while women of course know that they are performed, they do not have access to the knowledge surrounding them.

Human beings are not only a generalised species; we, too, are earthborn, or autochthonous. In addition to the human being repositories to be discussed shortly, there are also people's many statements of Dreamings going into the ground and human beings coming out of the same place. Specific human beings trace their ancestry back to specific places aligned with particular Dreamings.

Human death, too, originates with the dingo. The moon has the Law of eternal life, and he offered it to the dingo. Stories about the moon and death are widespread, occurring at least from the Kimberley (Kaberry 1939:128) across the top end (Berndt 1979:20–1) to Queensland (Bruno and Alpher 1988:16). In the Victoria River District, as in the Kimberley, the moon wanted to marry 'wrong-way'–he was wildly eager to make love with his mother-in-law. An argument arose between him and all the animals/people, including his mother-in-law (sometimes identified as the black-headed python), who told him that he was wrong. Out of spite he decreed that he would live forever and they would all die. As the story is told in Yarralin, the emphasis is less on the moon's sexuality, although that is well known, and more on his argument with the dingo. This story, too, is told in elusive terms, concealing as well as revealing. In Daly Pulkara's words:

> Dingo and moon, those two made a culture. Moon said: 'I'll stop three, four days dead, and I'll [be] coming back again!'
>
> *Walaku* [Dingo] said: 'I'll got to die forever. I'll lose my self, bone and dust . . .'
>
> Moon been say: 'I'll come back every four days.'
>
> *Jarkulin* [moon] been say: 'You can drink my wee wee, we'll make [become] same life.'
>
> *Walaku* reckoned: 'I won't drink your wee wee, too dirty.'
>
> Moon dead first, he's going to work first: die and come back. [He came back laughing and singing]: '*Kilikilir* [his song] . . . I'm here again, I'm home,' he said. He's come back. Dog say: 'If I'm dead, I'm dead forever.'
>
> Next one, Dog been dead and couldn't come back. [He] tried and tried.
>
> *Jakulin* said: 'I didn't like that [death]. I can make myself old and come back new.'

Through the actions of dingo and moon, death became a fact of human existence, inescapable and irrevocable. However, dingo developed another Law which, while not defying death, asserts that death is not as final as bones and dust. According to Old Tim:

> Moon been talking:
> 'What I gonna do? I not dead for good!'
> Moon there, still there today.
> 'I dead today, three day, three night, I come back.'
> We all gotta follow longa dingo . . . we be dead for good. We follow that dingo. That kid find new father, new mother: that's the Law belong that dingo. Dead man come out of the hole in the ground [grave]; [that's the] word of the dingo. His skin come up–no bones, but skin [and] guts come up . . . *Kaya* [custodian of the dead] come and take him longa river. Dead man look around think about him Dreaming . . . Make himself kangaroo, goanna, bird, crocodile . . . [Law] From that dog.

One's life will be extinguished; according to Dreaming Law, it must finish. But life itself is an on-going process, and as participants in that process human beings share both in the particularity and in the continuity of life.

Woman and man

In Dreaming there were also Dreaming human beings–women and men who travelled separately, making their own separate rituals, usually referred to as 'business'. Men and women are now interdependent, but this was not always the case. In Dreaming men and women walked separately and women had most of the 'Law'. Men have Law now which Dreaming men got from Dreaming women; women continue to have their own Law which is quite distinct from men's. Dreaming women carried all the knowledge of reproduction, and many, if not all, of the ceremonies. The only knowledge women did not specifically have, apparently, was the knowledge of making men and the knowledge of sex. They did not need this knowledge for they had no need of men or of sex. Walking across the earth singing, naming, giving birth, hunting and gathering, they were fully independent in ways that nobody is now.

In the end, men appropriated or were given some of women's knowledge. Walujapi, the gentle python (Namija subsection) who is called *Ngamayi* (mother), was accosted by two poisonous snakes who she called uncles (Japarta subsection). They taught her about sex, making her a woman in the human sense of becoming a woman through sexual activity. She kept her private women's things and kept on travelling to the east, but the males took men's secret song cycles (*kujingka*) and men still have them today. Men who are living now know that the knowledge was stolen from women. They say it was not right that it happened, but it happened in Dreaming and so it stays that way. Song, dance, story, knowledge, and access to visual testimony are now divided between men and women.

One group of women, the Nanganarri women, travelled through Malngin, Bilinara, Ngarinman and Mudbura countries. Starting from the west, they came carrying firesticks and yamsticks, calling the names of places, giving birth, and performing rituals. At many of the places where they stopped they left 'babies'–unborn humans needing only a mother in order to be born.

They, too, met men, and their encounter resulted in the *Pantimi* ritual for men's initiation which defines a large tract of country and people. According to Hobbles, who is a 'boss' for *Pantimi*, the women's adventures began when they found a shady place to sit and rest. Two dogs came up to them and they were frightened. The women started dancing and when they next looked they saw young men. As the women were engaged in secret 'business' they told the young men to go away, but the men were persistent, so the women started moving again, still singing. They turned themselves into possums and then, later, into women again. All this time the men were following them and cutting themselves. After a long time the women began to get 'really sick and tired for dance' and threw spears to make the sun come up. Just as the sun rose there was a 'big mob' of men, all of them 'really' (fully initiated) men. The women disappeared into a rockhole and stayed there.

In their negotiations the women agreed to allow the men to sing their songs. In effect, women allowed men to carry on the Law that was initiated that night–to continue to make themselves into 'proper' men. Hobbles characterised the women as *Pantimi* and the men, who travelled parallel to the women, as *Marntiwa* (men's secret business):

> *Pantimi* talk: 'You can be singing me, head, eye, when I walk and when I sing out, and when I dance. You can be use all my body. No matter [don't pay attention to] what I [am] carrying, but you can sing it body. You can have the song, that's all. But I can't give it you my side. Man can't look.'
>
> That's Dreaming been have that one now, [at] Nijpuru [Pigeon Hole].

> Only women been find dance and told *Marntiwa* he can sing it. But women corroboree all up to women mob. Right from beginning . . .

Yarralin men, and other men throughout the Victoria River District, recognise that much of their secret ritual and Law ultimately derive from women Dreamings, just as all life originates in mother earth, and as they themselves are born of women. Dreaming women gave or lost some of their power to men, but women today still hold their own Law and ritual which have been handed down to them from Dreaming women.

Through Dreaming actions, certain geographical areas are now defined in relation to gender, having been acted upon in Dreaming in such a way that they are now inbued with the essence and secrets of femaleness or maleness. What people must or must not do in regard to gender-defined areas varies from place to place. Some are so heavily restricted that persons of the other gender cannot even approach; others allow access but restrict knowledge. One highly restricted place is on the track of the Dreaming women. Because of the women's actions men cannot go to that place, and if they go near they must cover their heads and look the other way. Men cannot drink the water that flows directly from that place, nor may they eat any food that the women hunt there, nor ought they to look at smoke rising from that country. This area–its food, water, sites, smoke, its visual imagery and its knowledge–is defined as women's country totally and absolutely.

Allan Young and Jack Jangari spoke of this area when they were discussing the Nanganarri Dreaming track:

> AY: Only that one [name omitted] there now important, you know. Like when you go every morning, you can see the long pocket there now; you can see smoke get up. But we don't go la that place, you know.
>
> JJ: Sacred ground.
>
> AY: Sacred ground belong to women. But we just turn back from half way. We know. We can see smoke from long way. But still they [are] walking there yet.

There are also men's countries. Women cannot go directly to them, and if they go near they must cover their heads and avert their eyes. Sanctions for breaking the rules vary. Women say that their areas will harm men who intrude. What the women's country discussed above does to men is private knowledge. In addition, women have the right and the power to cause men who intrude on certain places to become sick and to die. Similarly, some men said that if women or children strayed into the most secret of men's areas they would be speared. Other men said the place itself would kill the intruders.

That each gender is independent as well as dependent is assured by the fact that each has its own Law and its own Dreamings. Secret business preserves this independence: one cannot take over what one does not know. Secrecy is also a public assertion of autonomy: when the women go away for secret business the men are told to stay in camp; they must not walk around, and certainly they must not come near. Often secret business is conducted very close to camp. Sometimes when women sing their songs they are close enough for men to be able to hear the sound of their voices but not the words. Since one of the main features of secret business is to demonstrate autonomy, the demonstration must be public while the knowledge is kept secret. In this complex combination of public demonstrations of secrecy, difference and independence are asserted and maintained.

Strings

Dreamings determined the differences that matter and the conditions of existence for all living things. One such condition is the boundaries which transform the original undifferentiated mother earth into specific localities, defined by Dreaming presence, language, cultural practices, plant communities, ceremonies, and by the fact that there are people who belong there and take care.

Dreaming travels are celebrated in song, dance, story, and ritual. Tracks and songs are the basis to Aboriginal maps and are often called 'boundaries'. To say that there are boundaries is to say that there are differences; the universe is not uniform. Unlike European maps on which boundaries are lines that divide, tracks connect points on the landscape, showing relationships between points. These are the 'boundaries' that unite. The fact that a Dreaming demarcates differences along the line is important to creating variation, but ultimately a track, by its very existence, demarcates a coming together. Dreaming creativity made possible the relationships which connect by defining the differences that divide.

Yarralin people sometimes refer to these tracks as 'strings' (cf McConvell and Palmer 1979:45; McConvell and Hagen 1981:57). Like string figures (which people now rarely make except for the static ones used in ritual), in which a single string can be formed into any number of different figures, strings are webs of connection. Dreaming strings connect and divide, cross-cut and re-converge. The particular 'figure' one sees depends in large part on how one defines the context of looking. And as these strings are also songs and stories, the particular 'figure' depends too upon who is singing or telling, who the audience is, and what the purposes of the performance are.

One type of boundary is the demarcation of ecological zones. Distinct plant communities serve as particularly salient markers of difference and of Dreaming activity. The black-headed python travelled from the salt water in the west to the salt water in the east, carrying in her coolamon, and scattering along the way the seeds of a variety of types of plants. The portion of her travels which Yarralin people know, tell, sing, and dance takes her from a coastal region into the big river country of the inland. She deposited the seeds of plants which are confined to coastal regions along a portion of the track; then she left her coolamon behind and moved into a different zone which she marked with a different set of plants.

Dreamings spoke languages as they travelled, defining localised Dreamings, people, and country. In a discussion of origins with Jimmy Manngayari, Jack Jangari, and Allan Young, Jimmy explained that emu (*Dromaius novaehollandiae*), corella (*Cacatua pastinator*), and Jurntarkal (a 'cheeky' snake whose species is usually left unspecified) were three great travellers giving Law and language to a vast tract of big river country, as Walujapi (python) did further to the north. Allan Young is the youngest of the three (born about 1932); gifted with an inquiring mind, he is always keen to understand more fully. Once he described himself by saying: 'I'm a bit of an anthropologist myself, you know'. He used the term *maluka*–a term of respect for an older man–in addressing Jimmy:

> AY: *Maluka,* let me ask you, what that emu, *yiparatur* [emu], that one been give it Ngarinman?
>
> JM: Them three. Them three been give it you and me, don't matter whanim [what or who] you and me tribe, what language, them three been give it we. All the tribe. Give it language; what country you. Them three been give it now.
>
> AY: Like that Namija [python]
>
> JJ: That tribe, they been talk one and one. That's why they been talk language way. '*Niyuntu kanka Malngin. Niyan kanka Bilinara. Niyan kanka Ngarinman.*' That's the way been talk language way, early day. Just like: 'You Chinaman, Malayan, Indian,' see? They told people what language. Give it la alabad [everybody].
>
> JM: This is the one, threefellow boss for every group.
>
> JJ: That's the mob been talking language all the way.
>
> JM: Give it longa don't matter where. From that end [west] right up, give it.

Human origins are more complex than Old Tim's stories of the dingo indicate. All of us, including Jesus, share the privilege of being the offspring of female dogs, but now, equally, we are all born of woman. My understanding is that when the Dreamings changed over they became the animal or plant relatives of people with whom they share intimate relationship. Jimmy is intimately associated with the emu and the corella, and it was of them that he spoke when he discussed his own origins and responsibilities: 'That's why people been breed. They got to go back to that two; go back to where they started.'.

Dreaming strings fix country and people, demarcating human and geographical identity. Some Dreamings belong to a particular locality while others travelled through many areas establishing connections between them. In Jessie Wirrpa's story of her own owlet nightjar (*Aegotheles cristatus*) Dreaming, Jirrikit (a local Dreaming) travelled north from VRD to get a particularly hard wood for making spears. Among his numerous mishaps, he encountered the black-headed python as she travelled through: ' "This one might kill me. I'm too small",' he said, according to Jessie, and he flew away home.

Many of these lines cross-cut and overlap each other. An example, sketched on Map 5, will help clarify this point. The pigeon Dreaming,

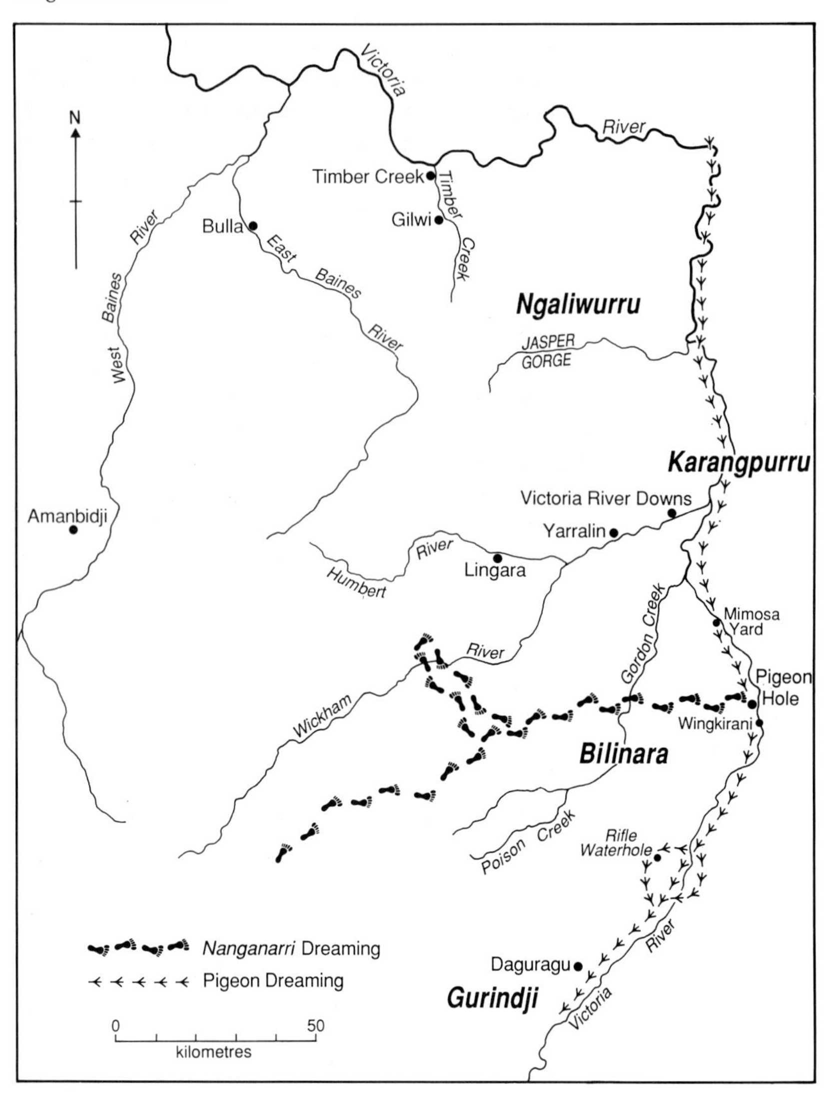

Map 5 Dreaming 'strings'

insofar as Yarralin people speak of it, runs from the desert fringe to the coastal region, following the Victoria River. Two pigeons, a brother and sister, started at Buchanan Spring where they were speaking the Gurindji language. The brother was carrying a grindstone and, as he did not have a hairbelt to tuck it into, he placed it on his head. As he travelled he lost bits and pieces of the stone which are still to be seen as massive sandstone outcrops. From Buchanan Spring to Rifle Hole in the Victoria River, the pigeons spoke the Gurindji language. From Wingkirani (another waterhole) to Mimosa Yard they spoke the Bilinara language. Near Camfield, in the Bilinara language area, they turned away from the river but were stopped by other Dreamings speaking the Mudbura language. After speaking the Bilinara language they changed to Karangpurru, and later again they changed to Ngaliwurru.

We can see that several different geographical regions and languages are brought into a relationship of joint responsibility as a co-owning series. Gurindji and Ngaliwurru people were traditionally 'strangers'; their countries do not adjoin, their languages are not mutually comprehensible, and they did not intermarry. Yet they could come together as 'mates' because they stood in a similar relationship to the pigeon Dreaming.

A second point is that the Aboriginal type of boundary, expressed as strings, creates sets of identities which cross-cut each other. The geographical regions based on desert, river, and coast are clearly distinguished through ceremony lines of initiation. *Pantimi* (brought by the Nanganarri women) belongs to the big river country, *Yalaju* to desert country, and *Wangka* to coastal country (chapter 9). Each ceremony demarcates a series of languages which is differentiated from others. Bilinara people, for instance, are responsible for both the pigeon and *Pantimi*. Ngaliwurru people are responsible for both the pigeon and *Wangka*. In relation to the pigeon, Bilinara and Ngaliwurru people are 'the same' in that they maintain their own responsibilities with respect to a single Dreaming. In relation to young men's initiation, however, they are 'different'. A string forms a set which, in other contexts, is broken up. Every string defines both difference and similarity, and as the tracks cross-cut each other, forming elaborate webs and stories, so people assert their rights and obligations both to differ and to come together.

Relationships based on strings are often referred to as 'fifty' relationships. This is one of the most eloquent of Kriol terms, clearly highlighting the difference between Aboriginal and European concepts of boundaries. I think this term probably derives from the English expression 'to divide things fifty-fifty'. In Kriol, 'fifty' has to do with sharing; people come together, generating each other as equals through exchange. Where people come together along a Dreaming track, there they are 'fifty' for country.

Countries are autonomous. No country, however defined, is dependent upon any other country for its Law, its livelihood, its right to be. The English definition of autonomy as the 'liberty to live after one's own Law' accurately expresses Yarralin people's sense that country defers to no external social authority. Autonomous countries were established in Dreaming, and that is how they remain when all is well. String imagery includes the concept that each node is its own centre of the figure. People know that others see their own nexus as the centre; indeed, they expect them to. To be a centre is not to dominate, but rather to have one's own perspective. Each country is, from its own viewpoint, its own boss. There are no 'orders from above' because there is no above. There are only interrelated parts (chapter 13).

Dreamings frequently did the same things over and over. Some keep emerging across the landscape with the same stories. The moon, for example, does not have a track that is public knowledge. He has place after place after place: where he chased women, where he argued with the dingo, where he chased more women, where he had more arguments. The Law of death applies to all people in all countries because it happened everywhere. No country or group imposes this Law by virtue of being in a privileged place. All places are privileged. In the following chapters I will be referring frequently to group (or country) and individual autonomy. I use the term with this limitation: that while every unit which is autonomous is its own boss, all are mutually dependent on each other. As David Turner (1987:14) says, Aboriginal Australia was made up of a plurality of promised lands each with its own 'chosen people'. The coherence of plurality is effected by redundancy, and by the many strings which connect.

The Law is in the ground

Doug Campbell, one of the senior Yarralin men, explained to me early on in my time there that I must observe Aboriginal rules because there could be no exceptions under the Law:

> You see that hill over there? Blackfellow Law like that hill. It never changes. Whitefellow law goes this way, that way, all the time changing. Blackfellow Law different. It never changes. Blackfellow Law hard–like a stone, like that hill. The Law is in the ground.

Law is often expressed as rules about behavior. But what Law seems most fundamentally to be about is relationships. Dreamings determined sets of moral relationships–country to country, country to plant and animal species, people to country, people to species, people to people. Individuals of any species come and go, but the underlying relationships persist. Law is a serious life and death business for individuals and for the world; it tells how the world hangs together. To disregard the Law would be to disregard the source of life and thus to allow the cosmos to fall apart. Doug defined Law (*yumi*) this way: '*Yumi*: Law from Dreaming side all the way. What Dreaming been done before, you can't lost that Law. Our Dreaming been do that, we got to hang on.'.

Beginnings, creativity and fixity: Yarralin people have struggled to maintain an unbroken set of links from Dreaming to this time now. Jack Jangari and Jimmy Manngayarri explained this:

> JJ: Well he can't wash out, that map. He's on the ground, map. You know, map in the paper, he just wash out, he got to go make another one. He might be a multimillionaire, that's all right.
>
> JM: He can make him that way, all right. But no! We watch him by what the Dreaming been do. We follow that Law. We never change. We follow one Law. Number one Law. No more two Law, no more three Law, no more four Law, no more five Law. No! Only number one! One Law! Number one. That's the way.

Jimmy's and Jack's words may have had a concealed agenda, for they followed from an earlier discussion about God. The two old men did not want to provoke an argument, and they chose their words carefully. Hobbles, in contrast, was never tactful about these matters:

> Everything come up out of ground–language, people, emu, kangaroo, grass. That's Law. Missionary just trying to bust everything up. They fuck em up right through. Gonna end up in a big war. Before, everything been good–no war, no missionary.

Through their continued observance of Law, all species sustain the relationships which were developed in Dreaming. It is implicit that all living beings have a choice in following Law. They can do what is necessary to maintain life or they can turn their backs on responsibility and, in so doing, allow destruction. Yarralin people often do not express this as a matter of choice because, for them, to follow the latter course would be an act of madness. It may be that their encounters with European society have highlighted types of perceived madness and waste that formerly would have had little salience, but it is equally true that they see themselves as people with *both* responsibility *and* choice. Burridge (1973:80) states that 'Aborigines did not take their powers of intellect, mind, and will for granted . . . They are and seem always to have been much concerned with the proper exercise of intellect or mind or will informed by moral awareness: in sum, the implementation of the Law'. In their own view most Yarralin people choose to uphold the Law out of concern for life. All species have Law and culture, free will and choice; the burden of responsibility is shared among all living things.

To us alive now, one of the most important aspects of Dreaming is that the marks do not wash away. In this sense, Dreaming is quite literally 'grounded'. The earth is the repository of blood from Dreaming deaths and births, sexual excretions from Dreaming activites, charcoal and ashes from their fires. Dreaming life has this quality which defies change: those things which come from Dreaming–country, boundaries, Law, relationships, the conditions of human life–endure. Compared to the ephemeral existence of living things now, Dreamings carry on forever. Riley Young of Lingara compared Dreaming Law to a European pastoral lease:

> This thing been start from beginning. We follow that same rule. We never change him rule. We on the same road all the way, all the way, till we gonna die, this nother man gonna take same rule . . .
>
> Belong to white man, you might have that bit of paper, that's what white man call that lease belong him. Him have him over there, bit of wind come up, him blow him out, him gone. He got to get another one and write him down. That's his Dreaming. We can't changem that one. No!
>
> Why that government reckon he gonna changem everything? Change him round? How you going to change him round? You can't change . . . that big hill there. You can't change him this ground. How you going to change him? How you going to change that creek? . . . Put that creek this side, he'll come back to flood this side. You can't! No way! . . .
>
> I know government say he can change him rule. But he'll never get out of this ground.

4 *Living and Dead Bodies*

Human life is enriched through birth, depleted through death. Where we live is the earth. We walk this ground, and our feet mark our living mother who feels and knows. We are bodies of a particular shape and culture, and our spirits both connect us to other living things and mark us as uniquely human.

There is no dogma among Yarralin people on those portions of a human being which exist before the person is conceived and which separate at death. My social science training and my Western religious background predisposed me to expect that proper research would reveal a cohesive set of beliefs. It was with some difficulty that I came to accept that there is simply no consensus on these matters, and that Yarralin people are not troubled by this.

I use the term 'spirit' with some trepidation. The English term cannot but signal a body-soul dichotomy which is inappropriate to the Yarralin context. Were I able to find a better term, I would avoid 'spirit' altogether, but as it is, I must state emphatically that spirit is immanent in body and even death does not wholly disrupt this immediacy. Death terminates the unique, separating out different parts, but spirit lives and continues to be embodied. As we will see, Yarralin people believe that a human being embodies several spirits at least one of which remains embodied on earth; this idea is widespread across Aboriginal Australia; (cf Warner 1969; Reid 1983; Tonkinson 1977, 1978; Montague 1974 provides an overview of conception beliefs which are closely entwined with beliefs about spirits).

Living Bodies

Human bodies are microcosms of larger systems (cf Schebeck 1978). Kin are mapped onto the human body through sign language: my brother is equivalent to my right calf; my sister to my left calf. My right thigh is my mother's brother; my mother is my left thigh. My mother's mother and mother's mother's brother are my forehead (brain); my mother's father is my belly (indicating liver); my breast is my child (and sister's child), and my chin (whiskers) is my father.

Formerly when a boy was made into a young man his sister had narrow lines incised on her calves. Evidence of the brother's state was borne on the sister's body. When a woman's son was made into a young man, scars were incised on her belly, and scars on her arms indicated her husband's state. Like the earth which bears the evidence of Dreaming action, people's bodies change over time, and physical wounds are not necessarily to be feared. Being as state and being as body are not separate. Visual evidence and the state of existence are a coherent system.

Human beings also are identified with parts of the cosmos. All human bodies maintain a stable temperature when they are healthy, but women are thought to be hotter than men, particularly during their fertile years. Associated with the sun and with fire, women's heat 'cooks' or grows babies much as the sun 'cooks' the earth and grows life. Men are associated with water and with the rain which cools the earth. Both rain and sun are necessary to the continuity of life on earth, as, of course, are men and women.

In these ordinary non-Dreaming days, a human being begins its existence as a baby growing inside its mother. Prior to its presence in its mother, life exists, but is not entirely human. *Yimaruk* is one of the terms for life in its continuity. It is not confined to humans, and is frequently absorbed through eating. Extremely fat fish or animals are thought to be most likely to contain *yimaruk*. Baby centres, increase sites for human beings, are also sources of human life. From one of these centres a baby enters its mother and grows into a human being. People say that the baby stones at Pigeon Hole, many of which are in the water, give women fish. If a woman goes away feeling particularly happy after eating a fish it may mean that she has gotten a baby. That is, an unborn baby has entered a fish in order to find the mother who kills and eats the fish. There are other ways in which women can get babies, and babies may wander about looking for their mother. The significant point is that a human being has origins in the world beyond its immediate parents.

Yimaruk may be glossed as life itself. It endures as part of an ongoing life process which infuses the whole cosmos. It is universal in the sense that all living beings share in it, but it is also specific in that it is identified with particular individuals and often bears a close relationship to country.

The *yimaruk* which a person has now was another person or animal before, and will become another person or animal later. All Yarralin people know something about who their *yimaruk* was before it came to them. Most people have a mark on their body which gives an indication of the most recent past life of *yimaruk*, and the mark too is called *yimaruk*. Hobbles has a little indentation by his ear which is where the barramundi that he was before was speared. Young Cedric has a birthmark which indicates the leprosy of the former life. I have a

Ivy Kulngarri (centre) and other Pigeon Hole Bilinara women, holding one of the baby spirit stones; Pigeon Hole, December 1986.

brown birthmark which, I learned, shows that the person my *yimaruk* was before was burned to death.

In those instances in which a person's *yimaruk* derives from another person, some contact with the surviving relations of the deceased is in order. For example, one of Mirmir's and Daly's daughters has or is the *yimaruk* of a person who lived near Timber Creek north of Yarralin. When we visited a community there in 1980, relatives of the dead person rubbed the girl with red ochre and cried over her; they gave gifts of fabric to Mirmir and Daly because they had given that *yimaruk* another life. Daly and Mirmir responded with gifts of fabric to mark the transaction.

This much is public knowledge. Further details of the Law by which human beings are brought into their mothers and into the world are secret. Both women and men have their own ideas about these matters, but they all agree that life in both a general and specifically human sense exists prior to birth.

Whilst in the womb the baby is nurtured by its mother, and after birth it is nursed on its mother's milk. Through milk our mothers give us body or flesh (often termed 'meat' or 'beef'; *ngarin*) which we share with all of our siblings out of the same mother. We share body with our mother and all her siblings (male and female) and with her sisters' children. When we drink of our mother's milk we partake of the life of

Maggie Wilinkarri of Timber Creek cries over Julie (Mabel's daughter) during a brief ceremony to mark the fact that 'spirit' which once lived in one of Maggie's deceased relations now lives in Julie, December 1980.

our mother and her brothers, of their mother and her brothers, and so on back to Dreaming.

When women grow babies and give birth to them they bring something totally new into the world. This is an ultimate gift, and because it is the domain and responsibility of women most men say that certain things simply cannot be done. Hobbles spoke of people further to the south in the desert who, he said, have a Law by which women who intrude on men's business may be killed. He was contrasting this Law with the Law of the big river country, saying that Yarralin and other people in the area do not kill women because women are mothers: 'Mother gives life. White woman, Aboriginal woman, half-caste woman–all give life. We drink that milk, we drink that life. Women [are] good to have babies, [to] give life.'

A similar relationship obtains between people and the country in which they grew up. Formerly a child's first solid foods, usually provided by its mother or other maternal relations, were vegetable foods which grow directly from the earth. Now a child's first foods are likely to be store bought, but with time it begins to eat 'bush' foods. Food of the country gives a child body–one shares flesh with country, and country, like the earth more generally, can be understood as a life-giving and nurturing presence.

Women's nurturance is expressed in a ritual called 'cooking the baby' (*julpara*) which women perform for their children and daughters' children during the first year of life. Carried out without ostentation, and frequently in the presence of men who witness but do not participate, this small ritual brings the child out of the ground, 'cooking' it to make it strong, healthy, and 'grounded'. The first and essential stage of the ritual is usually organised by the infant's maternal grandmother. She collects some termite mound (called 'antbed'; *martumartu*), cooks it on hot ashes, crushes it, and mixes it with water to make a slurry. She rubs the infant with this mixture, and gives some of the murky water to her daughter to drink, for antbed is said to bring down the mother's milk. Usually a fragrant grass is also mixed into the slurry, although this is not essential; women from different areas use different grasses (*Cymbopogon bombycinus*, Ngarinman; *Sehima nervosum*, Bilinara). In later stages the child is placed in the ground, first with only its head above ground, later with its upper torso above ground. Other items are used to make the slurry for these later stages, usually ashes from particular plants such as pandanus (*Pandanus spp*) which are said to have healing and strengthening qualities. The bark of the *jangarla* tree (*Sesbania formosa*) makes the infant very black, and there are some indications that women formerly used this slurry on half-caste infants in the hopes of deceiving the police and welfare officers who were supposed to take such children away to institutions.

There are many symbolic resonances in this ritual. 'Cooking the baby' replicates the process by which Dreamings emerged from the ground. Detaching the child from its extra-human origins and delivering it both from and to the earth as a complete (cooked) human being, this ritual seems also to autochthonise the person. Born of woman, and by woman 'born' of earth, the infant becomes a person with specific attachments to country. The fragrant grass may also give to the person the smell by which country and Dreamings will know the person (chapter 7).

Women now give birth in hospital or at a local clinic. Until about 1970 many babies were 'born in the bush', as women say. Being 'cooked' in or on the ground, and, formerly, being born onto the ground, confer rights to place, expressed as rights to knowledge. Riley Young stated:

> Because this ground belong to Aboriginal people. Aboriginal people been born la this ground. What they call it this ground, he's [she's] the mother. He's the mother. Used to be born la this ground. No hospital, no needle, no medicine. Used to be working by cooking by ashes. Make this. Any boy been born la this ground, him been makem strong by cooking by ashes. Make it strong. Because this ground is the hospital. Even me, [I] been born la this ground. My mother been used to rub me with the ground, makem me black one, same as that coal. Used to get that coal, grindem up. Or get a pandanus, or spinifex. Put em in and roastem up in the ground, making me strong. That's what they been do: this Law, la this place. Early days. Because I never been born by top of the hospital. I been born by ground. Because I know this Law.

Life, strength, place, and rights all derive from birth and women's nurturance. In addition, every person has at least two social identities which are associated with skin and hair and, like flesh, derive from the mother (chapter 6).

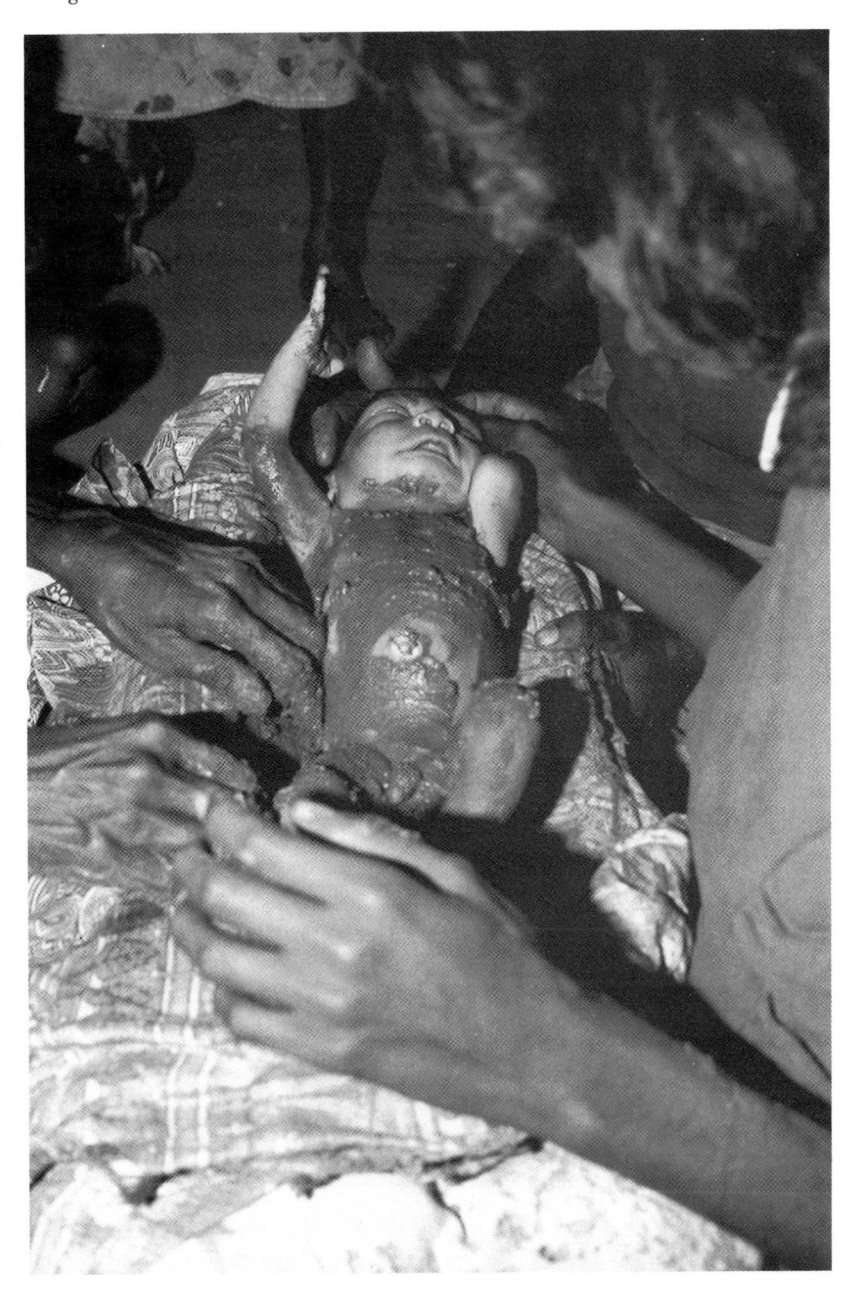

Little Harry, Mabel's grandson, being rubbed with slurry, April 1982.

Mabel Mirmir is cooking the termite mound which she will use to make a slurry in which to 'cook' her daughter's son, April 1982.

Other identities, types of strength, place, and rights derive from the father. People say that blood 'follows' the father. Just how this happens is not public knowledge in Yarralin, but it is taken to be fact. Fathers do have rights in their children and their sharing of blood is one basis for these rights. So while we belong to our mother and mother's brothers because we share the same body (milk, life), we also belong to our father by sharing the same blood.

In contrast to milk, blood is diffuse. It can be used as an identifier for many kinds of belonging, and at the most general level people say that we all have the same blood–we are all human. According to Hobbles, 'all people can come together. We all one blood. One blood, different skin, one land'.

'Women's blood'–the blood of menstruation and childbirth–

belongs to women totally and absolutely. Men rarely refer to it, except perhaps to say that it is dangerous to young men. Women discuss it only privately; their knowledge is secret.

Living and dying

When a human being is fully alive Yarralin people say that the person is *punyu* (Ngarinman language). *Punyu* is variously translated as good, strong, healthy, happy, knowledgeable ('smart'), socially responsible (to 'take a care'), beautiful, clean, and 'safe' both in the sense of being within the Law and in the sense of being cared for. This is a complete state of being. The person who is knowledgeable is best able to live within the Law and can expect to be strong, healthy, happy, and so on, while the person who is at odds with the Law is in physical as well as social danger and can expect to become ill as well as to face the anger and retaliation of others (Reid 1983 provides an excellent analysis of social and cultural management of health and illness among Arnhem Land people).

I understand *punyu* to be a state of being which involves living in the fullness of life, maintaining one's own health, promoting that of others, and promoting the health of the whole world. *Punyu*–the fullness of life–is a state which must be nurtured. When Yarralin people talk of 'growing people' they refer to actions which include feeding, protecting, singing, and teaching. The term does not distinguish between physical, mental, social, and spiritual being, nor does it distinguish between country, Dreamings, and people: these are all part of being alive.

Healthy relationships can be reversed through inadvertant damage to country or Dreamings; they can also be damaged intentionally. Sorcery is initiated by humans and causes another person to 'lose body' rather than gain body. Body loss is 'sickness'; it may be accompanied by vomiting and diarrhea, or it may consist of pain accompanied by an overall weakness including lack of appetite.

Near Daguragu there is a grasshopper Dreaming site which can be used in this way. If a person wants to diminish or destroy another, they go to this site and draw a picture of a human being on the stone, calling out the name of the person to be afflicted. Not long after, the person under attack will begin to feel pain in the belly like something eating at their vital organs from the inside. The Dreaming is at work: a human being is in the process of being consumed by grasshoppers. If the intent was to diminish but not to kill, the sorcerer will stop the process before death occurs by going back to the Dreaming site to wash out the drawing. Alternatively, any interested person can wash out the sorcery drawing and stop the sickness, but it is important not only to halt the physical symptoms but also to locate and deal with the cause of hostility.

There are many other ways to kill people which involve similar

Figure 5 Line drawing of a sorcery painting

processes. People can sing songs, insert objects into other people, draw pictures on any one of many Dreaming sites; the result is that life drains away from the victim. Fat, as we have seen, is a major indicator of life; *yimaruk* is often transferred through fat, and fat animals are prized because to eat them is to become strong. In humans and other animals the kidney fat is especially significant, and some sorcerers are said to specialize in stealing people's kidney fat. The result for the victim is inevitably death.

Men say that women can perform sorcery, but I have no indications of women ever doing so. While nobody ever admits publicly to trying to kill another person surreptitiously, there are many stories about these practices, all of which involve men as the actors, and many men claim to have halted the process on others' behalf. There is no doubt in anyone's mind that women can and do kill people, but their methods may be different.

There are also various means by which sorcery can be reversed. With the grasshopper method, the sorcery painting can be washed out. Clever people can remove foreign objects from the body, or, in earlier times, insert new replacement body parts. But in many instances sorcery is successful, for it is not always possible to remove the intent to kill. If the appropriate means have been used, there may be nothing that the victim and their relations can do about it. An important part of halting sorcery, then, is to seek for causes of hostility and attempt to repair the damaged social relationships which inspired the act.

In 1985 the prehistorian Darrell Lewis, Allan Young and his family, and I visited a boab tree ('bottle tree'; *Adansonia gregorii*) that is a

Allan Young Najukpayi rubbing out a sorcery design from a Dreaming tree in his father's country, September 1986. (D. Lewis)

Walujapi (black-headed python) Dreaming. As we walked around the base looking at the various initials and brands that had been carved into it by Europeans over the years, we were surprised to see a small human figure. Allan Young was immediately concerned that this might be a sorcery figure, and he began speculating about who might have put it there and for whom it might be intended. The tree is in his country; it is his and his countrymen's responsibility to assure that harm does not come to others from his country. Later that year he identified the probable victim, and this gave him some insight into the probable perpetrator and his motives.

Later still he returned to the tree, scraped off the image, rubbed the scar with animal fat, and spoke to the Dreaming, telling her not to kill anyone. The victim recovered.

People do get sick and die; the evidence of sorcery is always at hand. There are a number of ways to test the proposition that a sick person is a victim of sorcery. The first step, of course, is to consider possible motives. Usually these are not hard to come by; there is no one who can honestly say that they have never offended anyone. An analysis of dreams may also contribute, for people say that a victim may dream of the Dreaming species identified with the killer. In extreme cases, an ordeal may be organised. I saw one ordeal which was held for a man who had been sent home from hospital because the European prognosis was that there was nothing to be done for his overtaxed heart, high blood pressure, and diabetes. His relations saw the matter differently; his father and father's brother asked that all the men in the surrounding communities come to the dying man's camp. There each man rubbed the dying man with fat and with their own sweat, while speaking softly in his ear to remind him that they were friends and relations who did not want to harm him.

The men explained to me that if one of the men present was the killer, the victim's body and Dreamings would recognise him. The dying man's hair would stand on end and he would fall over in a faint or coma. I was told, as a general principle, that the relations of the sick person would then intercede, asking the sorcerer to save their countryman's life and promising to make good whatever wrong the sorcerer had perceived that had prompted such action. In this case the fathers said that they intended to corral the murderer and force him to save their son's life. None of the men who rubbed the victim with fat and sweat was identified as a killer; the conclusion was that the killer was not present.

Punyu is not confined to humans. When people are attacked, country suffers, and when the country is damaged, its people suffer (chapters 6, 7). When people and country are *punyu* life is nurtured, and both remain strong, healthy, and fruitful.

Once an achievable state for all portions of the cosmos, *punyu* is now more an ideal than an actuality. It is, nonetheless, the way things ought to be. Very little of Yarralin people's social and ecological environment can be characterised as *punyu*. Few individuals are genuinely healthy; the country is suffering from degradation caused by European land use, and many Dreaming sites are under threat or have been damaged or destroyed by Europeans. Furthermore, many Yarralin people are not certain that they can manage these threats, and this is an even more debilitating absence of *punyu*. Daly referred to the Christian God, expressing the deep concern for dying relationships in a damaged and suffering earth that was characteristic of many adults when worry and despair came upon them: 'God can make you die. He'll take all the soul, you lose your body. Next time he'll take your spirit.'

People frequently say the the world is dying because of the way Europeans have grasped and managed both country and people. Their assertions have a political component, of course, but they also indicate that while knowledge is, in one sense, inherent in humans, it is primarily learned and managed. Yarralin people point to knowledge as a marker of their rights of 'ownership'–rights which they believe to have been in no way abrogated by conquest. They do not say that Europeans have no rights or knowledge; rather, Europeans' rights and knowledge are located elsewhere, and they have never taken the trouble to learn from the people who know this place. In the words of one of the Bilinara men at Pigeon Hole: 'We follow father, *jawaji* [mother's father], *kaku* [father's father]. That's the Law from beginning day. *Kartiya* [Europeans] got no brain like that. They don't understand, when they come from big city'.

Dead Bodies

Death separates the body: life leaves and the flesh decays. At death the person fractures into a number of different portions. Most frequently a dead person is referred to as a dead body, and it is up to the listener to determine the context which would specify what portion of the dead body is being referred to, or to accept the ambiguity of the statement. Specifics relating to the numbers of, and terms for, portions of the dead body are subject to considerable variation among individuals, and include Ngarinman, Ngaliwurru, Gurindji, and Mudbura terms, as well as Kriol, and English terms which are not used consistently. Some people have accommodated Christian teachings within a general framework of ideas about spirits, but few people use Christian ideas in precisely the same way, and some people have no interest in such accommodation.

The other side of this story is that when confronted with a specific death, Yarralin people do come to a set of conclusions about the likely fate of the portions of that person, although it may take some time for the final determinations to be made. Learning about the process of interpretive decision-making is hampered in this context by the fact that it is believed to be dangerous to talk about a recently deceased person. I found that the context in which my questions were most pertinent was also the one in which people preferred not to speak openly and explicitly about these matters. The following discussion necessarily expresses some of the range and variation of terms and explanations, while seeking grounds of similarity so as to draw out the underlying beliefs.

In Aboriginal English the terms for 'dead' are 'finished', 'washed away', 'gone', 'lost', and 'home'. In Ngarinman the terms are *tampang* (lacking life; finished), and *lurpu* (go back). These terms refer to two processes. 'Finished' 'gone', 'lost', and 'washed away' refer to the termination of that which is unique and will never be replaced. This is the first part of the dingo Law; unlike the moon, who dies and comes back as himself, human beings finish and stay finished forever. The second part of the dingo Law of death is that human beings do not terminate only in bones and dust. 'Home' refers to the disposition of parts of the once living human: bones should be returned to a person's home country, another part will remain on earth, and another part is likely to leave this earth. In the context of life human individuals are for the most part inseparable; death is the context in which parts separate and in which the separate parts endure forever.

When a person dies their *yimaruk* 'goes free'. A few people suggested that *yimaruk* goes 'two ways': one part stays on earth and one part goes to heaven with the missionaries. I have never been certain whether this assertion represented a belief or a speculation. Nor have

I been certain that it is regarded as an improvement over the old way. A few people treated this idea as an acceptable alternative; others treated it as a concession to the missionaries. Some rejected it entirely, and others felt that they would like to have a look at heaven before they committed their dead body to it. Daly appeared to consider it as yet another form of European appropriation.

Some people identify *yimaruk* most closely with bones, for like bones it endures in the world. Before Europeans came into the Victoria River valley, dead bodies were placed in tree platforms while the flesh fell away and the wind scattered the traces of that person. When only bones were left, people returned to the tree and removed them. Skulls were rubbed with red ochre, and the remaining bones were wrapped in paperbark. Bones were sent around for all the dead person's relations to cry over. Finally they were returned to earth: placed in a cave in the dead person's country. Occasionally they were taken out and rubbed with fat and red ochre to improve the health of the country. As country grew the person, so bones nourish the country that gave them life, and some people say that part of the reason why the country is not as rich as it used to be is that people no longer put bones back as they did formerly. Big Mick explained: 'We never think about that bones, [we] not take 'em out [anymore] and put red ochre and fat. That [used to] make it good for anything, goanna, sugarbag, that makes fat food that country.'

Yarralin people say that bones endure forever. They are well aware that bones disintegrate over time, but in their view this process is not one of destruction. Rather, bones remain even though they are no longer visible, and traces of *yimaruk*, or whatever named form of life people identify with bones, also remain. As bones disintegrate they become part of the earth, as does life. In this way country contains its own life, Dreaming life, and the traces of all those other lives that belonged to that country. Plants, fish, animals, and birds and people are all made healthy through the presence of bones.

Some people distinguish between *yimaruk*–life that becomes new life–and *yingyingamanu*: life as it leaves the dying person. The terminology is not crucial. What matters is the understanding that part of a person's life is identified with their breath, or wind, and that as they die life leaves with the wind. It may be seen as a shooting star, returning to its own country if the person died far from home. If it is already home it may still be associated with a star as it passes over to another body to be born again.

Old Tim's account of his father shows some variations: his father appeared with a rainbow rather than with a star. Old Tim Yilngayari and his wife Mary Rutungali told me about Tim's father's death:

OT: They been put him on the gravy [in the grave], I'll tell you. You savvy that big hole? That big hole right longa store, Katherine store? You been look?

DR: Yeah.

OT: That's the gravy belonga my old man.

DR: Oh, true?
OT: And him been, him been get up Rainbow now.
DR: Him been get up Rainbow?
MR: Yeah. Get up.
OT: That my daddy longa Darwin now, alive.
MR: Him there now.
OT: Him there longa Darwin la buffalo shooter, Marrakai [Station]. I was been there. My old man still alive. Him been dead there [Katherine], and that thing been come out, Rainbow, and him fly up. Him been there too, going longa Darwin. You know my old man too fucking too clever. Really clever.
MR: Him been come back, isn't it? Him been come back now?
OT: Him been go over Marrakai, and sit down about longa Marrakai. I was went out from here. I been sending telegram, and I said my old man been come la Bagot [Aboriginal reserve in Darwin] . . . Him been takem me longa Marrakai, longa buffalo shooter . . . I been go down there, longa Bagot, I been send word, telegram, that my old man been come. My mother been come, all my brothers, they been come see em him. And mother been go and cry longa him. Old man been cry longa me. Finish. They been take up me, take me longa same place. I been tell all the government [this was in the days when Aborigines had to have permission to travel]: 'I'm go down to my old man. Oh, I just go longa daddy, stop for four more weeks.'

In contrast to *yimaruk,* there is another spirit which embodies all that is unique in a human being. *Manngyin* is a term which many Yarralin people use to talk about this part of a person once the person has died. *Manngyin* is connected to flesh and organs, and when a person dies and is buried this portion of the body gets up again. Old Tim considered himself to be an expert on *manngyin.* In his words:

When him dead, his body, he leave his bones, he get up from hole longa grave; long hair, body still in ground. He get up, look around country, up to chest, the rest underground. Come up more, up to waist, [the] rest under ground. Come up, look self: 'I'm born. I'm here.'
Talks to himself in graveyard place. Get up to thigh, look around country, look around: 'Where my wife? I like to go down to my wife.'
Nother little boy come along back behind. Dead man [talk]: 'I've gotta go back to my wife.'
Little boy talk: 'No. You gotta go that way.'

There is considerable diversity of opinion as to where 'that way' might be. Old Tim spoke of the dead body, *manngyin,* being taken by an unborn baby back to a baby centre and waiting there to be born again in a few years' time. Others thought this interpretation was rather idiosyncratic. Far more people spoke of the *manngyin* going to the sky country. Some people, including Old Tim, say that the *manngyin* meets its previously deceased relations in the sky country, joining the sky or lightning people and eventually losing all personal relevance to the living. Once on top, *manngyin* is referred to as *yimungaya.* According to Big Mick: '*Yimungaya*–spirit goes on top. That's the dead man way. He's gone for good.' Some say that if the dead person had failed to co-operate with its relations in life, the relations would reject it in death. Under such circumstances, the *manngyin* would not go to the sky country, but rather would remain on earth (chapter 6).

The most salient feature of this part of the dead person–*manngyin* or, more rarely, *kaya* (chapter 6)–is that it can be dangerous. My understanding is that this is because it is the unique individual with intimate ties to people and all the passions of life. Unless a person dies shortly after birth or at an extraordinarily advanced age, Yarralin people believe that death is almost certainly caused through malevolent human agency, and that the dead person is angry about having died. Like the living, *manngyin* experience both sorrow and anger at death. They long for the people they love and want to kill those who made them die. Yarralin people believe that out of love and loneliness a *manngyin* may return to take its relations or spouse with it on its journey to the sky country, thereby causing them to die. Conversely, if a *manngyin* feels that its family has not shown proper concern to prevent or avenge its death, it will turn its anger on its own relatives, killing them one by one.

When a death occurs, all traces of the dead person are removed. The personal effects are buried with the body, and the community is swept with fragrant green leaves to clear away the tracks and the smell of the dead person. These are signs of individual identity which must be removed both so that the relatives of the deceased will not be reminded of their loss and so that the *manngyin* will find no traces of itself to remind it of having been a living person. The camp in which the person died is smoked out with green leaves, and everybody moves out of that house. The person's name cannot be spoken.

Yarralin people now bury dead bodies rather than putting them in trees. If the person died in the hospital, or if the body was sent to town for an autopsy, the body is buried in a standard European coffin. Otherwise, if the person dies at home, the body is covered with the person's personal belongings such as clothes and the whole bundle is wrapped in the deceased's swag (bedding plus tarpaulin) and taken to the graveyard. A few men dig a hole for the body and when it is ready all the men, women and children go into the graveyard where the body lies in the coffin or wrapped in the swag. Adults, particularly those who were close to the deceased, cry and attempt to gash themselves with stones or whatever else is at hand. Other relatives restrain them so that they cannot do themselves serious injury. After each adult has had the opportunity to cry over the dead body, the children are brought forward. One by one they are held over the dead body and the dead person is told 'this is your kinsman (specifying the relationship), you'll have to leave now', or words to that effect. There is no set formula; the intent is to send the *yimaruk* home and at the same time to remind the *manngyin* that it should feel pity for its young relations and not come bothering them.

Women and children leave the graveyard before the body is buried, although a few close relations stay, at a distance, to continue the haunting crying which is women's expression of grief and loss. As the last of the women leave they brush the ground behind them with green leaves to clear away traces of footprints and smells. Men remain behind to discuss and assess the causes of death.

Relatives of a dead person do all they can for their lost loved one. It is only when someone else dies, not a relation at all, but a possible killer (or close relative of one), that they begin to feel 'satisfied' with respect to vengeance. And still, as long as family members feel the pain of their loss the dead person is very much present. As long as the memories are fresh and raw the dead person is there. It may be years before people will again whisper the name of a dead person, saying, 'no matter, him only *yimaruk* now'.

Yarralin people also believe that dead bodies continue to live in their own country. Neither the depersonalised form of *yimaruk*, nor the dangerous form of *manngyin*, bodies in country are a life form which is benevolent, personal, and localised. Although sometimes identified with bones because they keep the country productive, most people simply refer to these forms as old people, dead bodies, or *ngurramarla* which is glossed as 'owners' (chapter 5). When Yarralin people go out hunting, fishing, collecting, or simply visiting country, they call out to their dead relatives, identifying themselves and telling the bodies to make the country good for them. They usually call out for what they want, and mention that they have children with them. Hector Wartpiyarri of Pigeon Hole gave an example: 'I'm hungry. I want your goanna, sugarbag, bush yam. I got all the the *karu* [children] here hungry'.

Many people stress the importance of living near the dead relatives, both for the sake of remembrance, and for the care they provide. Historical remembrance is vital to people's sense that there have been too many deaths, far more than have been avenged. To be near the dead is to remember the invasion which brought about so many deaths, and to sustain the will to resist. Living near the dead also indicates the intention to die in one's own country and to join one's forebears as benevolent and responsible 'owners' of country.

Allan Young spoke most eloquently about the benevolence of the dead, and his words would find agreement among other Yarralin people:

> At night, camping out, we talk and those people listen . . . When we're walking, we're together. We got dead body there behind to help . . . Even if you're far away in a different country, you still call out to mother and father, and they can help you for dangerous place. And for tucker [food] they can help you.

5 *An Emu is not a Catfish*

Yarralin people define themselves with reference to a number of social categories which, like Dreaming strings, cross-cut each other to provide a rich set of identities. These categories are said to derive from Dreaming; their existence is defined as Law. Some categories form sets which are abstract and elegant closed systems–an intellectual delight for those who enjoy puzzles. Others form sets which involve a profound sharing of physical being. Yet others depend on geography as the nexus of shared identity. Together they span the major parameters of intellectual, social, physical and spiritual relationships within the cosmos.

Skins

Yarralin people use a system of social categories which anthropologists call subsections. These categories of people are called 'skins' in Kriol; there are sixteen skins which can be grouped into eight brother/sister pairs. Many anthropologists treat this system as an eight-part system in which sisters are subsumed under the brothers. This is a reasonable approach given that the system works on an eight-part division and that there are numerous contexts in which brothers and sisters are grouped together. However, when this system is examined over time it is evident that brothers and sisters reproduce their categories differently. Accordingly, I do not conflate brother and sister.

In a system of eight brother/sister pairs, in which each skin is related to every other, diagrams can be drawn in a number of ways, depending on the emphasis and explanation required. We will start with the basic question of who gives birth to whom. This is how I was introduced into the system. On my seventh day in Yarralin the oldest woman, Gracie Kanku, came up to me and said, 'You are Namija. You got to call me "mommy". Me Namira. You can come to my camp and bring me sugar.'

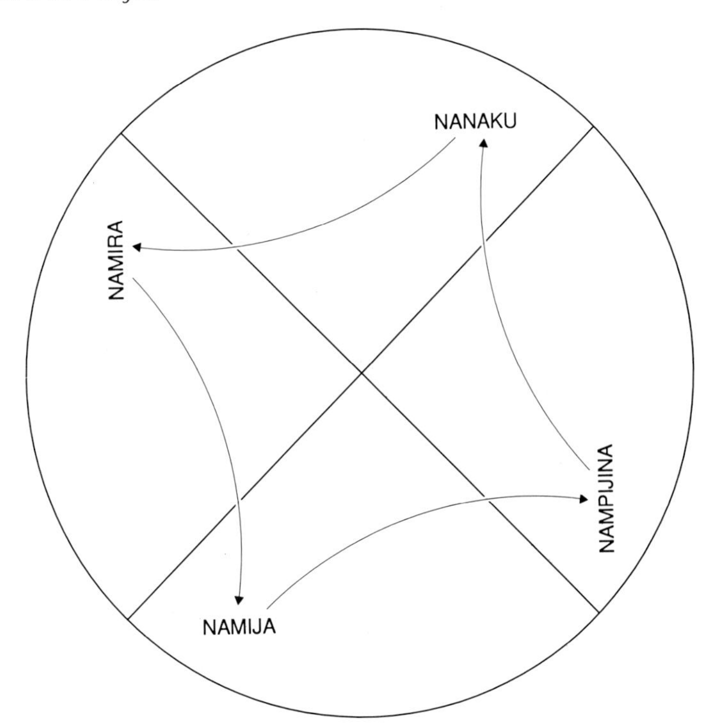

Figure 6 Circle of women, showing who gives birth to whom

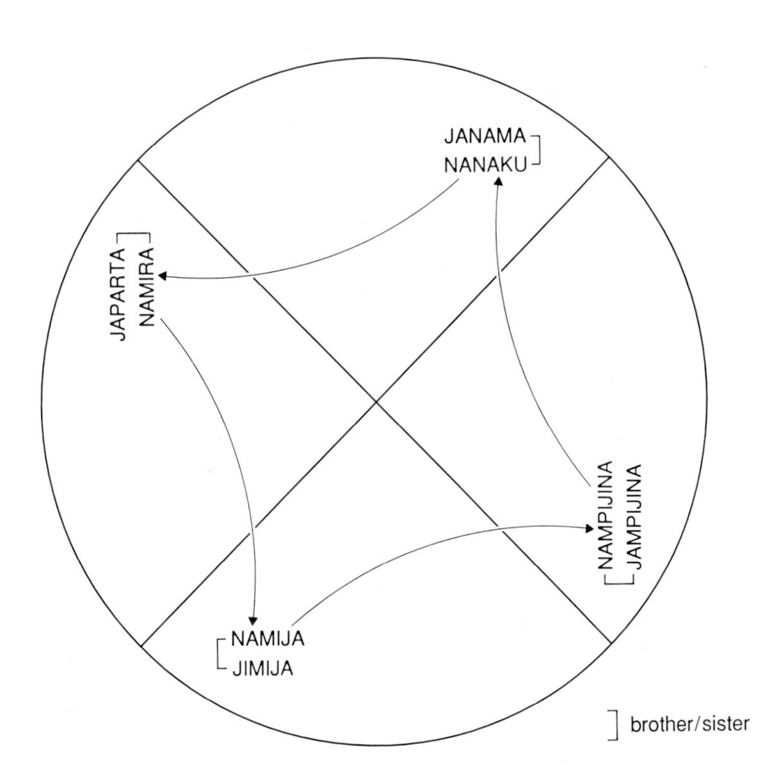

Figure 7 Circle of women, including brothers

Women give birth to women in a never-ending circle. Namira gives birth to Namija, Namija to Nampijina, Nampijina to Nanaku and Nanaku to Namira. Namija's mother is Namira, her grandmother is Nanaku. Her daughter is Nampijina and her granddaughter is also Nanaku. This is one of two circles of birth. Neither circle ever gets 'mixed up' because women always give birth correctly: 'Children always come out of the right one mother.'

Namija's brother is Jimija. They are conceptualised as sharing body as they are both born of Namira. Nampijina is the daughter out of 'their belly', the belly belonging to brother and sister.

As shown in figure 7, these four brother/sister pairs make a circle: Namija/Jimija, Nampijina/Jampijina, Nanaku/Janama, Namira/Japarta. All eight belong together, sharing a set of matrilineal identities.

This circle constitutes one half of the subsection system. The other half consists of marriage partners. Namija's 'proper' or 'straight' husband is Jangala. Her brother Jimija marries Jangala's sister Nangala. Sister and brother marry sister and brother, bringing together the two halves of the system into one whole.

This other half forms another circle of women: Nangala gives birth to Nalyiri and Nalyiri gives birth to Nawurla, Nawurla gives birth to Nangari, Nangari gives birth to Nangala.

When Yarralin people explained how the parts of this system relate to each other, they emphasised the idea that the system, as a whole, is complete. That is, over time, through marriages and births, all the different categories circle back. This is best seen by looking at an example. In structural terms, Namija's brother Jimija marries Nangala while Namija marries Jangala. Out of two brother/sister pairs

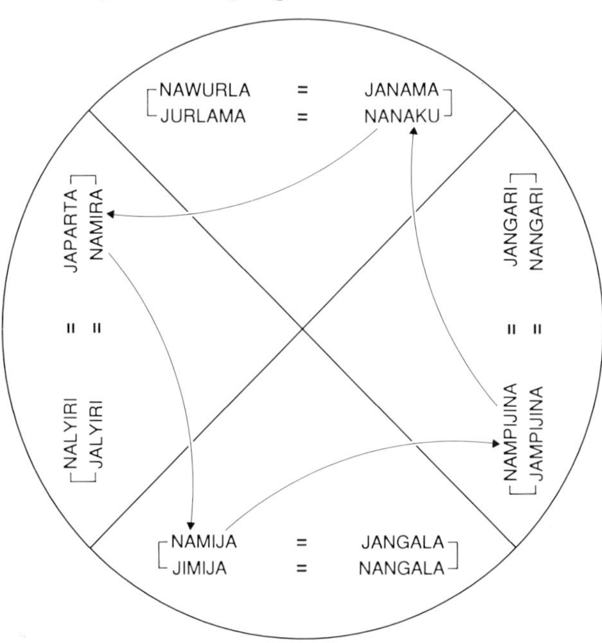

Figure 8 Circle of women, including brothers and marriage partners (= indicates marriage)

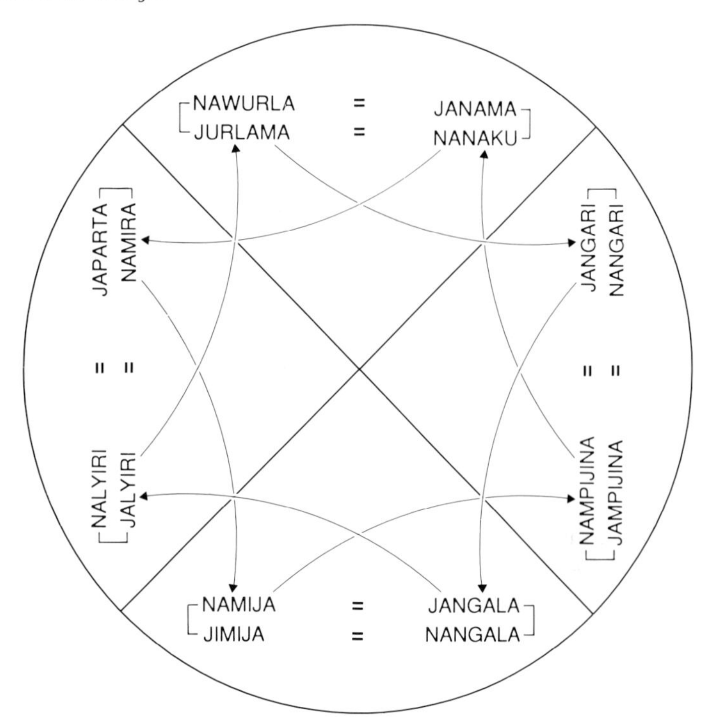

Figure 9 Sixteen subsection categories showing circles of women, brothers and marriage partners

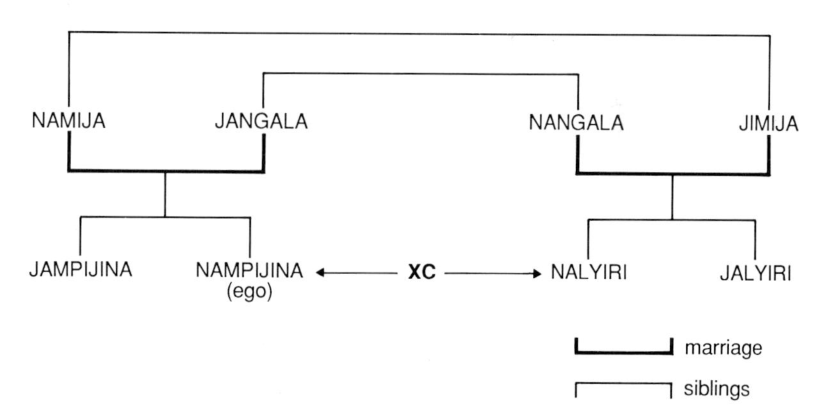

Figure 10 The cross-cousin relationship

come two sets of children. This second generation consists of cross-cousins; from the viewpoint of Nampijina, Nalyiri and Jalyiri are both her father's sister's children and her mother's brother's children.

These cross-cousins do not marry each other. Rather, each brother/sister pair marries a different brother/sister pair and the third generation marries back. Out of a brother and sister in the first generation, the second generation consists of one set of cross cousins. Out of these individuals the third generation consists of two sets of cross cousins and these sets marry each other.

Through a process of marrying out and having children, brother and sister initiate new generations. These lines do not ramify forever. Structurally they must return for the system is closed.

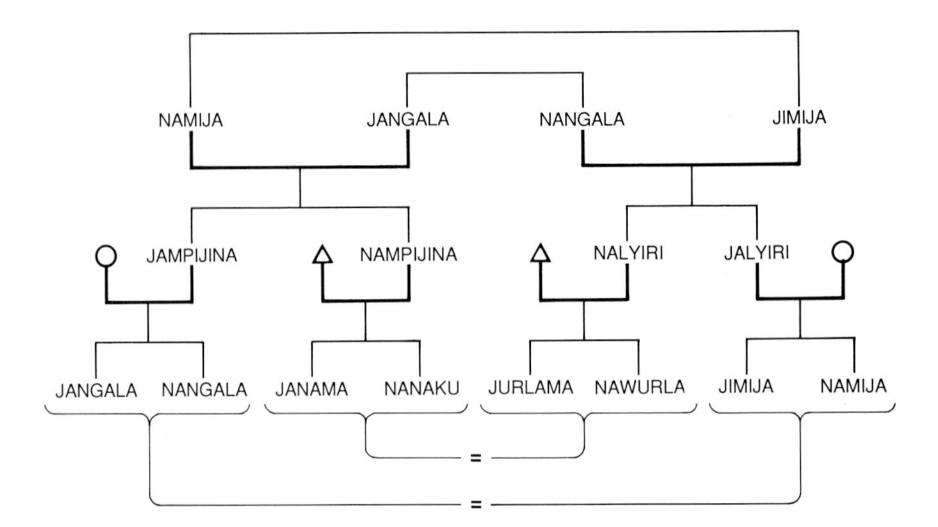

Figure 11 Three generations, showing marriage partners out of cross-cousins

Lines of women move in circles. When we look at lines of men we see a different pattern. Jimija's wife gives birth to Jalyiri, Jalyiri's wife gives birth to Jimija, and so on.

Out of the brothers comes a pattern that repeats in alternate generations, so that each line of men consists of two skins. With the eight male skins, there are four lines of men.

The system as shown in figure 13 obtains when people follow the marriage rules, but frequently they do not. A person's skin identity always derives from their mother. This means that a man must marry a woman of the right category if he wants the children to be of the right category in relation to him. If a man marries a woman of the 'wrong' skin then his children will be 'wrong' skin in relation to him.

Categories are linked to, but not coterminous with, kinship. Each skin stands in a particular kin-defined relationship to each other skin. The categories are widespread, and people who have never met before can, by identifying each other's skins, know how to address and behave with each other. As Namija, I call all Namija women 'sister'. All Jimija men are my 'brothers', all Jangala men my

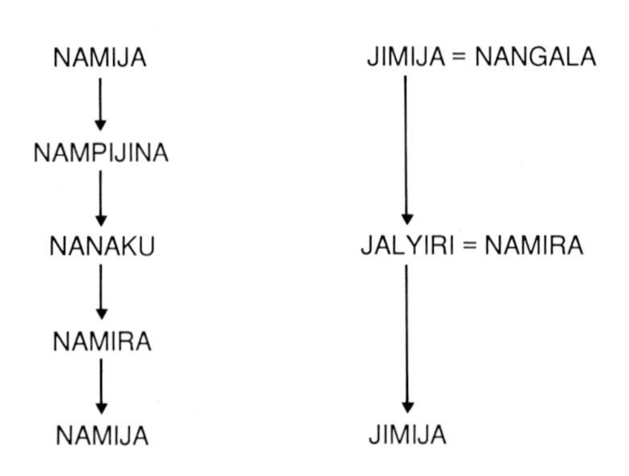

Figure 12 A line of men contrasted with a circle of women

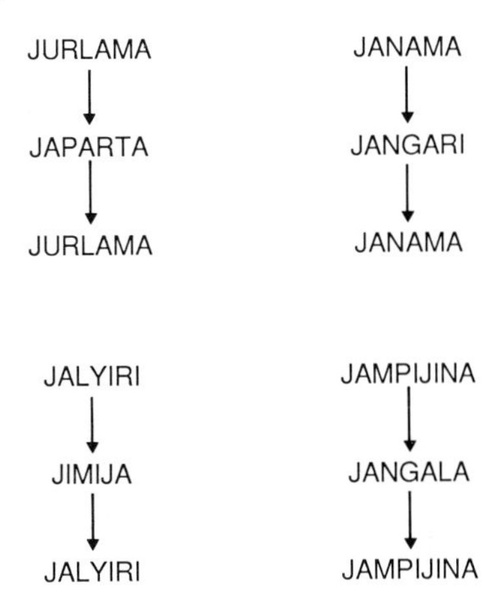

Figure 13 Lines of men

'husbands', and so on. Categories, however, do not supplant kinship (chapter 7). Rather, they are a way of classifying people, and kinship provides the mode through which classifications are socially expressed.

There is a further point to be made here. In figures 12 and 13, I have shown the relationship between a man, his son, and his son's son. In generational terms this is quite correct. Yet I believe that Yarralin people conceptualise this relationship somewhat differently. As an analogy, let us suppose that 'lines' of men are something like a light switch: if Jimija is 'off' then Jalyiri is 'on'; the succession of men always moves back and forth between the two. Diagramming them in a line may imply some sort of progress. In contrast, the analogy of a switch implies only a change of state. From Jimija to Jalyiri is a change of state; from Jalyiri to Jimija is a return to the former state. Men are frequently named after their father's father. Jimija X may have a son Jalyiri Y who has a son Jimija X and so on.

These four 'switches' are four oscillating father/son pairs which constitute one model of human perpetuation. The other model is that of women's cycles of birth: cycles which return, over time, to where they began. Each person has a place in each model. Men are placed in the circles of women alongside their sisters, while women are placed in the father/son pairs alongside their brothers. When men's and women's reproduction through time are put together, one finds the one big circle–a total system (see figure 14).

Generations and other moieties

Analytically there are two closed circles defined by birth. Together they encompass the social world as it is organised by skins. The technical term for such a bi-partite division is moiety. As a general rule, one might expect moieties to form well-recognised, perhaps even named, categories. Yarralin people do not name these circles, nor do they use the inherent division as a basis to social action. Matrilineal moieties are implicit, but, as we will see shortly, there is

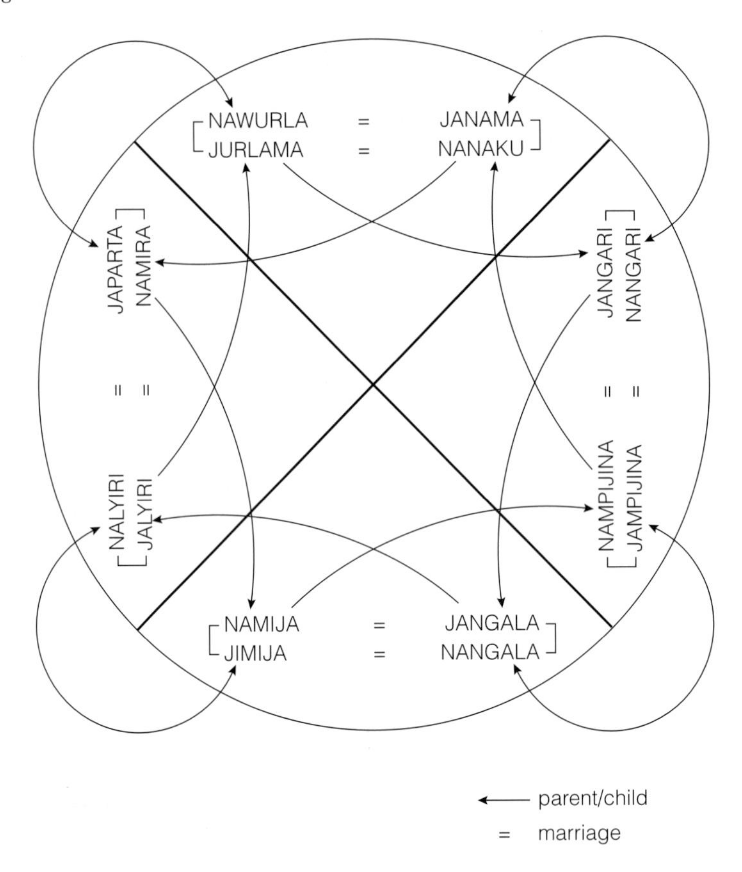

Figure 14 Circles of women and oscillating sets of men

another set of matrilineally inherited identities which add substance to the internal logic of a moiety division.

Another type of implicit moiety is that composed of paired lines of men. Neighbouring people recognise patrimoieties (McConvell and Hagen 1981; McConvell and Palmer 1979; Bauman, Akerman, and Palmer 1984), but I have been unable to elicit any information on these categories. There is no local term to specify this type of organisation. Other researchers indicate that their primary salience is in the context of men's secret 'business' and it may be this fact that has limited my attempts.

Yarralin people do articulate a type of moiety division which anthropologists frequently term generation moieties. The Ngarinman and Ngaliwurru term is *purnturtu.* While everybody agrees on the existence of *purnturtu* and on the composition of the two moieties, different people explain the categories differently. Women, for the most part, define *purnturtu* in terms of birth: a woman always gives birth to children of the opposite *purnturtu.* In contrast, several men spoke of it in terms of marriage: one should always marry within one's own *purnturtu.* One man, like many others who had married wrongly, joked about it saying that he had 'married for bullet'–men of the

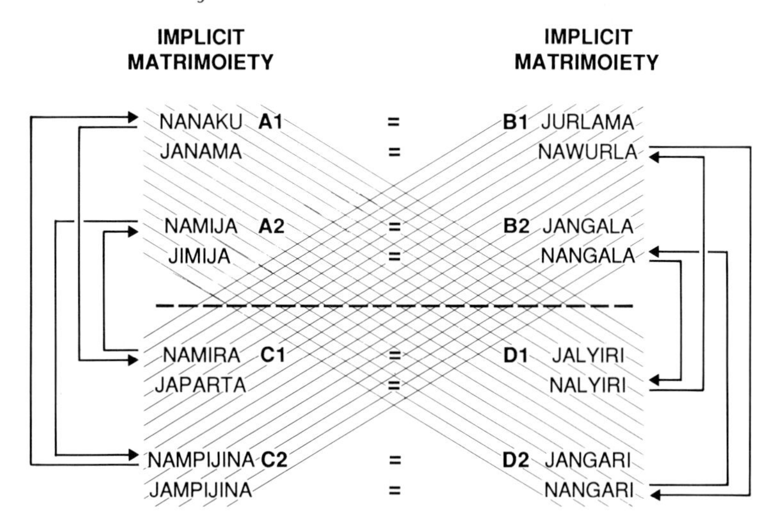

Figure 15 Moiety divisions (adapted from Bauman, Akerman and Palmer 1984:44)

opposite *purnturtu* could have shot him for 'stealing' one of 'their' women. His joke was only funny because people would never take a breach of *purnturtu* endogamy to be a matter requiring bullets. There are rules which are taken so seriously that they are never joked about, but *purnturtu* endogamy is not one of them.

Another man spoke of *purnturtu* in terms of 'business' which belongs strictly to men, saying that it is an organising principle in that context. Yet another man spoke of it in terms of paired cross-cousins. That is, each *purnturtu* is made up of two separate sets of cross cousins; each set marries another set (cf. figure 11) and has children who make up the opposite moiety.

These differing explanations do not contradict each other. Rather, they show some of the variations in how one set of categories may be thought about differently by different people or in different contexts.

The diagram shows how various moieties cross-cut each other (figure 15). A1, A2, D1, D2, etc. here are standard anthropological signs designating subsections, allowing people to consult technical literature without having to depend on localised terminology.

Earth and water, flesh and hair

Circles of women are further articulated through a system which may be termed matrilineal identities or Dreamings. The Ngarinman and

Ngaliwurru terms are *ngurlu* or, more rarely, *kartpi*. Patrick McConvell, a linguist, suggests that the term *ngurlu* may be derived from a word meaning 'seed' (McConvell and Hagen 1981:28), but there seems to be no overt sense of this connotation. I have found that Yarralin people sometimes use the term *ngurlu* to refer to skins (subsections), and that sometimes they use the word for hair–*kartpi*–to refer to *ngurlu*. A few Yarralin people associate hair colour with *ngurlu*, and say that old people used to be able to look at one's arm hair and know one's *ngurlu* (see also McConvell and Hagen, ibid.).

Ngurlu is a relationship between people and one or more plant or animal species. People of the same *ngurlu* share the same flesh with each other and with their *ngurlu* species. This category of identity is inherited through women, and one's *ngurlu* is identical to one's mother's. Men and women all have a *ngurlu* which they acquire through their mother; the sisters of a sibling set transmit their *ngurlu* identity to their children, while the brothers marry women of different *ngurlu* and thus have children whose *ngurlu* is different from their own.

Ngurlu are localised within the matrilineal circles, and each circle contains more than one *ngurlu*. Namija's circle contains flying fox/rainbow, and catfish/brolga. These circles run concurrently: out of all the women in the Namija category at Yarralin, some are flying fox/rainbow and some are catfish/brolga. Nangala's circle contains emu, sugarbag (honey), sugarleaf (an insect exudate which Yarralin people class as a form of vegetable food), and a seed bearing tree called *yimiyaka* (*Brachychiton* spp).

My skin is Namija. I was also assigned flying fox *ngurlu* on the basis of my close relationship to my 'sister', Mirmir. She is flying fox because her mother and her mother's mother were flying fox. Mirmir's children are all flying fox, as are mine, and her daughter's children are flying fox. There is a relationship of sameness between catfish Namija women and flying fox Namija women in that they are all Namija, all sisters; yet there is also a relationship of difference in that some are catfish and some are flying fox. Those who are both Namija and flying fox are closer to each other than they are to catfish Namija.

Ngurlu categories classify various portions of the cosmos. Catfish is 'fish-kind' (*yawunyung*); sugarleaf is 'plant-kind' (*mangarinyung*), emu is 'meat-kind' (*ngarinyung*); and sugarbag is honey or 'sweet-kind' (*ngalunyung*). Flying fox and rainbow are also classed as light rain; in this context flying fox is also termed *walijitpari*. Yarralin people gloss this term as 'hanging upside down looking into the water'. Brolga is classed as *kulumarrangarna*, glossed as 'on top' (sky-dweller, according to McConvell and Hagen 1981:31). Brolga and catfish together are classed as dark rain. Emu, in contrast, is also termed *yarnanganja*– 'ground' or 'earth'.

Relationships within and between *ngurlu* open outward to plants, animals, the elements, and seasonality. For example, the particular catfish identified as *ngurlu* is a dark one called *jarlalka* which is associated with flood waters. Brolgas come to the Yarralin area in the early part of the wet season, and they, too, are associated with rain and flood. Rain and the wet season are the connecting links between water and sky, associated with the Namija moiety, and the rainbow and flying foxes are both intimately connected to rain. Within the opposite moiety, emu, the earth, is related to vegetable foods and honey through wind. For example, people say that the spots on the emu's legs are where the wind blew sugarleaf onto them. This moiety is related to land, wind, sun, and the dry season when sugarleaf is harvested and emus hatch their chicks.

This level of understanding, of identifying the relationships between elements, goes right to the heart of Yarralin people's cosmology. It is not the boundaries which divide but the relationships across difference which are, ultimately, what knowledge is all about. Daly Pulkara, who is catfish *ngurlu*, said that when the brolga sings out in the sky the *jarlalka* starts to move. He explained: 'You didn't know that? That's really culture, that one.'

'MATRIMOIETY' A/C	'MATRIMOIETY' B/D
flying fox / rainbow	emu
catfish / brolga	sugarbag
	sugarleaf
	yimiyaka

Figure 16 *Ngurlu* and 'matrimoieties'

There is a pattern to *ngurlu*: All of the Namija circle (implicit matrimoiety A/C) identities relate to rain, water, and sky, while all the Nangala circle (implicit matrimoiety B/D) identities relate to dry land, sun and wind. One set of *ngurlu* signals the dry season, just as the opposite set signals the wet season. Together they comprise the totality of the annual cycle and the interactions which make possible continued life on earth.

The *ngurlu* classification is untidy compared to the subsection system. Where the subsection system is elegant, logical, and symmetrical, *ngurlu* categories are non-symmetrical. The subsection system is closed; its parts relate essentially to each other. *Ngurlu* constitute an open system; the parts relate not only to each other but also to the cosmos.

The particular species with which one's *ngurlu* is identified is called one's *warpiri*. The feelings and behaviour associated with *warpiri* are most intense with animal species. Some Yarralin people will neither kill nor eat their own *warpiri*, sometimes specifying that for them the smell is too human. Others treat it with special care if it has been killed. A few seem relatively indifferent. All Yarralin people, however, are reluctant to kill a *warpiri* species if a person of that *ngurlu* has recently died. A loss is a source of both sorrow and anger, and people prefer not to inflict further losses until those who are bereaved have had time to recover.

On the way back to Yarralin after a visit to Lingara, we spotted an emu near the road and pulled up because one of the men, a flying fox Jimija, wanted to take a shot at it. His shot wounded the emu, and the children all jumped out of the truck and raced to kill the animal. After considerable excitement with sticks, stones, guns, a wounded emu, shouting children, and barking dogs, the emu was 'finished' and brought back to the truck. All the way home Jimija protested that he had not meant to shoot the emu and had only wanted to use the gun for fun. His protestations were interrupted as other people discussed to which emu person we should give the dead bird. We took it to Allan Young (an emu man), but he said he would not have it and suggested that we take it to Old Tim. While not an emu person himself, Old Tim's wife Mary is the oldest emu person in Yarralin. Tim agreed to accept the emu. By then it was dark, which was good because people say that emus ought to be butchered in the dark; they are also related to a darkness Dreaming site. He rubbed himself with red ochre, butchered, and cooked the emu. The next day most of us ate some of it, but none of the emu people ate, for they do not like to eat their *warpiri*.

This was the first emu to have been shot following the death of an emu person at Pigeon Hole, and responsibility for the killing was consistently denied. Jimija always maintained that he had shot it by accident, and when others suggested that it was not much of an accident to have loaded the gun, pointed it at the emu, and pulled the trigger, he reminded people that the gun had no sights and that its value in hunting was something of a joke. Jimija was respected in all the other contexts of his life, and people did not hold it against him that he had shot the emu. Neither, however, did they forget. The question of his relationship to emu people surfaced again, briefly, a few years later as he lay dying. There was some suggestion then that emu people might have been angry with him, but this suspicion was quickly dispelled by emu people.

Even without recent deaths, many people treat their *warpiri* with special consideration. Once on a fishing trip, Mirmir caught a dark catfish which is her husband Daly's *warpiri*. She presented it to him with regret. He said that it would be all right to cook and eat it, but he made certain that afterwards the bones were buried in the ground. In this context he explained that *warpiri* means 'biggest sorry'. That is, the death of one's *ngurlu* species is like the death of kin–one feels sorry (sorrowful), and therefore gives the body special care.

Ngurlu categories are exogamous: one does not marry one's own *ngurlu*. This is a rule that is taken so seriously that it rarely requires discussion. Rather, *ngurlu* exogamy emerges from a set of attitudes and actions that pervade many contexts of peoples' lives. The reluctance to eat one's *warpiri*, for example, is a mirror image of the reluctance to engage sexually with people of one's own *ngurlu*. I have encountered every possible combination of 'wrong' marriages within the subsection system, but I have never heard of a marriage within the same matrilineal identity. Even in the private arena of extra-marital affairs, where people are free to express their personal preferences and individual will, they appear to observe *ngurlu* exogamy. I cannot speak with certainty, for of course I only know of those affairs which have become common knowledge; not one has involved people of the same *ngurlu*.

Through *ngurlu* a person stands in a special relationship to people of the same category and to the particular species associated with it. Being of one flesh, person and species participate in a relationship of nurturance and care. We have seen that shared body is the equivalent of shared life. With *ngurlu* it becomes clear that to share specific life places people and species in relationships of mutuality such that what happens to one member of the category has ramifications for other members of the category. The dingo Law which created humans as a particular type of being, is thus cross-cut by other 'laws' which align people with other species, creating categories whose members share flesh and life.

Ngurlu run in families, and families are related to country, so that *ngurlu* can be seen to cluster geographically. Often this appears to be the effect of other forces and interests at work, and I have yet to discern any rule or principle that associates *ngurlu* with country (cf Spencer 1914:198–9; Stanner 1979a). On the other hand, if *ngurlu* were not linked to country, we would expect them to be equally distributed, and this is not the case. At Yarralin, Lingara, and Pigeon Hole (the only communities for which I have comprehensive information) the emu people are all descended from a set of Bilinara women. Emu is an important Dreaming in Bilinara country and while it is not confined to Bilinara country it seems to define a set of people who are descended from emu Bilinara women.

Most frequently a person's *ngurlu* does relate to the country of one of their ancestors. Dreamings travelled through country, people are located in country, and it is not unusual for a person's *ngurlu* species also to be a Dreaming being who was active in country to which that person has rights. Where *ngurlu* and other sets of identities coincide, people often express a particularly strong feeling for that country and that Dreaming being, but I do not know of any instance in which *ngurlu* identity confers rights to country independently of a genealogical link to country.

Locative identities

There are several identites which Yarralin people acquire from their fathers. The most significant in public life is *kuning* which is glossed as 'Dreaming'. *Kuning* is the term for a species that shares country and responsibilities with a set of people who are related to each other through their fathers. Usually, *kuning* is one or more Dreaming beings localised in one's father's country. Where skin categories relate people to other people, and *ngurlu* categories relate people most specifically to other people and to plant and animal species, *kuning* relates people to other people, to species, and to country.

With *kuning,* the nexus of shared being is country. All of the people who share a *kuning* are believed to be descended from related fathers who took responsibility for a particular area and associated Dreamings. These fathers are likely to have married women of different *ngurlu,* so that the category of people who share *kuning* do not necessarily share *ngurlu.* People who are related to each other through *kuning* ought not to marry each other, and my information on marriages shows that this rule of exogamy is regularly observed.

People and their *kuning* share rights to, and responsibilities for, particular country. Some Yarralin people say that a set of people and their *kuning* species are 'countrymen': they are all descendants of the original people and species identified with that country. Jessie Wirrpa, Allan Young, and their father's brothers' children are referred to occasionally as 'Jirrikit mob' because Jirrikit (owlet nightjar) is their *kuning.* It can hurt people's feelings to see their *kuning* species killed, but there do not appear to be any formal requirements concerning handling the dead bodies of that species.

For many people, *kuning* carries connotations of authority. Allan Young compared his *kuning* to a boss, saying that if he were to do something wrong, such as kill someone without reason, his *kuning* would take action against him. Equally, he could expect that if he were killed for no reason his *kuning* would take reprisals against the killers. The other side of authority is nurturance, a fact which Myers (1986) has analysed most eloquently with reference to Pintupi people. Person, Dreaming, species, and country share a relationship of care and nurturance, and *kuning* connotes safety and security as well as authority. However, in the context of security Yarralin people usually use the term 'Dreaming' which has a broader set of referents than simply the patrilineal *kuning*; other referents include the localised Dreamings within one's mother's father's and mother's mother's countries. Most of what can be said about *kuning* is also true for these other relationships.

There is another patrilineal category of identity which I first learned of from a Bilinara/Mudbura man at Pigeon Hole; my attempts to follow up the information with Ngarinman and Ngaliwurru people were not markedly successful. On our way back from a trip to map country we stopped at a billabong so that we women could collect some lilies and mussels. As we were leaving, one of the men said that this billabong was a crab place, and did a delightful imitation of how Dreaming crab talks. He explained that the crab belonged to him from his father, and said that the term *jamaran* denotes this category.

McConvell (McConvell and Hagen 1981; McConvell and Palmer 1979) has analysed the *jamaran* category in defining land ownership for the Gurindji and Mudbura land claims. He associates *kuning* with a local descent group or lineage and *jamaran* with a clan. In McConvell's terminology, a clan is a set of father/son pairs, skin categories identified with a particular geographical area. According to this model, a *jamaran* group, or clan, is made up of people of different *kuning*. Yarralin people spoke of these identities in ways that indicated a recognition of this type of system, but they volunteered very little information and, indeed, preferred not to emphasise these aspects of their relationships to country. It is clear that at this time people to the south and east of Yarralin organise themselves in relation to country in ways that show a stronger patrilineal structure than do Yarralin people.

McConvell's work derives from land claims, and it is important to note that the land claim procedure impels both anthropologists and claimants to define their models of local descent. 'Clan' and 'local descent group' are terms which have gained public credence as identifiers of 'traditional ownership'. Outside of the land claim context, I found that while people speak, frequently with pleasure and invariably with deep emotion, about their country and their Dreamings, they show little enthusiasm for articulating social divisions. *Jamaran* seems to be a category which is too broad to be intimate and too narrow to be politically useful. In this time of recovery from a disastrous history, Yarralin people may find that such divisions are neither sustainable nor productive.

Dora Jilpngarri is a woman who is politically astute and strong in the Law. She vigorously rejected my questions on these matters, and she declined to participate in land claim proceedings for precisely the same reason. Land claims require that at some level people sort themselves into those who will act as claimants, will assert primary responsibility for the country, and will, if successful, receive title to land. The process of sorting necesarily means that some people will be excluded. Dora and her husband Jim Wright Winkulkarri made their position absolutely clear on one occasion when I asked them about a local land claim:

DJ: Mudbura, Ngarinman, Gurindji. Everybody relations. Same language. We can answer back language [understand them, and make ourselves understood in response].

JW: Well, this is the way. This Mudbura, Gurindji, Ngarinman, Bilinara.

DJ: Bilinara, yuway [yes]. Four way.

JW: And all the same language. We hear him. We all relations together. We hearem language.

DJ: We no more chuckem [throw out] mijelb [ourselves; each other].

JW: We no more chuck it away. We right. We know the Law. Ngaliwurru, and this one.

DJ: Nungali.

JW: Nungali. All different tribes, but they understand. We understand too.

DJ: Language.

JW: Language. We give it answer back. We talking about: 'That's right. We mean like that.' We different different language but we hearem. We hearem. That's right.

DJ: We don't want to chuckem away.

JW: We don't want to chuck it away mijelb one another.

DJ: We all relations.

JW: We all relations. We living together by language. We understand. No different.

DJ: Olden time people do same.

JW: Olden time people been our relations. They been wash away. When they been wash away, same tribe, same language. They been allday living together. We here today top of that. From beginning, we here. We understand that Law. We know the everything. We know the country, we know what's that all the people, all the children, everything. Same language. But we only know the part of it [here he notes distinctions in access to knowledge], that's all. All the country ... But we still same language. We understand. We hearem one another. We give it back, answer back. We know. Because before all been footwalk all around. Travelling.

Dreaming beings walked in the shape of human beings. Their descendants include the species they became and the human beings who are intimately attached to the country which they defined. Yarralin people use the term Dreaming as a gloss both for *kuning* (patrilineally identified relationships) and for other relationships between person, species and country which are not necessarily patrilineally defined, or localised, but which are characterised by the same social, intellectual, emotional and spiritual content. Sometimes people use the term 'Dreaming' to refer to *ngurlu*, the matrilineal category of flesh, but most frequently they reserve 'Dreaming' for relationships which have a specifically spatial component.

Dreaming beings associated with one's father's country identify species, geographical sites and responsibilities; they are a matrix of mutual care and well-being. So, too, do the Dreamings associated with one's mother's country. Dreamings and country on the father's side are often referred to as 'whiskers' (with the hand sign designating 'father'). Dreamings and country on the mother's side are referred to as *ngapalu*–milk and breast–and are indicated with the appropriate hand sign. Yarralin people are adamant that they are responsible for the well-being of both their mother's and their father's country. They most frequently use the terms 'my Dreaming' and 'my country' to express these relationships. Patrilineal identities, with their geographical and Dreaming denotations, are an important part of a person's identity, usually marking special relationships of authority and care, but they by no means exhaust the range of a person's identity, responsibilities, and rights.

Dreamings who confined themselves to small areas are often termed *ngurramarla*, as are the dead bodies in country. *Ngurra* means country; *marla* is not productive of meaning in and of itself, but probably derives from a suffix in other languages which means 'dweller' or 'native to' (McConvell, pers. comm.). These are the Dreamings with whom humans have certain kinds of intimate ties.

Daly stated the case eloquently. He was speaking for his mother's country, Lingara, and referring to a Dreaming which he relates to through his father, but which is not his *kuning*:

> We want to see white man talking right way for this Lingara. We're going to get a lease for this, excision lease. Up here, I'm the man called Daly Pulkara. I'm talking to you now. This [is] not [an] argument. We just tell you all the story what we been doing longa this country. You know all this Dreaming around here? Dreaming: that's my power. Kangaroo Dreaming right along the top here, that's kangaroo Dreaming. Well kangaroo right for me. No good for white man. I don't like someone shooting everything like that. I don't like that. You hurt me.

When Jessie Wirrpa told the story of how Jirrikit (owlet nightjar) travelled, met the black-headed-python, and came home, she was telling the story of her own *kuning*. Home, for Jirrikit, is around the area of the Victoria River Downs homestead, and it is in that area that Jessie and her sisters and brothers have worked for much of their lives. It is not the only place where they have rights and responsibilities, but it is an area in which Dreaming identities carry an intense social and emotional load.

In 1985 Darrell Lewis and I made a trip with Jessie, her brother Allan Young, and Allan's wives and infant daughter to visit some Jirrikit sites. We drove as far as we could, and then walked to the rockhole where Jirrikit had doused himself when his whiskers caught fire. We ate food from the country as we went along, and we looked at remains–old camp sites; abandoned stone tools. Jessie and Allan called out to the country, the Dreamings, and the dead people. They had walked this country with their parents when they were children, and their father had taught them the significance of the area, admonishing them always to remember that it is their country, their responsibility. Jessie and Allan are no longer youthful, and their parents are long dead. On our 1985 trip the dead people walked with us; they watched and listened, as did the country. 'Old Man Jirrikit' would take note of our actions, Jessie said. For her and her brother, remembrance, dead bodies, responsibilities, country, *kuning* and other Dreamings fused. And as we were documenting sites and country for purposes of a land claim, all of us had hopes for the future which we wove into the journey.

6 *The Gift of Life*

I understand Yarralin people to be saying that life is good; they offer no justification for this assertion. Most frequently they take it to be self-evident and fundamental: the earth gave birth–both earth and life are good. There is a certain circularity to this contention which I believe is implicit in Yarralin people's stories: the cosmos as it exists, or as it existed before European invasion, is good because it works–it does not fall apart. And the cosmos works because it is good; it could not continue to exist otherwise.

The circular assumptions contained in the notion of goodness indicate the participatory quality of life. Yarralin people pay close attention to what people, country, and cosmos are 'telling' them. The point is not to find reassurance of order there, but rather to note any disturbances so that problems can be corrected and order maintained. The meta-rule which I have labelled 'response' speaks to this issue of participation.

Who was that masked cockatoo?

To be alive is to act, and to act is to communicate. Anything which is alive communicates, and in Yarralin people's thinking, everything is alive. Boundaries between species are immutable; they are not, however, impenetrable. Clever people and clever animals can change their shape, disguising themselves as other species and learning to communicate with them. This is what it means to be clever–to be able to cross boundaries.

In a world where anything may be something other than what it appears to be, knowing and acting take on a particular kind of significance. Once Hobbles and I stopped during a trip so that Hobbles could shoot two turkeys (*Ardeotis australis*) he saw by the side of the road. He first shot from the truck, a distance of about three metres. His bullets missed, and the turkeys, looking slightly disgruntled, stepped behind a conkerberry bush. Hobbles left the truck and, using the bush as cover, moved to within two metres of them and fired. Again the bullets missed, and again the turkeys walked away. This sequence was repeated for about half a kilometre through the scrub. By that time nearly a whole box of fifty bullets had been used up, and the turkeys, looking decidedly peevish, flew away. Hobbles came back to the truck muttering that they 'must have been clever'; it was probably a good thing, he said, that they had not been shot, for there might have been dire repercussions.

All animals perceive and evaluate. As conscious and responsible beings, they must. The clever turkeys may well have thought that Hobbles was a bit of a 'turkey' himself for having wasted so many bullets on them. Had an accident occurred, and one or both of them been killed, they would have been angry that he had failed to understand them and had allowed himself to persist beyond the point of reason.

Animals observe and interpret humans; they also evaluate each other. I had a cockatoo that some Yarralin people had found in the bush and given to me because they wanted him to learn to speak English. He was a wonderful pet but not a skilled speaker. He learned to say 'hello cocky', and he had a laugh that was absurd. When 'Cowboy' learned to fly he went out daily to try to mix with the bush cockatoos. He would land in a tree with all the other birds, and sometimes he would screech. The others took no notice of him, but after half a minute or so they would spread their wings, en masse, and leave him. My good neighbours Clipper and Tawil used to sit by their fire every morning and watch Cowboy's overtures and rebuffs, just as I sat by my fire and watched. Eventually Clipper said that maybe the bush cockies had heard Cowboy speaking English and thought he was a clever person dressed up as a cockatoo.

Intersubjectivity, ways of knowing and relating to others, is founded in direct communication, Dreaming stories, received knowledge, observations, and informed interpretations. The fact that there are clever people and clever animals introduces the necessity of interpretation into Yarralin people's environment: one cannot know, with certainty, what a thing is just by looking at it. One must also observe behaviour and events and deduce the quality of being in this light. Yarralin people do this consistently, and in their view all parts of the cosmos are doing the same thing.

Old Tim was one of the few people who claimed to be in regular and direct communication with another species. He said that his dogs spoke to him telling him that dogs are not happy these days. ' "We don't come bash up people", they say. "What for people want to bash up we?".' Or again: ' "I been make them man and woman. Now you been drop me, put me in the rubbish dump".' Tim added: 'Anyone reckon dogs too dirty to lick my pannikin [cup], and kill [hit] him, kill him–we come out of that dog. No good kill him, no good shoot him. Dog's a big fellow boss. Got to leave him. No more touch him.'

Other beings and worlds

Yarralin people's cosmos includes other worlds and beings which Westerners might describe as supernatural but which Yarralin people believe have their origins in this earth. Natural in this sense, they are also extra-ordinary in that they are not subject to the same laws of birth and death as are ordinary species. They, too, interact with us.

Much of the information concerning other worlds and beings first came to my attention through Old Tim. Many people told me not to bother with Tim because he was boring and always got things mixed up, but he was the kind of persistent orator who is nearly impossible to avoid. He was a bit hazy at times, yet there was a curious cunning to the style in which he managed to keep me listening to him for hours. It often happened that when he had pushed me to the very limits of fatigue and frustration he would say something so rivetting that almost against my will I would again pick up my pen and start writing. Old Tim had been a clever man of the old style; he had actually been to the lightning country in the sky and been given objects of power. Although he said that he had lost his power, he was still relied upon to assist people in crises. When one old woman was critically ill, Tim went on a metaphysical journey to fetch her spirit (breath) back; later, when he saw that there was no hope, he told her spirit to go.

I found that while Tim did mix up many details, his stories offered remarkable access to underlying structures. He also offered voluminous and scattered bits of information which I then explored with other people; and others explained things to me very clearly and patiently because of their conviction that Old Tim would have got it wrong. A fluent speaker of English, a Christian, and a competent stockman in his youth, it seemed to me that European ways of thinking and doing had washed over Old Tim like the tide over great boulders. He was immensely generous in his teaching, and after he died I felt sorry for not having been more generous myself.

Death is an ending leading to a variety of continuities. The dismantling of a human being necessitates a transfer of parts between worlds. In earlier days, there was a ceremony to effect the transfer of the spirit (*manngyin* or *yimungaya*) from our world to the *kaya*, who would then escort it to the sky country. Sometimes at sunset great long streaks go across the sky from the setting sun. These streaks are *wuma*: 'roads' or 'strings' that the *kaya* make so that they can go back and forth between earth and sky.

I translate the term *kaya* as 'custodians of the dead'; the term is sometimes used to indicate human 'spirit', and in those cases this translation is inappropriate. The Kriol gloss is *debil-debil* (devils), and it may be that this has contributed to European notions that Yarralin people engage in 'devil worship' or are concerned to placate 'evil spirits'.

Kaya live in caves on earth where they guard the bones of the dead. They are described as skeletons although they are able to take other

Wuma — the roads or strings which connect earth and sky. Europeans know this phenomenon as 'false sunrise'. This photo was taken at sunset, facing east, May 1982.

shapes as well. *Kaya* do not live their lives according to ordinary time; they do not give birth nor do they die, but their business is with ordinary time, specifically with death. They exist in our world, walking the earth as we do, and eating many of the same foods but, having access to the sky country, they are not bounded by this earth.

People are frightened of *kaya* because their business is death, and because they steal living people and transform them into *kaya*. In addition, people whose sky country relatives reject them must stay with the *kaya*, becoming *kaya* themselves, and if the mortuary rituals are incomplete there is always the possibility that the dead person may become *kaya*.

A small bird, often identified as the willy wagtail (*Rhipidura leucophrys*), is 'boss' for the process of transferral. The knowledge of willy wagtail Law allowed human beings to control the potentially dangerous transferral of spirit. I do not know much about this Law, partly because I never saw it in action and partly because it impinges upon men's secret knowledge.

Big Mick Kankinang saw the old funerary rites when he was young, and he remembers them well. He described them this way:

> Corroboree for *kaya*, corroboree for new dead man [or woman], they make a fire with paperbark. They chuck those light around everywhere, that means no devil [probably *manngyin*] come. Dead fellow can't come back longa *ngumpin* [people]. They been hunt him with that fire. They [*kaya*] come up in a line, that dead fellow behind. Boss *kaya* hold him by finger [take him by the hand] to take him away. Him worrying, but that *kaya* boss hold him. Corroboree give him power . . . When you got to make them [*kaya*] come up, that's the corroboree you got to sing.

The essential point is that while *kaya* manage the interface between worlds, between death and what comes after, they are, in turn, managed by people. Those who knew the willy wagtail Law called up *kaya* when they were needed and dispersed them to do their job. The custodians of the dead did not invade and overwhelm the world of human life.

The sky world, above the stars but below the sun and the moon, is the home of the lightning people: Jangala men and Namija women who live 'on top'. When we on this earth see lightning in the sky we know that the lightning people are active: probably fighting. This is the home of dead people (*manngyin* and *yimungaya*) and this is where they stay forever, except on the rare occasions when they make contact with this world. People who are recently deceased are, of course, remembered, but with the passage of human time they become part of the collective: *Kalangka*–lightning people.

Old Tim was taken to the sky country when he was young and it was lightning people who made him clever. He described the place as peopled by women, men and children, and said that the women had long hair, smooth skin 'like a snake', and 'very strong eyes'. Inside they are different, according to Tim. His 'granny' (mother's mother or mother's mother's brother) opened up and showed him: 'no fat, just grease; no blood'. Tim described his experience:

> Alabad [everybody] reckon this sky close up. But no, him long way place. Really dark there. You can look back this land but can't see much; can't see people or much anything. Too far away. That time at Carroll Yard [where Tim was taken up], string everywhere from on top. Clever string that one. I go high up, water been come out from eye. Can't look now . . . That country wind get into your nose, eye, everything. Look down. If somebody make a big fire here on bottom you can see that light just like a star, from on top. I was fortnight there. [They] Really make me good, clever now. And [they] put me back, right back same place. Same mother and father right there now. I got clever longa lightning.

People who are made clever by lightning have powers of healing. They know how to look inside a sick person, identify what is wrong, and remove the sickness. Lightning is connected with rain, and power from lightning people also gives power for water: to stop floods, to dive into flood water and rescue people, and to revive people who are drowned. According to Tim, lightning power also allowed him to prolong people's lives:

> When spirit [breath] been walk away, I been bring it back . . . And *tulpu* [heart], *yayiya* [lungs], rubbish ones–gone. Clever man can bring back

> new ones. Got [a] big fucking country that way. Clever man know. Big mob *tulpu*, big mob *yayiya*. That's country on top. That's my country.

Lightning people do not die. Their world is separate from ours, connected by the *kaya* roads or strings, and by strings (lightning) which they drop to our country in order to climb down or to pull people up. They sometimes bring corroborees to their relatives on earth, as one deceased man had done for his daughter who was an elderly woman when I met her at Yarralin. Other times they simply walk around, usually in the area of a lightning Dreaming site. And sometimes they come to heal their sick relatives, as Old Tim's father did. This was not the part of his father that went to the buffalo-shooters' camp at Marrakai, but the part that went on top and later took Tim up to the sky country. He pulled a four-inch stick from Tim's shoulder blade and gave him new lungs.

Tim's power is finished, he says. Formerly he had tools which were given him by the lightning people which he stored in his belly:

> Lightning put wood and iron inside, just like a clothes needle, but solid like a finger. Can go right through trees, anything. Go through and come back again longa body. But gone now. Nothing now. Me empty. [I] got no good eye, I got nothing now to help me. All lost now, finish.

Water constitutes another world. There are water 'people': the *miriripana* women and *karukayin* children. Unfortunately I know very little about these beings. The major force is the Rainbow snake who walked in human shape during Dreaming, and was an ally of the flying foxes. Later it changed over to the Rainbow snake form as it is now, but it is not ordinary. Changing size and shape, it sometimes looks like an ordinary snake; sometimes it is described as having an animal head with ears, and 'spines' on its back like a barramundi. The Rainbow snake is neither precisely male nor female, mammal nor reptile, nor is it species specific. It lays eggs, gives birth, moves about the sky 'chucking rain' in what can best be described as a phallic manner, and suckles its companions such as flying fox and budgerigar.

To irritate a Rainbow snake by trying to kill it, or to damage its eggs, is to invite disaster by flood and there are songs and actions which usually can stop the rainbow. Clever people penetrate the domain of water with impunity, diving into floodwater to wrestle with the Rainbow snake. Many old people who are now dead are said to have had that power, but today nobody in Yarralin has it. Tim says that lightning people are not giving their power any more, and in general Yarralin people say that there used to be more of this sort of power available in the world. Nobody claims to understand why it is declining.

Another category of beings is that called the *mungamunga* women. *Mungamunga* are much like humans; Ivy Kulngarri, contrasting them with the Nanganarri Dreaming women, described them as 'proper girls [women] just like us'. Other people say that they differ in having webbed feet and hands. *Mungamunga* do not give birth, and they do not die. They stay young and lovely forever, roaming this earth at will.

Mungamunga make friends with humans and teach them songs, dances, and designs. Hobbles had direct experience of the *mungamunga*. It was his misfortune to have been working as a stockman at the time, and his experience was cut short by the demands of the job. He was with a stock camp, mustering, and as he was going to sleep that particular night, he woke up again:

> Still awake, but not much. Bit of a tree, I see them go round and round:
> 'Hello, I'm no good longa brain. I must be hurt.' Because that thing hit me right here [below the ear]. Make me mad now [dizzy]. Ground kept coming up, coming up. Lay down, ground turning over. That's thing for that *kajirri* (women: *mungamunga*). Can't sit up. Can't lay down: 'Well, better get my brain quiet.'
>
> Nother side they been hit me now. Settle me down and bit of a full sleep . . . [I] Touch him [her]. Really cold-fellow binji [belly] and milk: 'Hello, somebody here longa my camp. Who this fucking woman been come out? This woman going to give me trouble tomorrow!'
>
> That nother people wake, look around. That woman . . . know I gotta get up, well him [she] gone now . . . That's *mungamunga* we call them. Can go longa woman too, make them talk ordinary language and *mungamunga* language. Make them clever . . . If him [she] stay [could have stayed], [she would have] give it me language and I [would have] give it him language, ordinary one. Got no husbands, that mob. [They] Look for husband, boyfriend.

In making friends with ordinary people *mungamunga* provide an entree across boundaries, making ordinary people clever, or giving them new corroborees. The songs and dances which they teach people are personal property, handed on from parents to children, and performed to the pleasure of large groups of people. There are two such corroborees in regular use at Yarralin; one is secret for women, and one, which was given to a man, is public.

While new things come into life because of the *mungamunga,* they are not the only beings who give people songs and dances. Any Dreaming being can act as a source of creativity. So, too, can people who are now dead and have gone to the lightning country. *Mungamunga* are not unique in this respect, but they are one of the most consistent sources of creativity.

Kaya, *mungamunga*, and Rainbow snake all prey on human beings. *Kaya* and *mungamunga* are most feared because their prey is specifically human. *Kaya*, the custodians of the dead, do not confine themselves to waiting for death, but actively seek out the living, stealing people in order to consume their body and make them *kaya* too. *Kaya* take people out of our world/time and incorporate them into their own so that a person who becomes *kaya* remains *kaya* forever.

One little girl was stolen by *kaya* many years ago. Her family had been travelling on foot through an area that is *kaya* Dreaming. When they noticed her disappearance they followed her tracks to a big cave, and inside they found her surrounded by these cannibalistic beings.

Luckily they had a clever person with them. They lit fires and sang to hunt away the *kaya* and the girl was restored to her family.

As *mungamunga* do not give birth, they seek human children whom they raise, making them *mungamunga* too. When they steal a child they carry it in their arms, and because humans cannot discern *mungamunga* foot prints there is no way to follow up the child. Hobbles' sister's daughter was stolen by *mungamunga* on a rainy and windy night when the family was crossing a river. Her mother had her arms full and told the little girl to hold on to her skirt, but when they came to a stopping place they found that the child was gone. They called to her all night long, and in the morning they tried to follow her tracks, but no trace of the child was ever found. People concluded that she 'must have' been taken by *mungamunga.*

Such children never die, but once gone, they are gone forever. These losses are bitter not only because of the sorrow but also because people who feed other worlds become part of a different life process which cannot be reversed or negated. This loss is more final than the loss through death because *yimaruk,* bones, and body do not stay in this world. And it is a loss without the satisfaction of revenge; there is no way of paying back *kaya* and *mungamunga.*

One of the facts of human existence is that we are both predators and prey. The relationship between our world and others is reciprocal in the abstract, but no one wants to lose their children. *Kaya* perform the necessary tasks of removing the spirits of the dead and of guarding the bones. However, no one wants to become food for *kaya,* or to lose one of their relations in this way. Similarly, *mungamunga* give new songs and dances back into our world. There is no idea of direct reciprocity: the *mungamunga* will not take a child in exchange for a song any more than a parent would offer a child to gain a song. Rather, they take what children they please, as the appropriate circumstances arise, and they bestow their gifts as they please irrespective of past events. I never heard anyone suggest that *kaya* and *mungamunga* predation is morally wrong, only that it is terrifying.

Rain and sun

Each part of the cosmos has within it the potential to expand; each is potentially a runaway part, pushing and testing until it is stopped by others. But each part, as it becomes active triggers other parts which are interconnected to it and which stop the runaway process. Human beings have a responsibility to intervene where they consider intervention necessary and to leave things alone where they consider that necessary. Humans have the ability to adjust the system, as well as to throw it out of kilter. But looking at the system without human intervention we see that each part is alive, and each part in communicating itself elicits responses which restore balance.

The seasons are conceptualised as the actions of the sun, the wind, and the Rainbow snake. Since any starting point is arbitrary, let us start with the late dry season. At this time (October-November) the earth has become so hot that it can hurt people's feet to walk on bare soil. The wind is blowing from the south-east–hot, dry, and dusty. The country is parched, the animals have grown thin, the waterholes and billabongs are drying up. The sun, which is necessary to life, is beginning to destroy life. Earlier in the year the flying foxes have been dispersed through the bush, eating blossoms which grow on the open-savannah eucalypts (*E. terminalis* and *E. confertiflora*). As the blossoms dry up, the flying foxes move to the river, roosting in the trees along permanent waterholes. When the Rainbow snakes see the flying foxes, their Dreaming allies, hanging above them they know that it is time to move.

Now the rainbow is young and restless. It gets up out of the water, opens its mouth, and shoots out lightning and saliva. The saliva is rain, and it contains tadpoles. This first rain alerts the lightning people. Lightning women flash their lightning with ever increasing frequency, aroused by the Rainbow snake. The rain brings steam up from the hot earth; steam collects into clouds which carry more rain. Tadpoles turn into frogs who sit up and call for more rain. The wind shifts, coming now from the north-west.

These early rains arouse other species. Various grubs, as well as frogs, are 'boss' for rain: they call on the rainbow to bring more. As the rains increase, the floodwaters rise, signalling the presence of the mature rainbow. The water becomes dark and muddy, forming whirlpools which are the rainbow in action. Careless people and animals can be sucked into these pools, drowned and perhaps eaten by rainbows.

After a few months the rainbow has expanded its influence enormously: floods abound, the sky has been cloudy for a long time; the sun has been eclipsed by the rain. The flying foxes are said to have gone underwater to join the rainbow, and frogs stop calling for rain. The rainbow has been roaming abroad and is becoming 'old and tired'.

The sun now asserts itself, burning the rainbow. At the same time, the wind shifts to the east and breaks the rainbow's back. Burnt and broken, it retreats to the rivers. The east wind clears the skies and brings up cold weather. Dingos have their litters, kangaroos and turkeys become fat; the whole emphasis of the world shifts from water to land, from rain to sun, from river resources to land resources. When the country dries out, the white gum trees blossom and the flying foxes return. Cold weather recedes as the sun takes over the sky and heats up the earth, and the whole cycle begins again.

Water, characterised most forcefully as the rainbow, is associated with all the manifestations of water and with all water resources. Fire, characterised most forcefully by the sun, is associated with ripening, growing, and cooking, as well as with land resources. The sun cooks the earth, making it hot and fertile; if allowed to go out of control, it would kill the world. Likewise, the rainbow waters the earth, cooling it, making it 'clean and new' again. If allowed to go out of control, it would inundate the world, killing everything.

People can and do intervene. There are ways to bring up rain and to stop it, and there are songs to bring out the sun and the wind. People and animals, particularly cattle with their weight and hard hooves, can accidentally interfere with these processes, irritating a rainbow or damaging a site. Unless there has already been interference, however, neither sun nor rain goes out of control because the other stops it. Yarralin people are usually reluctant to interfere because they know that they do not know everything. Nobody minds throwing dust at a storm to make it go sideways because it is just a local event. If people want to dance all night, and a storm threatens, why not send it around rather than have it come full on? But they do not attempt massively to alter these processes, and they are critical of people whom they believe do interfere on more than a local basis.

The actions of sun and rain exemplify a kind of relationship in which action triggers more action in such a way that a balance is maintained and the cosmos is kept healthy. Sun and rain exist in a relationship by which each brings the other into action by being itself. The process of knowing what is happening with the other is built up over time, and this knowing links these two beings into a relationship. Each has its own Law of being which includes knowing and responding to the other.

In the midst of life

Yarralin people see their country as a land of plenty for those who know how to use it. Virtually every adult in Yarralin said to me, 'it's good country here. Plenty tucker [food]. You can't [go] hungry in this country. Any bloke hungry in this country just silly'. Knowledge is the key to staying healthy in country–and to keeping country 'healthy.'

People have an encyclopaedic store of knowledge relating to resource management. They understand the workings of the food chain, both from their own perspective and from the perspective of many other species within the system; they apply this knowledge systematically as part of their own food quest and as part of their responsibility as living beings. Women, in particular, know a broad range of foods which are edible for humans, including the many varieties of fruits, vegetables and medicines, the locations at which they are found, the kinds of locations at which they are likely to be found, the correct seasons for gathering them, the signs by which their presence is detected if they are underground, methods of preparation and cooking, including methods to leach toxins out of certain plants, and methods of storage. Women know about plant propagation and are careful not to destroy by over-gathering. Areas which they define as 'gardens' were selectively tended in the past, but it has been difficult for me to learn more than generalities because cattle and horses have eaten and trampled all the gardens.

Women also know which other species are dependent upon the same resources and, when they are collecting, are careful to leave some food *in situ* for these other species. With regard to fish and shellfish resources, women in particular know their eating habits, the resources on which they are dependent, and how to go about catching them.

There is also a vast range of information concerning animal behaviour about which men are most vocal. Knowledge of animals, like that of plants, is tied into Dreaming Law and Dreaming identities. Associated with the emu, for example, is a set of small birds (finches) whose presence signals waterholes and springs; they tell the emu when it is safe to put its head down to drink. Coded both as Law and *ngurlu* (matrilineal identity), this knowledge also assists the hunter.

Yarralin people generally do not eat fully domesticated animals, although they eat the wild cattle that roam the stations. Dogs, cats, and chickens have been eaten when people were very hungry, but they are not thought of as food and are a last resort. Old Tim's efforts to raise chickens were complicated by this fact: neither he nor anyone else would eat either the eggs or the birds. Tim said he hoped to make money from them, but there was no one locally to buy. His dogs, however, were appreciative.

When it comes to killing it is usually women (particularly elderly women) who have the final say. Men have a say in these matters too, for resource management is everyone's concern, and there are no hard rules about decisions. As a general rule, people do not kill very young animals, saying that they should 'leave it for later'. Likewise, animals which have been in scarce supply are usually not killed at all. In my experience, when we saw animals within shooting distance, old women told us either to 'get it' or 'leave it'. Their decisions were based on a number of factors: how much food we already had, how many of us there were, and the condition of the animal population. Categories of identity such as *ngurlu* also pose restrictions; many people do not like to eat those animals who are their 'flesh' or 'countrymen'.

Predation depends upon knowledgeable management of ecosystems. Prior to invasion burning was an essential feature, but now, in the Victoria River valley, Northern Territory regulations prevent people burning the country as they would choose, and this has been so for decades. My discusssion of burning is necessarily based more on conversation than on observation (see Jones 1969; H. Lewis 1982; D. Lewis 1988 for discussions of burning). When people burn off the tall grass, as they do around their own settlement, they say they are making the country *punyu,* and everything will come up new and fresh: it makes the country happy (*punyu*) to be taken care of; it makes the country clean and good (*punyu*); it makes it easy to walk around without fear of snakes and without the nuisance of grass seeds; it provides new and good food for kangaroos and wallabies, making them *punyu*; and it facilitates hunting, allowing people to see animal tracks and burrows.

Relationships of care and killing transfer life from one species to another. This is not a hierarchical ordering of transfers which leads to humans. Rather, every species is seen to have its own right to exist of and for itself. Less a chain than a network, feeding and taking care nurture all life. Yarralin people believe that if they take care of country (burn it, perform increase rites, sing the songs, visit and use it), country will take care of them. This is a cyclical process in which the knowledge and care which humans put into the system, including the former deposition of bones, form an essential part of human survival in the system, making people, other species, and country *punyu*.

Within the embracing concept of a system that is good are these basic facts of human life: birth, and death. Ideally balanced and reciprocal, founded equally in predation and care, these relationships can become dangerous. A lack of balance can occur in two directions. Over-hunting, over-gathering, or a general lack of care can deplete species. Extinctions have occurred in Australia in the past. The giant animals that formerly inhabited the continent are now gone; the causes are not yet understood scientifically and Aboriginal knowledge, if it exists, appears to be locked away in men's secret business. Others are more recent: the dingo, which archaeologists and zoologists believe has only been in Australia for the past four thousand years, was probably introduced from Asia. It seems likely that the dingo took over the foods and habitats of the Tasmanian tiger (*Thylacinus cynocephalus*), causing its extinction on the mainland. In Tasmania, where dingos were not introduced, the Tasmanian tiger lived on to be exterminated by Europeans early in this century (Breckwoldt 1988:49–53).

Since the arrival of Europeans, extinctions have been occuring at a vastly increasing pace. As the rate of extinction is faster than the rate of European documentation, many species will almost certainly die even before they have become known to Europeans. All up, over two thousand species of plants are known to be extinct or on the verge of extinction. Dozens of species of animals are thought to be extinct, and close to two hundred are endangered or vulnerable. It is not possible to make any statement about insects for there is simply not enough information (Gould League nd:3; 53).

In addition to loss of life, there is also drastic loss in life-support systems. As early as 1945 the geographer Maze estimated that four to twelve inches of topsoil had been lost in the Ord River area (adjacent to, and subjected to similar pressures as, the Victoria River); he warned that soils and plants subjected to such pressure could not sustain an industry (Maze 1945:7–19). His voice was ignored. Nearly forty years later, the Conservation Commission of the Northern Territory warned that 'signs of deterioration through fertility loss and erosion is [sic] already evident' (Melville 1981:vi).

Erosion at the site of one of the early VRD yards, June 1986. (D. Lewis)

Those who know the country well see a more complex and serious process. Yarralin people experience losses directly and personally. Local disappearances are all around them all the time, and for the most part they are powerless to stop them. The topsoil is being eroded, river banks are badly degraded, the rivers are silting up. Many springs and small billabongs have dried out; the plants that once grew there are gone, and the animals that depended on them have had to seek water elsewhere, putting more pressure on surviving systems. Changes in plant communities suggest early signs of desertification, and a number of plant and animal species are locally either extinct or in severe decline.

People's physical and spiritual being is bound up with many of the species, plant and animal, which are lost or threatened, and many apprehend loss in a very immediate way. During a trip in 1986 to examine damage that Europeans with bulldozers had wrought on a set of Dreaming trees, Daly asked me to pull up next to some tall white eucalypts; still standing, and still alive, they are Dreamings. He said when he was a young man, about fifty years ago, the European boss had wanted to have some of these trees cut down. His Aboriginal workers had told him they should not do it because they were

Dreaming, but he insisted. Daly said that the trees' cries were terrible to hear, and in the end the men could not go on with it.

While extinctions, at least at the rate at which they are now occurring, are something relatively new in the world, the idea of an overwhelming lack of balance is not new. The most explicit examples have to do with floods. There are many flood stories, often relating to people who mistakenly killed, or tried to kill, a Rainbow snake, or who mistakenly damaged Rainbow snake eggs. The result was major flooding to the point where people had to take refuge on top of the highest hills; many people are said to have died in such floods, and at least one Dreaming site is also a site of human bones which the Rainbow snake regurgitated after having swallowed its victims. Clever people are said to have been able to stop floods, but sometimes the Rainbow snake is too powerful (chapter 12).

The other direction in which a lack of balance can occur is that of self-destruction (chapter 10). A group of people who belong together by virtue of country, Dreamings, and family ties are expected to take care of each other. When Yarralin people told me of things they heard of people doing which they felt to be terribly wrong, one thing that inspired horror was non-legitimate violence within this group. Part of the wrong is a question of boundary; if all violence, everywhere, were sanctioned, there would be no particular safety in a group, and people are most explict about their desire for the safety assured by countrymen (chapter 7). Part of the wrong is also a question of balance: if a person attacks a countryman, the countrymen cannot take revenge without further weakening their own group. Taken as a whole, such violence simply does not make sense: a person who attacks his own attacks himself. Such an act is, according to Yarralin people, frightening and shameful.

'Good' and 'bad' are all part of life on earth, and what is 'good' in one context may be 'bad' in another. Moral actions are those which sustain balance, immoral ones are those which violently threaten it. Human intention is considered in moral evaluations, but usually it is the act and its results which determine the context. Morality and immorality are most consistently identifiable at this very abstract level: to act, to respond, and to take responsibility within a cosmos in which life is inextricably bound up with death.

What we hear in Dreaming stories is not so much about good and bad as it is about balance and order. Dreamings make 'mistakes', but others right the balance so that mistakes do not accumulate to the point of becoming destructive. Stories are not so much about rules as they are about types of actions and responses; they demarcate relationships through recounting events. It is up to individuals to identify the choices and consequences, and relate them to their own living experience. As Berndt (1979:28) says of western desert people, they 'did not get all of their myth-interpretations ready-made. Something was left to *them*, to put the implications together in the course of their *own* lives'.

Daly once reflected on the story of the moon and the dingo. He was brooding about death at the time because the last of the old men he called 'father' was dying, and because we had been talking about his warrior ancestors. Being responsible for moon Dreaming sites, Daly usually articulates a philosophical attitude toward death which may reflect his proximity to such a fatal decision. On this occasion he queried the conditions of human life, but also found some comfort:

> Yeah. Well him [Moon] been talk: 'You want to die, die! Bones to bones. *Kujilip.' Kujilip* mean where he got to go back to bones. That what it really means now . . . [He was being] Cruel. That *walaku* [dog; dingo] said: 'You try, learn me how to go.'
>
> *Jakilin* [Moon] been die, and him come out for four days. And him [dog] been say: 'You can't see em me come out four days. I'll go forever.' And this *walaku* been die, and forget altogether. Nother *walaku* been talk: 'We gotta go like that.'
>
> And there, we go like that, all right. And he couldn't make a change. I don't know why. That *jakilin* should have been say, Moon should have say: 'Ah, that's bad. No good you stay back, like that. Why don't you come back again?' That *walaku* been do wrong. Yeah. Nother dog been there: 'What's the good, poor bugger. Come back, come back, make a new life. And you'll die and come back with new life.'
>
> Nothing good. He made a mistake now, *walaku* . . . You think. What's a good life? *Jakilin*, that Moon. That one we had to miss out. We been follow that dog. We never make change. We should have followed this Moon.

Like most other people who discuss the moon, Daly went on to point out that the dingo Law is not as final as it appears:

> *Ngumpin* [humans] been follow that dog way. Where we going? We'll die. *Walaku*, he'll die too, dog, well he got a two life . . . When he die he got another life. Still alive, one *kaya*, one God.

One notices immediately that the messages contained in this story are contradictory. The dingo is blamed for having made a mistake, and by implication, so are we. Because he missed out on eternal life, we must miss out too. But equally, although more circuitously, the moon is at fault. Indeed, the whole tone of this story heaps blame upon the moon in a manner that is quintessentially Aboriginal: by eliciting compassion for the dingo. Daly says that the moon should have been more generous; by implication, he should have gone back and helped the dingo. He was so entranced with his own triumph that he was heedless of others.

There is a story within this story which becomes more apparent if we consider the larger frame. Many stories tell of the moon's rapacious sexual appetite, the ribald humour conveying a serious message. We see the Moon night by night, month by month, growing big, dying, and returning. When he appears as a crescent shape, some Yarralin people say that he is having sex, the shape being an indication of two people engaged in that act. And while I have listened to a single man speak longingly of the moon's activity because his own desire was restless and unsatisfied, there is also a recognition that the Moon is stuck, as dogs become stuck, locked forever into his sweetheart.

Nothing new comes into the moon's world, as nothing old goes out of it. His sexuality is sterile. There is no change, no choice, only static repetition.

This story can tell us that without death there is no birth, no past, no history, no human time. As the moon's arrogance has prevented him from engaging with others, so he becomes a closed system. The moon, we can say, was holding the Law of perpetual self; he offered this Law to the dingo in offering him his own urine. There are many ways to understand this offer, and I would suggest that one of the things being offered was another form of obliteration. The cost of the moon's Law was the dingo's loss of his own independence. The dingo refused, and the result was death. Dingo, like his human descendants, is open to life, sharing the finality of death and the continuity of parts.

We can hear this story as the dingo's bid for eternal life; we can also hear it as the moon's bid for others with whom to share his Law. As the story makes clear, this is not a Law that can be shared; the cost of perpetual self is perpetual closure. The moon tells of desire; sexuality provides the configuration, accommodating most profoundly the desire to dominate. His is the ultimate effort to perpetuate one's own life at the expense of others. Closed to the world, he lives forever. We can say that the moon's position is one of total dominance over nothing. It is a failure of intersubjectivity based on the proposition: 'I, and maybe you, but only as part of me.'

We are not descendants of the moon; he has none. Our ancestor, dingo, opens us to the world, requiring that we come to an understanding of our place in it which is radically different from the moon's. The meta-rules of balance, response, symmetry, and autonomy concern relationships in which the ever-present desire to dominate is contained. Death and its corollary, birth, open humans to time and to the sharing of life. As I have said, we are participants in processes of life: we kill and eat, we die and our bones nourish country, giving life back to the places and species that sustained us. We are part of a system which, in its totality, is probably closed, but which, from our perspective as participants, is very much open. We are participants, but we are not the ultimate focus of this system. And death, for all that it may be unwelcome, is one of life's gifts.

To hunt, kill, and eat, is a bloody business with the potential to go out of balance in any number of directions. It is one thing to say that all beings have the right to exist, that existence depends on birth and death, continuity and closure, eating, growing, and dying. It is another thing to know that the potential for disaster is built into the structure of the cosmos, and that prevention depends upon all living things taking responsibility. The autonomy of country, species, and people is sustained by an intense interdependence. This is a non-human being-centred cosmos, in which one aspect of interdependence is eating, and thus in which controlled predation is part of the structure of the cosmos.

The gift of life, like the fact of death, comes wrapped in blood.

7 *Dream Country*

So this is a human being: sharing flesh with country and with other species; killing and taking care; loving life, and required to die; born of woman, and of earth. To be located is to have a ground from which to know, to act, to invite and deny, to share and ask, to speak and to be heard. Old Jimmy Manngayarri, a Bilinara emu man, expressed this groundedness through an analogy with trees. Both people and trees, he said, have their roots in the ground. If the roots are gone the tree, or person, cannot grow. As the tree grows it produces seeds which fall down and grow new trees. But if this new generation, of trees or people, is not grounded then it, too, cannot grow. Jimmy said that younger generations who did not understand their origins would be like a tree without roots; they would have to say: 'I don't know my reason; I can't find my Dream country'.

Locatedness–identification with place–is fundamental to Aboriginal people's understanding of life all over Australia. For Yarralin people, a great deal of social and cultural life acquires its spice as people manage the tension between producing and reproducing the ties that bind while yet sustaining and manipulating the flexibility that prevents bonds from becoming shackles.

I will look at what it means to be an owner of country, to belong to a place and to be responsible for it, before turning to the issues of how people become owners and how they manage multiple affiliations to country.

To take a care

People who own country are responsible for it. Responsibilities to country include:

- Keeping the country 'clean', i.e. burning it off properly.
- Using the country by hunting, gathering, fishing, and generally letting the country know that people are there.

- Protecting the country's integrity by not allowing other people to use country or Dreamings (in ceremonial contexts) without asking.
- Protecting the country, particularly Dreaming sites, from damage.
- Protecting the species related to that country.
- Protecting dangerous places so that harm does not come out of that country.
- Providing a new generation of owners to take over the responsibilities.
- Educating the new owners to the knowledge and responsibilities for that country.
- Learning and performing the ceremonies which keep country and people *punyu.*

Like many Aboriginal people, Yarralin people have great difficulties fulfilling their obligations. Until the Sacred Sites Protection Authority (NT) came into being in 1979, they had no Australian law to back up their assertions that certain areas not be touched. While this law offers some legal redress in the event of damage, and may actually prevent some damage, it barely begins to address the responsibilities which people have toward country.

Learning is a life-long process which takes place formally and informally. As people become increasingly knowledgeable, and assert their knowledge ever more vigorously, they also become increasingly responsible for teaching the new generation who will take over from them. The most informal trips in the bush always involve teaching. Adults tell the appropriate children: 'this is your country', and children (whether it is their country or not) learn the placenames and Dreaming sites and activities. Although informal, this form of education is serious; adults impress upon their children that they must learn so that they can take over when the adults die.

Yarralin people often use the terms 'caretaker', 'boss', or *ngurramarla* to indicate the person who is living in their own country, taking care of that country on a regular basis. The term *ngurramarla* (*yakpali mulula* in Ngaliwurru) refers to those people (past and present) who actively exercised their rights and responsibilities, as well as to the localised Dreamings of a given area. When used to refer to living people, the term can be modified by the adverb 'really' so that those who actively exercise their rights and carry out their responsibilities are referred to as 'really' *ngurramarla.* The term can also be used to refer only to the dead bodies in country–those people whose sole continuing purpose is the care of country. According to a Bilinara man: 'he's the *ngurramarla* when he's dead–to take care of the country'.

At the most intimate, the potential is for a completely reflexive relationship: the person takes care of the country and the country takes care of the person. Such a relationship is built up over time through knowledge and the assumption of responsibility. The relationship so developed is an individual achievement; a person is born with rights, but each must choose further to develop their own relationships with country.

Damage to people is damage to country. Old Tim told me: 'when old people die they kill the country.' He gave examples. When Allan Young's father died, a Walujapi (black-headed python) Dreaming tree broke in half and the water it contained all ran out. When the last of Allan's father's brothers died, another Walujapi tree died too. It was from many such statements, concrete examples, and correlated behaviour that I developed the abstract proposition: the relationship between people and country is reflexive.

The reciprocal proposition is also true. Damage to country, and to Dreamings in particular, causes death or injury to people. Intention is not a factor. If damage occurs, it ramifies; hence the overt need to protect the integrity of country and Dreamings. In the course of the Kidman Spring-Jasper Gorge Land Claim, Allan Griffiths (Allan Young's classificatory brother) told of damage to Jirrikit (owlet nightjar) places and of his father's brother's death. This discussion, taken from the transcript of the hearing, involves Allan Griffiths and the claimants' barrister Ross Howie. Ross repeated many of the statements in order to facilitate their comprehensibility:

AG: One place they knock them out right on the road.
RH: Eh?
AG: They knock one on the road, right on Kangkiji Creek [near VRD head station].
RH: At Kangkiji, that's [Site number] 108. What happened there?
AG: They knocked one rock, Jirrikik.
RH: They knocked a Jirrikik rock down.
AG: Yes, in the middle, right on the creek.
RH: And what knocked it down?
AG: The bulldozer.
RH: And how did you feel when that happened?
AG: No good.
RH: Why not?
AG: Well, that's when as soon as we tell the old falla, Old Dan, that's when he died from the Dreaming . . .
[discussion of identity of Old Dan]
RH: And why did he die?
AG: Well, he was thinking around for the Dreaming . . .
[clarification of actual words]
RH: What's happened to that place now where that Jirrikik was knocked down by the bulldozer?
AG: Well, they put the fence–they got the fence right down there on the road, right at the bore.
RH: All right, and is that Jirrikik–is he still there?
AG: Yes, he's still there, but he's been moving from the tree.
RH: You moved him?
AG: Yes. We lift him up and put him in the tree. He's standing up in the tree now.
RH: He's a stone, is he?
AG: Yes, a stone.

RH: And who made that place?
AG: Jirrikik.
RH: And was there a tree down there at VRD, too?
AG: Yes. One been get knocked off right in the middle, right [at] the airstrip. . .
[discussion of where and when]
AG: We still using a photograph [design] every year on the [ceremony] time, on the ring place time, tell [young men] that the bloodwood [tree] be still gone but we can dream.
RH: You've still got the dream.
AG: Hold it up [take care of it], yes–photograph, yes.
RH: Yes, and use the photograph.
AG: They shouldn't touch the tree, but they done it. We still got the photograph. (Transcript 1988:162–4)

Countries, or the Dreamings in country, take notice of who is there. Country expects its people to maintain its integrity, and one of the roles of the owners is to introduce strangers to country. Trespass–use of country without permission or introduction–is a threat to the integrity of country, Dreamings, and owners. Bilinara people, for example, use the term *kamariyu* to refer to strangers, people who come from far away and must be introduced to the country by the owners. The ritual of introduction, which is by no means restricted to Bilinara people (Gary Lee, pers. comm.), includes the following steps: first, the owner brings the stranger to water, calling out to the country as he approaches; secondly, he or she wets the stranger's head or arm and gives them water to drink. Hector Wartpiyarri, a Bilinara/Mudbura man, described the ritual:

> You [the owner] talk [to the country]: 'I got *ngumpin* [Aboriginal/human being] here from long way. I don't want you to hurt him, he's *jimari* [mate], he's all right'. [You] take him, give him water, wet him head. Now he can walk every way [anywhere in that country]. That's *kamariyu*–from long way.

A number of people explained that once a person has been introduced to the country through this means the country knows the person's smell. Without this introduction, strangers are at risk–the water may drown them, or they may become sick and die. In discussing this ritual of introduction, people used the English word 'water' as a verb. Jimmy Manngayarri said that it is the Dreamings in country who actually smell and identify people's sweat: 'Dream can smell other people. After you water him, that Dream knows hims.'

This ritual identifies owners and signifies their assumption of responsibility for the person they have introduced. It also marks strangers as people who, while no longer at risk simply by being there, are dependent. In acknowledging their status as strangers, they assent to these facts: that others are the owners, that their own knowledge is limited, and that the country has no real responsibility for them (Myers 1982a treats this issue with great sensitivity).

To take care of country is to be responsible for that country. And country has an obligation in return–to nourish and sustain its people.

Yarralin people take country's obligations seriously. They are thoroughly at home in country that Europeans define as 'wilderness', believing that they will never go hungry or thirsty for long. The nonchalance with which people walk or drive off into the bush has never ceased to amaze me. Where I have worried and planned ahead for a lack of food, Yarralin people have simply gone, confident that the country would take care of them. To my knowledge, they have always been right.

One country, one mob

Dora Jilpngarri explained the importance of person and place: 'your relations, that's one country. You can't marry.' Your relations are people in whom, if you are an adult, you have made investments, and who have invested in you. Investments are a kind of belonging. To give somebody life is to place that person under an obligation, and people belong together by sharing these obligations. This is a core group of countrymen: people who do not interact with untoward violence, and who share with, and defend, each other. Their futures are connected; to diminish each other would be a form of self-destruction. In defining these relationships for new generations adults situate young people in human/geographical/Dreaming space, expecting that this locatedness will endure throughout their lives and will generate further continuity.

Yarralin people use a classificatory kinship terminology: 'collateral kin are terminologically equated with lineal kin' (Keesing 1975:148). In practice this means that, for example, one's father and father's brothers are all classed as 'father'. Father's brother's children are classed as siblings; they are children of men one calls 'father'. The same is true for mother's sisters and their children. The terminology is also classificatory in the less technical sense of referring to classes. The subsection system provides the classes. For example, if one's father is a Janama (A1) man, then every Janama man will be classed as 'father' unless there is a genealogical reason to class him otherwise. Demonstrated actualities of a relationship almost invariably carry more weight than the category identities.

Frequently people mark their genealogically defined-relatives only if asked to do so. The set of people to whom one refers as kin, family, or 'full family' is often greater than demonstrated genealogical links can account for. It is, however, by no means random or based on category. Country, Dreamings, and matrilineal identity (*ngurlu*) are the key reference points: a 'full' relative is one who shares the same country and therefore the same locative Dreamings (patrilateral or matrilateral); sharing the same *ngurlu* may add substance to this sense of belonging together.

'Full' relationships also express the sense that people ought not to be deprived of kin. Kinship rights and obligations are shared among a given set of relatives, and as members of that set die, others take over.

When an older brother dies, the next brother takes over as 'father' for all of the children. When an older sister dies, the next one takes over as mother for the children. This process is carried out through all the people of the same genealogical relationship and the same country, concentrating kin responsibilities in the very old. Jimmy Manngayarri, for example, is the last of the senior generation of Bilinara Jalyiri men. For most people he is the sole surviving person in the relevant category: mother's brother, mother's mother's brother, and so on to a whole group of people. Because subsection categories are cyclical, the new generation of Jalyiri brothers for Bilinara are the small children who will one day replace Old Jimmy.

Yarralin people acquire rights to country from their parents: the woman who gave birth to them (and her sisters and brothers), and the man (and his brothers and sisters) who acquired rights to those children by marrying that woman. Formal adoption amplifies parental relationships, creating parent-child ties which are socially equivalent to those founded in birth and marriage. Descent (being the child of one's parents) and–its social equivalent–adoption are the only ways in which Yarralin people acquire the full set of rights associated with ownership.

Other rights, such as the right to learn about and to use country are acquired through marriage, residence, willingness to learn, and demonstrations of responsible management of knowledge. With the exception of marriage, that is how I came to be taught. But nothing other than formal adoption replaces descent; living, learning, and marrying do not generate ownership.

This system of transmission of rights along genealogical paths which are not gender-specific is called 'cognatic'. It is a system which is important both as a means to personal freedom and as a means to survival. Choice and flexibility allow people to place themselves in country according to the state of the resources and the state of the politics. As a system, cognatic affiliation is essential (see also Myers 1982a).

Countries are exogamous: they must look outward for marriage partners, and each person's father's and mother's countries are different. One's Dream countries are those of one's father and mother. Each parent also had a father and mother of differing countries, as did their parents. Such a system has an enormous potential to ramify; if pursued relentlessly, the intimacy which is the essence of groundedness would be destroyed.

In reckoning rights to country there are four lines of descent: from the mother's mother and her sisters and brothers (*jaju*), mother's father and his sisters and brothers (*jawiji*), father's mother and her sisters and brothers (*ngapuju*), and father's father and his sisters and brothers (*kaku*).

Relatedness is constructed for continuity, and must therefore be subjected to closure (chapter 12). One means by which continuity is achieved is through the way that subsections cycle back: alternating sets of father and son, five generations of women (figures 12 and 13). The patrilineal identity (*kuning*) and the matrilineal identity (*ngurlu*) specify particular lines of descent within the generalised subsection system.

The other major way in which continuity is achieved is through marriage. By subsection, by exchanges in marriage, and by the logic of substance being returned to its country of origin, a set of ideal marriages through time generates extraordinarily complex relationships. Figure 17 shows how generations can be mapped onto country assuming that children take over their father's country. This diagram is highly simplified; men's lines are shown staying in place while the lines of women move around and finally return; only four countries are shown, and 'correct' marriages are assumed:

Namija (country A) gives birth to children who affiliate to country B, etc. Each segment of figure 17 shows a line of men staying in place. The lines of women appear to move in opposite directions through country. The actual connections of exchange are more complex. Jimija (1; country A) gets a wife from country B (2), and from her he gets children (4) for his own country, A. Jimija's son Jalyiri (4) gets a

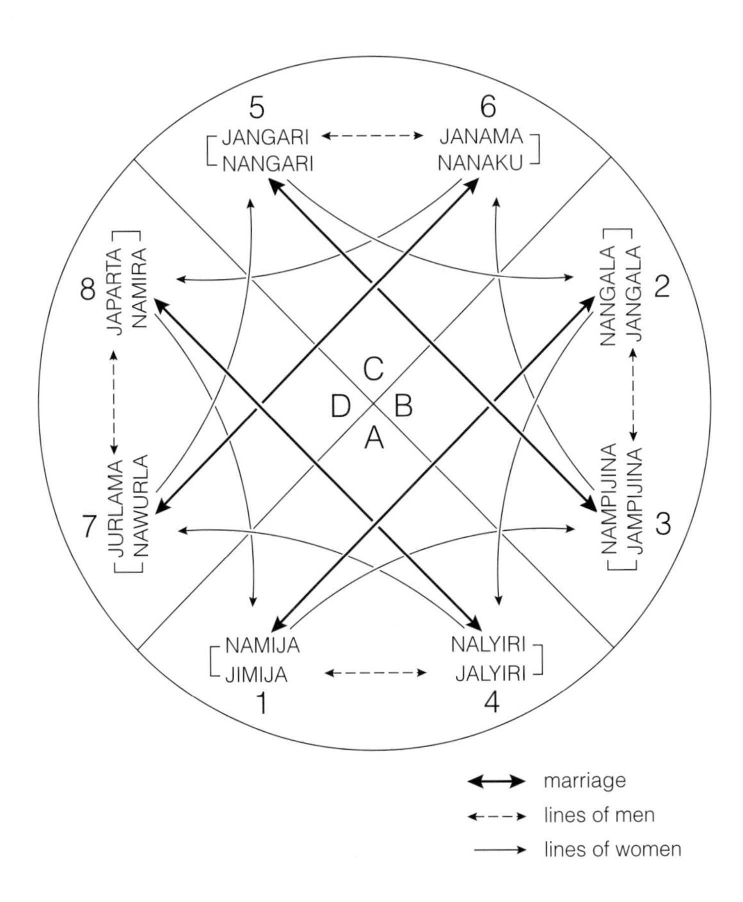

Figure 17 Simplified sketch of generations and country

wife (8) from country D and from her gets children (1) for his own country, A. Jimija's sister's children (3) belong to country B and one of these children, Nampijina (3), he must give to country C.

Yarralin people's concerns seem to have most to do with the maintenance of balanced reciprocity and the localisation of people in country. Over generations people attempt to effect a closure of space. Each group of people is involved in numerous marital exchanges. Each group can be seen as a node in a network. Networks overlap, forming a web of kinship achieved and sustained through birth and marriage. From the perspective of each group, situated at the centre of its own set of exchanges, the problem is to sustain the relationships without allowing them to ramify indefinitely. Yarralin people distinguish between genealogically close and distant kin; those who are close are (with some manipulation of concepts of closeness) ineligible as spouses. Marriages which return people to country fulfil the goal of keeping people in country, while yet sustaining ties between countries.

The art of closure is that of curtailing some lines of descent so that those countries produce spouses rather than relatives, and the ideal marriages are those which take women back as wives to their father's mother's country. Curtailment is context-sensitive and involves considerations of gender, available personnel, past marital histories, individual life histories, group needs, and individual abilities. The lines of succession which are most emphasised are those of the father's father (FF), mother's father (MF), and mother's mother (MM). For men, the MM line appears to be more context-sensitive than the others; for women, the MF line appears to be more context-sensitive. Women's rights to ceremony are inherited through women, and the matriline is particularly important to women. Equally, men's 'business' is transmitted through generations from father to son, and the patriline is particularly important to men. The FM line is the one least emphasised; many Yarralin people are not certain exactly which country their father's mother came from, and when people do act upon rights transmitted through that line they almost invariably speak of their 'father's country' without further qualification.

Selective forgetting is an important part of this process of continuity and return. A man is taught the knowledge of his mother's country; he has the right but not the obligation to continue to transmit this knowledge. In the past one hundred years or so, most men have chosen not to do so. In the course of preparing for a land claim, I asked Allan Young about his antecedents in considerable detail. He explained that his father had run men's business through his mother's country, but that Allan's generation did not 'hang on'. 'We just hang on to father and *kaku* [FF].' He went on to say that he has business for his mother's countries, but nothing for his father's mother's country.

Within any given country there are divisions between those for whom it is their father's and those for whom it is their mother's country. In the context of ritual, the divisions are complementary. In politics, people who take the country from their father are generally granted a stronger voice in decision making, although age, knowledge, personal ambition, ability, and strategic sense are factors which skew particular instances away from this general proposition. Within the context of day-to-day responsibilities, the division largely disappears.

In addition to the many contexts in which men and women teach younger people informally, there are formal contexts in which gender-specific knowledge is communicated. Two types of women's business are regularly used among Yarralin and neighbouring women: *jarata* and *yawalyu* (see Kaberry 1939; C. Berndt 1950; Bell 1983). *Jarata* is a set of songs, dances, designs, and objects which originate from, or are closely associated with, the *mungamunga* women. Because *mungamunga* give women (and men) new corroborees, their songs may incorporate aspects of recent times. In contrast, *yawalyu* ceremonies are, as far as I know, based only in Dreaming.

Jarata rituals are both serious and playful; *yawalyu*, deeply moving, is always serious. *Jarata* are inherited matrilineally; the rituals communicate and affirm women's matrilineal rights to knowledge and to country. It seems that *yawalyu* may be inherited either matrilaterally or patrilaterally (from one's father's sister), but I have not felt easy about asking many questions and so I remain less than certain.

Women's business is a potent force in sustaining person-country relationships. Secrecy is essential to potency. Prior to the Kidman Springs-Jasper Gorge Land Claim (Ngaliwurru and Karangpurru areas) the claimants' legal advisers and I discussed with women the option of performing a portion of business for the Land Commissioner, as had been done in other claims, so that he could see and understand for himself. The women discussed the various options and decided that in the interests of the claim they would invite the Land Commissioner, his counsel assisting, his consulting anthropologist, their own barrister, the Northern Territory Government's barrister (representing government interests in opposition to the claim), and any other legal advisers who had a right to be present during evidence. All of these people were male.

The event was agreed upon for late in the day so that the women would have most of the day to make their preparations; the men took the Land Commissioner and all the others on a series of site visits which were more conveniently made without women. As soon as the men had left, I went to ask the women how they wanted to organise the day. There was a problem, they told me. They had decided they could not do it. One of the women explained: 'From Dreaming right up till now no man been look that thing. We can't lose that Law.' Not only did they not lose the Law; they speeded it up so that by the time the Land Commissioner returned the business was over and done with. There was nothing further to discuss.

Men's rights to country are formally transmitted in initiation when little boys are made into young men, usually shortly before puberty.

From a man's point of view, the appropriate and necessary set of people to take over care of country is a set of cross-cousins–one's father's sister's children and mother's brother's children (*pankurti*). They are co-owners of country, sharing mutual and complementary responsibilities with respect to ritual matters, and sharing equal and undifferentiated daily rights and obligations. This relationship is illustrated in the diagram, figure 18.

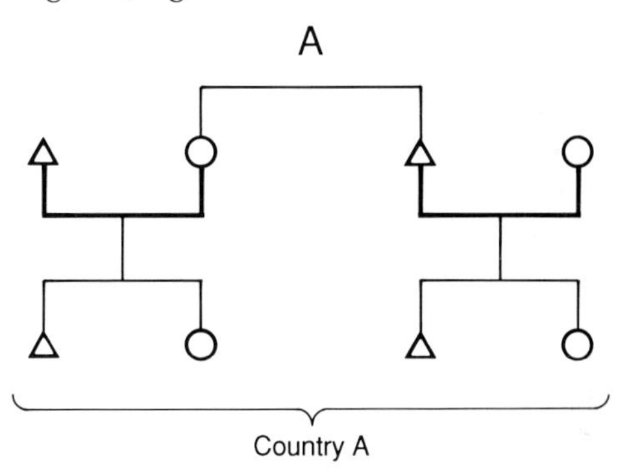

Figure 18 Cross-cousins replace a previous generation as co-owners of country

Usually people arrange marriages to maximise their ties to different countries, creating overlapping networks of rights and responsibilities, illustrated in abstract form in figure 19.

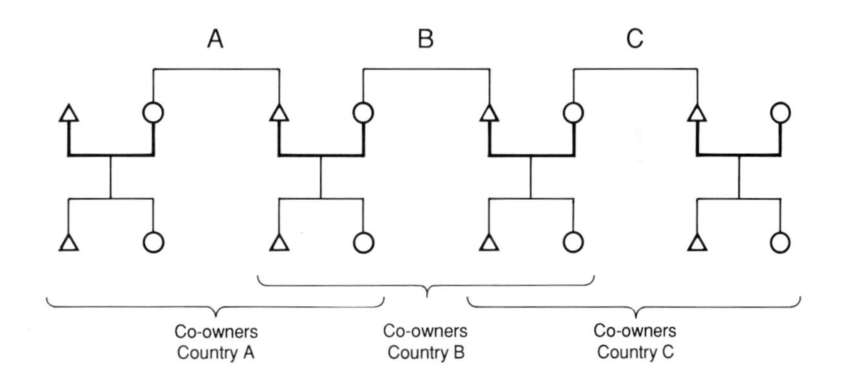

Figure 19 The cross-cousin relationship of co-ownership sets up overlapping responsibilities

During initiation, a boy is shown for the first time his father's father's and mother's father's Dreamings. He may also be shown Dreamings from his mother's mother's country in this context. Visual representations of the Dreamings in the countries to which the boy has rights are painted onto men, who then show themselves to the boy.

Cross-cousins are equal recipients of knowledge, but usually they do not transmit that knowledge equally; if they are to effect closure, they must not transmit equally. Figure 20 shows transmission through generations.

Jampijina receives the designs, and all that they represent, from his father (country A), who had previously received them from his father.

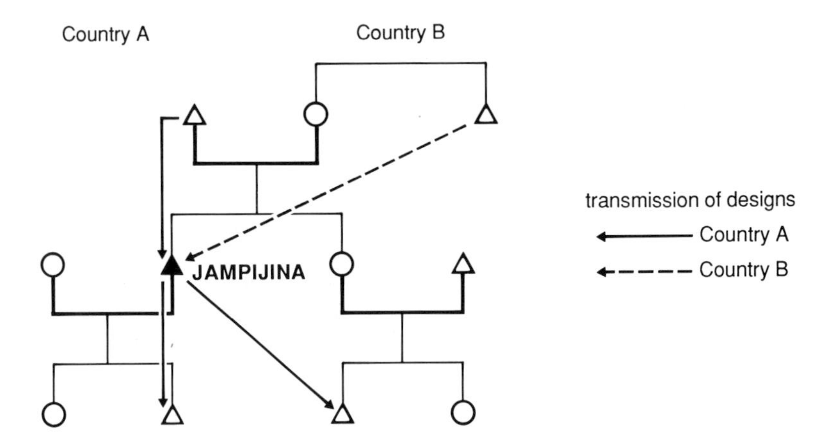

Figure 20 Transmission of rights in young men's business

John Daly (Daly's son) and Leo Young (Allan's son) having a quiet period during the 'young men's business' which will transform Leo from a little boy into a young man. John and Leo are cross-cousins and co-owners of country, December 1980. (D. Lewis)

Jampijina also receives designs from his mother's brother (country B). The set of designs from his father's father (country A) he further transmits, as a matter of obligation, to his sons and to his sisters' sons. In contrast, he has options with respect to transmitting his mother's father's (country B) designs, being under no direct obligation further to transmit them. In later ceremonies, when young men are made into 'full' men, they are taught more about ownership. I know very little about these later ceremonies because most of the knowledge is strictly for men.

Yarralin people are far more concerned to include rather than to exclude, and they emphasise their concern that every option be taken up. The salient point here concerns the patrilines through which the transmission of men's business is not optional but rather obligatory. These lines are conceptualised as forming a continuous chain of men from Dreaming into the future. They can be constructed only through marriage (chapter 8), because only marriage gives a man formal rights to his wife's children.

Which country?

Anthropologists have for decades debated the question of what kinship is 'really' all about (Lévi-Strauss 1969; Schneider 1972; 1984 and Keesing 1975 are some of the key figures in the debate; see Keen 1988 for an overview of the whole topic of kinship). The information presented here does not resolve a debate which may, in any case, be unresolvable. It does indicate, however, that for Yarralin people kinship is all about the matrix of country, Dreamings, flesh, and people. The purpose and meaning of families emerge from the achievement of continuity and closure in the Dreaming-country matrix.

I can state this dogmatically, but then I must return to the flexibility of context. As we have seen, Dreaming strings differentiate, connect, and cross-cut. Country is a geographical nexus of Dreamings and people. In Ngarinman the term for country is *ngurra*. Specifically, *ngurra* refers to:

- a person's own camp (in this context the location shifts as the person shifts; camp is where one has one's fire and one's swag);
- family area, usually marked by one or more *kuning*;
- *jamaran* (clan) area;
- geographical region;
- language area;
- ecological zone.

The term *ngurra* is thus used in many contexts, and allows ample manipulation of definitions of countrymen (chapter 10).

The group of people who are identified with a family area can usually demonstrate genealogical relationships. The patrilineal identity *kuning* is usually an identifier of family area, but because both matrilateral and patrilateral rights to country are recognised, the group of people associated with the country is not a patrilineal group.

The *jamaran* area is comparable to McConvell's 'clan area', but, as discussed earlier, Yarralin people rarely give social significance to this fact, and are reluctant to speak of it.

Geographical regions also form a basis to country distinctions. For example, the Ngarinman language area is divided into three geographical areas which correspond, roughly, to the drainage systems of the Wickham, East Baines, and West Baines Rivers. These regions are all part of one language group, and are linguistically marked by different accents (in Yarralin people's view) and the inclusion of loan words from different neighbouring languages.

Language, too, is a way of defining country, and thus of defining people who belong to that country. Speaking the language of one's identity is not an issue here. People belong to the area defined by the Karangpurru language, for example, because one or both of their parents were Karangpurru, and this is so regardless of what languages they speak.

Ecological zones based on coastal, riverine, and desert environments are also a basis of country distinctions. Coastal regions incorporate an area which Yarralin people call 'salt water country'; it includes the coastal fringe and follows the big rivers inland to the point at which they cease to be 'salty' or tidal. Riverine country lies between desert and coast and is characterised, by Yarralin people, as having plenty ('too much') of fresh water all year round and plenty of trees and shade. Desert country begins around the headwaters of the big rivers and continues inland.

One type of marker of these ecosystems is plants. Ngaliwurru (salt water) country is forcefully distinguished from Ngarinman (riverine) country by *kakawuli*: a non-toxic tuber (*Vigna radiata*) which the black-headed python carried and deposited in Ngaliwurru country. The break between coastal and riverine seems to be the more distinctive, while the riverine/desert distinction follows a cline. Differing varieties of the edible seed-bearing kurrajong (*Brachychiton*) trees mark the distinction between riverine and desert countries, and, although less salient, also mark the coastal region. These ecological distinctions also seem to conform fairly closely to linguistic distinctions, as they are defined by linguists. Ngaliwurru and Ngarinman, for example, are sharply differentiated ecologically, and are members of two very different language families. The coastal/riverine/desert contrast also corresponds to different ceremonies for young men's initiation. Dreaming 'strings' connect regions; ecological and linguistic breaks are cross-cut by social clines.

Ngurra are like nesting boxes, and to belong to a country is also to belong to the larger areas of which it is a part. However, people who are 'full family' are necessarily related by country and are usually defined as 'the same', and it is in this context that Yarralin people express their most intimate relationships.

Being the same is a minimal context which can be defined as that area within which no further social differentiation exists. In some places family area, or a cluster of family areas, is minimal; in others language area is minimal. Bilinara affords a clear example of a language defined area which is minimal. Loss of population, and the warfare which forced many Bilinara people to flee their country and through which others were 'stolen', have resulted in an identification of Bilinara people as all 'one mob', among whom finer distinctions are usually ignored. Bilinara people show some traces of internal differentiation, and people's different life histories mean that some are particularly knowledgeable for certain parts of the country, but they insist that these undeveloped differences do not matter because Bilinara people are all one mob. As there is no context in which Bilinara people divide themselves with respect to Bilinara country, so the Bilinara mob is a minimal context. Social and geographical boundaries are reflexive. A minimal geographical unit is defined by social coordinates.

Country is the nexus of individuals, social groups, Dreamings, nourishing relationships, birth and death. Conversely, an individual is a nexus of countries. Jessie Wirrpa and her brothers Allan and Barry Young, and her sister Nina Humbert demonstrate this in their own lived responsbilities. They have no involvement with their father's mother's country. Their father's father's family area is defined in part by Jirrikit, the owlet nightjar, and they are intimately associated with the country where Jirrikit walked in Dreaming and where he lives still. Jirrikit is in the Karangpurru language area, and while there are some internal differences based on other Dreamings, Karangpurru people identify themselves as all one mob.

Jessie's (and her siblings') mother's father's family area is in the Ngarinman language area, and is identified with possum (apparently locally extinct) and other Dreamings. There are two women's areas in or near their mother's father's country, and Jessie and Nina have particular responsibilities for them.

Their mother's mother's country is Bilinara, and they are all emu people. Jessie and Nina are always called for when Bilinara women's business is being organised; Allan and Barry are key participants in men's business for Bilinara. None of them has lived consistently in Bilinara country, but they are indispensable to the country's wellbeing.

The story of their multiple ties to country is a capsule history of the region. Both Bilinara and Karangpurru language-defined groups were decimated during the early years of European settlement. Jessie's mother's mother was stolen from Bilinara country by marauding Ngarinman warriors and was married to one of them. Her only surviving child, a daughter, was given in marriage to a Karangpurru man, probably to foster ties to people who were safely established at the VRD head station. There she gave birth to six children, four of whom survived to adulthood, and only one of whom has had children who have survived. Jessie's generation of siblings has kept up their ties to Bilinara country in part because there are very few Bilinara people

Mary Rutungali, Lizzie Wartalila, Mollie Nampijina, Jessie Wirrpa, Nina Humbert Ngapitayin, and Dora Jilpngarri have just erected a sign marking a women's registered Sacred Site near Yarralin, June 1984.

to maintain the knowledge. As well, they note a lack of reciprocity. Their grandmother, Jessie and Allan say, was 'stolen'; proper exchanges were never made. In the absence of relationships of return, it is up to her descendants to remember their origins and to carry on.

This history requires us to ask: who are these people? If answers can only be exclusive singulars, then there is no answer. In Bilinara country they are Bilinara; in that portion of Ngarinman country which is theirs from their mother they are Ngarinman. In Karangpurru country they are Karangpurru. In all these places they are essential members of the group which is responsible for the country, running the appropriate business for each country. In these places they can call out to the 'dead bodies' who are their relatives; these countries know them, welcome them, and need them. At present there is no Aboriginal community within the whole of Karangpurru country, but if they are granted legal title to a portion they will probably live there most regularly, for this is the country in which they were raised, which they walked with their parents, which they know best and are most intimately identified with, and in which they want to die.

Multiple affiliations may be confusing to outsiders who expect boundaries to set up either-or distinctions, but Dreamings know their people. Allan Young and I discussed his relationship to Bilinara country just a few weeks after the land claim hearing in which he had argued passionately for the return of some Karangpurru land, identifying himself unambiguously as Karangpurru. It seemed like a good time to ask him if he had ever been watered for Bilinara country. He looked shocked and said 'No. Not me. Never. I'm Bilinara myself.'

Hobbles spoke to this issue, saying:

> I talk about boundary. They put that boundary to stop that cattle, but not men [human beings]. Cattle get branded and sent back, but people can go. Like, Mudbura married to this country, got children here now; we don't worry because all family. Mudbura can come visit. Whitefellow put these boundaries for cattle and horse, but people all one mob. Calf follow longa mother, drink that milk and stop longa mother. But not men. Men can go anywhere. Men can stop for three, four, five, six years, and come back.

He, like others, also noted the potential for chaos:

> Those Dreamings never go in and mix up. They keep out one from another. Because people owning and hang on . . . Still their father got to teach: 'this your country; this your Dreaming'. So they know, and don't make a mistake now.

Belonging

By Dreaming Law no country is dominated by another. Autonomy, the right to be self-governing without reference to a higher social authority, (chapters 9, 12) informs the reflexivity of person/group/country. Within their own country, mature adults expect not to be dominated by others (chapter 10). This is where they are needed and wanted, and this is where they have the indisputable right to be. While people have ownership rights in a number of different countries, they must live somewhere, and people who lack residence options feel themselves to be deprived. When people speak of having nowhere to live they speak of the need to be needed, of the security that goes with being in one's own, known, country, and of the right to a life in which they are not dominated by others.

Usually a person can live and hunt in, and take active care of, only one country at a time, although now that most people are settled in communities they often have greater scope for taking care of several countries if the distances are not too great and if they have access to motor vehicles. For most people, as long as countries are exogamous it is not possible to fulfil all obligations equally, nor would people expect to. In general, people seek to sustain their ritual responsibilities most broadly, while directing the full range of caretaking activities toward the country to which they have regular access.

Knowledge is built up over a lifetime and it is the older people who have the most knowledge, the greatest confidence in asserting that knowledge, and the most intimate relationships to country. Ways of relating to country vary through a lifetime. From their earliest days on earth children are introduced to country, and some of these countries become familiar home places. From childhood people move into intensive periods of learning and travelling, followed by a fairly expansive period of asserting knowledge and rights to vast areas of country. Old people become increasingly like Dreamings, singularly fixed and enduring. While maintaining their far-reaching ritual obligations, they also become focused on the country in which they wish to die. The choice of place of death is a final statement on a person's own identity (chapter 12).

I have seen this latter process happening with Big Mick Kankinang. He lived at VRD and then at Yarralin for decades, away (but not far away) from his own home country (Kuwang, his father's father's country) which is in the Ngaliwurru language area. As his position at Yarralin became less tenable because of political disputes he began to talk about going home. He expressed all the longing and sentiment for home place by referring to the *kakawuli* tuber which distinguishes Ngaliwurru salt water country from Ngarinman riverine country, saying: 'I've been here for years and years helping all these people. I'm really old people [elderly] now. I want to go home to *kakawuli*.' A key witness in three land claims, Big Mick finally obtained a block of land which satisfied his desire to be home.

Dream country is belonging. Every person has a place in the world in which they are needed, and in which they are 'heathy'. The emotional involvement with country, well attested to in much of the literature, penetrated my senses most eloquently one night when I was camping in the bush with a small family group. Lying on the ground, with a fire burning to warn snakes away, the woman lying next to me told her father, who lay nearby, that she had decided to leave her husband after many years of brutal marriage. In the dark her voice sounded hurt and bewildered as she said, 'I don't know why, daddy. He always beat me'. Her father offered her his strongest and deepest consolation. He called placenames, verbally travelling first through his mother's country, which is where his children had grown up, calling each waterhole, each hill and creek, marking its extent and indicating the Dreamings. He spoke of places and Dreamings in his father's country, calling them by name. And he punctuated his words of comfort with this assertion: 'All that, that's all your country now.'

8 *To Have and to Hold*

Yarralin people would not agree with the proposition that marriages are made in heaven. Marriage is a key relationship, defining difference in one generation and constructing sameness in the next. Human demography in relation to country is a central issue: the allocation of country identities to an unborn generation of people. Women are strongly involved in marriage arrangements. Their critical role as ecological resource managers is matched by their responsibility for human fertility: both its promotion and its curtailment. Since European invasion, it has not been necessary to curtail human fertility; indeed many small areas have virtually no people who are responsible for them through genealogical links. The future for many countries looks bleak, and human beings are an extraordinarily scarce resource. This fact continues to inform adults' attempts massively to control marriage. They attempt to distribute women, and hence human fertility, to groups who desperately need people; and they attempt to sustain reciprocities between groups by making 'paybacks' for people who have been allocated to them.

Such matters are far too important to be left to the contingency of individual choice. Marriage is an institution which is fraught with tension because people's lives are controlled by others. It pits individuals against their own and others' groups, and young against old. Any society that values individual will, as most Aboriginal societies do, and also requires that that will be controlled by others, must generate these conflicts. Since the very early days of invasion, Europeans have provided added opportunities for Aboriginal people to exercise their will in defiance of others. The result is almost certainly a large increase in overt inter-generational conflict. The question is not so much as to how conflicts come about as to how they can be managed and contained.

One major purpose of marriage is to create a relationship between groups and countries. This is a group concern, a group effort. With formal contracted marriages both kin groups–that of the husband

and that of the wife–must agree to the marriage. The actual husband and wife need not be agreeable; they are essentially pawns in the affair. But while I know many girls and women who did not want to be married, or at least not to be married to their particular partner, I know of only two men who did not desire marriage to a promised wife. Men's and women's differing experience and strategies of continuity generate this asymmetry: virtually all men want and need wives, but many women neither want nor need husbands.

Men's and women's differing experiences of camp life and independence also create different attitudes toward married life. In camp women are surrounded by relations; this is a domain in which they are central. Women cook and care for themselves and each other. Older women expect their dependants to care for them, particularly their daughters and sons-in-law. In their own camp they are boss, and I know of no instance in which old women have felt that they were not cared for. In contrast, the appropriate person to cook and care for a man is his wife; single men are expected to fend for themselves. Older men who are not married, very old men in particular, do not have this same network of dependants to care for them. If they are unmarried they must either stay with the young men in the single men's camp or attach themselves to a household in which they are, to some degree, dependants. With one exception, the single old men with whom I discussed these matters were keenly anxious to get a wife to care for them if they became infirm, and to provide them with a place in camp in which they were not dependants.

The anthropological literature on Aboriginal Australians overflows with discussions of the institution of marriage: as it relates to, informs, or determines types of social categories; as sexual politics; as alliance politics; as part of the economic infrastructure of society; as part of the ideological superstructure (Burbank 1988 provides a good summary of many of the issues). My approach is to look at marriage first as a matter of relationships between countries, discussing the ways in which people attempt to fulfil their obligation of providing a new set of owners for their country. From this discussion it becomes clear that the burden of the plans which one generation develops is borne by the younger generation. Accordingly, I discuss individual strategies of co-operation with, and resistance to, marriage plans.

We must remember that a primary obligation is to provide a new generation to assume the responsibilities for country, and to replace people as they grow old and die. Riley Young said that he takes care of his Dreaming 'lease': 'Till I die, till another man will take over that lease. Same lease. That lease forever'. Many of men's obligations are set in the context of secret business; rights to country are transmitted along genealogical lines; and men have rights both to their sisters' children and to their wives' children. They acquire rights to the son who will take over for them through being married to the children's mother. Marriage, for men, is absolutely crucial to the human continuity upon which their country and, ultimately, the cosmos, depend.

A part of each in the other

David Turner's (1987:95–106) analysis of the mode of constructing relationships between Aboriginal groups defines confederation as a mode in which things (groups, individuals, ideas) defined as being different are brought into relationships of interdependence such that each contains a portion of the other without becoming subsumed. The operative terms are *pluralism*: a system that recognises numerous ultimate principles; and *accommodation*: exchanges through which each contains a portion of others without loss of integrity.

As I understand Yarralin people's ideas about relationships I see two types: symmetrical and asymmetrical. Symmetrical relationships are those in which the reciprocities are balanced. The group of mature adult owners stands in symmetrically-balanced relationships to their own country and to other equivalent groups. There is no greater social authority. Relationships betwen countries, like relationships between species, must be balanced. If one country were to annihilate another, the result would ramify to destroy the balance which is critical to continuity.

Asymmetrical relationships are those in which a person's options are limited and where obligations are not reciprocal. These are authority relationships. Within a country asymmetrical authority relations are thought to be legitimate between seniors and juniors. Between countries, legitimate authority relationships concern only individuals: mothers-in-law and other in-laws have some authority over sons-in-law; husbands have some authority over wives.

Marriage is predicated on exchange; brother and sister (putative or actual), marry brother and sister. An example of an actual case will help. Jangari's son, Janama, has married his FMBSD (father's mother's brother's son's daughter) and Japarta's son, Jurlama, has married his FFZSD (father's father's sister's son's daughter). Janama and Nanaku are brother and sister; they have married another brother/sister pair:

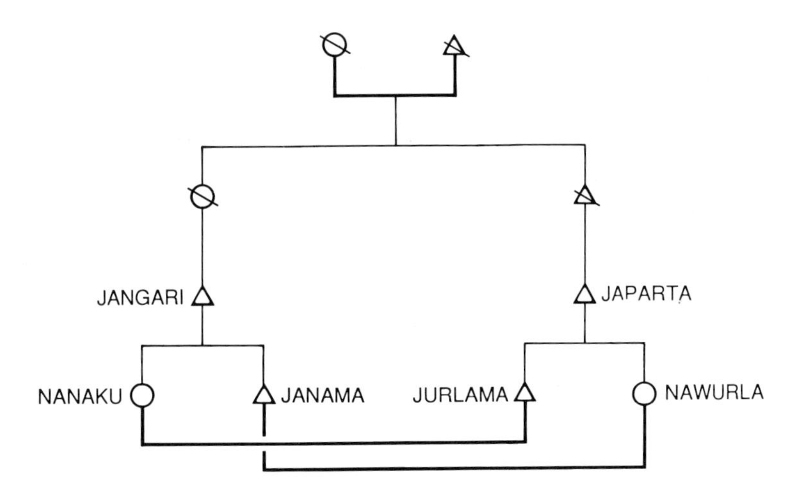

Figure 21 Sketch diagram: marriages between Jangari's and Japarta's children.

One country–the people one does not marry–can be bounded differently for different purposes. The example shown in figure 21 is one in which the Jangari/Japarta men define themselves as one country in relationship to ownership and care of that country. In the context of marriage they have chosen to emphasise their differences, becoming, as Marie Reay (pers. comm.) puts it, fictive non-kin. There is no contradiction here, but there is great sensitivity to context.

Subsections offer one way of talking about correct (or 'straight') and 'wrong-way' marriages. Each subsection category has its appropriate marriage partner. Because of the redundancy in the system, there are a number of genealogical paths leading to the correct category. From the point of view of the husband, his wife might be defined as his father's father's sister's son's daughter (FFZSD), his father's mother's brother's son's daughter (FMBSD), his mother's mother's brother's daughter's daughter (MMBDD), or his mother's father's sister's daughter's daughter (MFZDD). In practice, marriages among such close relatives are not common, but they are certainly present.

In fact, a great range of marriages is allowable (cf. McConvell and Hagen 1981:23–4; 1982:89; Stanner 1979a:58). Marriages among 'close' (usually genealogically demonstrated) relatives are rare. *Ngurlu*, as stated, effects an absolute constraint on choice of marriage partner: people do not marry within their own *ngurlu*. This rule is reflected in the permissible marriage categories: none is achieved through female links alone. *Kuning* also serves as a restraint; usually people do not marry within their own *kuning*. This too, is reflected in the fact that none of the permissible categories is based solely on links through men.

Many marriages are irregular with respect to subsection. McConvell (1982:90) estimates that 30–40 per cent of Gurindji marriages are irregular, and my census data indicate that over half of Yarralin marriages are irregular (see Hiatt 1965 for a good discussion of these and related issues). The fact that 'wrong' marriages occur is taken to be given; in Dreaming the moon engaged in an indiscriminate chase after women. Jimmy Manngayarri explained, as have others, that the practice of marrying 'wrong' is not new: 'That's moon been make the fault.' When other, more salient, rules are followed, this does not present a problem. Ultimately marriage is about country and people, and not about categories.

Marriages are contractual arrangements made between groups. They are intended to repay past obligations, to initiate future obligations, to create ties between groups, and to procure a new generation of people who will become affiliated to their parental countries and who will 'take over' the responsibilities when their parents die. Those which are arranged with due consideration of country affiliations provide great scope for strategies of consolidating a new generation of persons with rights and responsibilities for country.

In order for a man to obtain the right to deliver his rights and responsibilities to his own children he must first acquire rights to those children by acquiring rights to a wife. He does this through brideservice which has two major components: residential and ritual. A man must go and live with or near his wife's family for some period of time as part of acquiring full rights to his wife and her children. During this time he is expected to work for his wife's family and to learn something of her country. The ritual component involves carrying out a specialised role in putting his wife's brother(s) through the first stage of male initiation. This role includes guiding the novice through the various steps in initiation and providing the boy's family with goods.

There are among Yarralin people two models of how marriages are contracted. One stresses the relationship between a man and his daughter's husband, identifying the woman's father as the wife-giver, and linking patrilines to exchanges of marriage partners between countries. The other stresses the relationship between a man and his sister's daughter's husband, identifying the woman's mother and uncle (MB) as the wife-givers (see Glowczewski 1988a; Glowczewski and Pradelles de Latour 1987 for challenging analyses of the linking of matrilines to exchange of marriage partners between countries among the Warlpiri). I have found that the second of these models is more prevalent among Yarralin people than the first, but I have also found that actual cases depend upon the respective ages of father and uncle, and the particular strategies the group is pursuing. Frequently, marriages represent the working out of tactics which involve both models. And failed marriages, not surprisingly, are rarely anyone's responsibility.

My understanding of marriage arrangements derives primarily from the second model. In order to understand the rights which people have in arranging marriages, we must start with birth. In Yarralin people's view, children are not responsible individuals. Rather, they are dependants and as such are obligated to those who take responsibility for them; only gradually do they gain independence through paying back their obligations to others. They are primarily obligated to their mother and uncle (MB) for having given them life and body. Mother and uncle have rights to the life and body of these children; one of their rights is to enhance their own social relationships through their children.

As an example, Namija and Jimija (B/Z) are said to 'belong' to Namira (M) and Japarta (MB). They are the children out of 'their belly'–Namira gave them milk and body which they share with all of ther maternal relations. Japarta gave them food which grew their bodies. These two people, mother and uncle (MB) are said to be 'boss' for their sister's children: the children out of the sister. The children, sister and brother, are given first to the sister's husband. This is a 'promise'.

According to most Yarralin people, the mother and her brother decide to whom the daughter will be promised, but women downplay their authority in these matters, stating that the girl's uncle and father have the right to decide to whom she will be promised. All people live within a web of previous obligations and these must be paid off. If one country/kin group gave a wife to another country/kin group at some time in the past, then the recipient group owes a woman to the wife-givers and a promise may be made on that basis. The girl becomes the son-in-law's wife. Her brother is put through initiation organised by the son-in-law and is returned to the father so that he can take his place in his father's line of men.

Balance is formally built into the structure of arranged marriages. However, the final consideration with marriage is that people want to attract to and hold in their country as many people as possible. We have seen that residence is a critical factor in people's sense of intimacy with country, and that this sense produces long-term commitments both in life and in death. Holding one's spouse in one's own country means the assurance that the children will be raised there. To serve one's country–and by implication one's self and one's social group–well is to act in the present so as to provide for the future. In addition to social strategies, there are also extra-human methods. Both women and men, separately, have access to substances called *jirri* which they use to attract spouses and to hold them in the country where the user wants to be (cf Kaberry 1939; Akerman and Bindon 1986).

Making it work

Girls are promised well before puberty, and sometimes even before birth. The husband's age varies; people indicated that the appropriate age is about thirty-five years or older. The age at which men marry is declining, although promises are still most frequently made to older men. No man is too old to be a husband as long as he can persuade someone to promise him a wife. As a general rule a husband is at least twice his wife's age by the time that she starts to have children, although he may be much older. One effect of this age difference is that generations reckoned through women progress at a rate of about one generation every twenty-five years, while generations reckoned through men progress at a rate of about one generation every fifty years. Thus the amount of time it takes for a line of women (four generations) to circle back around is about one hundred years; the time it takes for the men's lines (two generations) to alternate and return is also about one hundred years.

Girls say they do not like being promised. Their relations say that they owe this obligation to their maternal relatives, and adults agree that it is important to promise girls at a time when they are really too young to resist. Young promised girls were far more open with my daughter than with me about their resentment toward their mothers and uncles, and their dislike of their promised husbands (see Burbank 1988 for a thorough and sensitive treatment of these issues). The questions they asked me about my experience with my first husband indicate some of their concerns: 'Was he awfully old, Debbie?' 'Did he stink?' 'Did he used to beat you all the time?'

Old men say that they are better husbands than young men because they understand the value of women and take care to treat them properly. As one man said to me, 'an old man will take care of you and give you money. A young man will only give you disease'. Many women agreed with the basic principle being asserted here. A young woman, for example, explained to me that 'an old man can save your life, but a young man will just give you a hiding all day and all night'.

A promise is a conditional gift. In essence, a son-in-law serves a probationary period while he is working for his in-laws (WM, WB, WF, and WMB). They may decide that he is not a good son-in-law and in that case they have the right to retract the promise. They need to be able to show his relations a good reason why they are 'pulling back' their daughter, but given sufficient cause they have the right to do so.

I know of one such situation. It was a sad and violent story of a man, who was much too young to receive a wife, being promised to a girl who was, herself, a bit young. The young man was subject to fits of violence, many of which focused on his little promised wife. Because the promise was interconnected to a whole series of other marriages, both families tried to pretend that it was a normal situation. But it clearly was not, and in the end the mother, father, and uncle took back their daughter and promised her to an older and wiser man who had already proved himself to be a good husband and who, as an added bonus, was an excellent fighter.

As I have said, the new husband has the obligation to put his wife's brother through initiation. It sometimes happens that a man puts a boy through initiation with the promise that the boy's kinsmen will provide a wife at a future date. Failure to do so is regarded as a serious breach of contract; one man, who has not yet received a wife in exchange for initiation work, talked about the problem as one which might require him to resort to sorcery.

Yarralin people often let time lapse between the promise and the return, allowing for flexibility and for the fact that some marriages just do not work. A man whose promised wife leaves him can honestly claim that he does not owe her group a wife because he himself has no wife. On the other hand, until he gives back a wife he cannot claim to have complete rights to his wife. Her relations can take her back, claiming that they have not received a wife in return.

A country-based group tries to assure new generations to take over. In order to retain access to the women's children, they attempt to hold sons-in-law in place. To do this they must enforce the daughters' marriages. In Yarralin it is most emphatically the case that a girl who runs away is in as much trouble with her own relatives as she is with her husband. However, once the husband decides to take his wife away from her own country, her relations may become less committed to the marriage.

I know of no instances, past or present, in which a husband chose to leave his wife. I mentioned two instances in which men did not desire 'promises' because they did not want to take on the obligations involved. Both men said that they did not want to live somewhere else. That is, they were unwilling to become sons-in-law. When I asked what would happen if a man wanted to leave his grown wife, people shrugged; some suggested that 'he must be a little bit silly'.

In Yarralin people's experience it is women who want to leave their husbands, and it is husbands who try to retain their wives. Attitudes towards divorce thus reflect men's and women's differing attitudes toward, and experience of, marriage. All women are married at least once. This is a fact of a woman's life, and in almost every instance the girls resent being promised. Women who were once married and who are now single by preference say that they do not want to leave their country and that it is 'too much nuisance' looking after a husband.

When a woman is promised she is fulfilling both her brother's and her own obligations to their maternal relations. Because of the symmetrical relationships involved, she is also securing a wife for her group. Her uncle has the right to give her away, and he stands to gain a wife. Her loss of independence is his gain of a human being. What is symmetrical from the point of view of the group is devoid of symmetry from her own perspective. Throughout her life she takes whatever she likes from her uncle–food, clothing, money, anything at all, and during certain ceremonies she is allowed to beat him quite unmercifully.

Her mother also had the experience of being promised. She too suffered a loss of independence. However, she has a strong interest in agreeing to her own daughter's loss of autonomy. Brother and sister are co-owners of their country. They are under the obligation to assure that there will be a new generation of owners for that country. To assure a full complement of owners–a group of cross-cousins–the brother as well as the sister must have children. When a woman and her brother promise the woman's daughter they are maintaining or initiating the reciprocity by which the brother will acquire a wife.

As girls mature they begin to spend more time with their husband and less time with their parents and siblings. Ideally the husband and young wife should spend time in the bush learning to rely on each other and to trust each other. In this context the husband becomes the only person feeding the girl; he thus begins to acquire more exclusive rights to her body. When a girl's breasts have grown full and menstruation has started, a husband begins to teach his wife about sex. Old women told me that nobody but their husband ever taught them anything about sex, and that they became women through sexual activity with their husband. This is the husband's right and obligation. A woman's sexuality is her own; she has the obligation to stay with her husband and this includes the obligation not to carry on sexual affairs which threaten the marriage. Married men and women of discretion who choose to have affairs, and some do not, conduct them circumspectly.

The husband's investment in the marriage assures his rights to his wife's children regardless of what westerners would define as biological parentage. A woman can fight her way out of marriage but she cannot obliterate these rights; some women are torn between their freedom and their children. Yarralin people expressed it as Law, that the children belong to the husband if the wife chooses to run away; but many women, while agreeing in principle, expressed the view that a woman should be allowed to raise her children until they are of an age to be given to others. The case studies which I have relating to divorce and young children are in no way conclusive. Every one of them involves a situation in which one of the partners to the marriage was a heavy drinker and in each case the children were kept by the parent who was sober.

A man who marries a woman who has been previously married must make some payment to her kinsmen in order to legitimise the marriage and thus establish his rights to her children. If she has had children between marriages, he also acquires rights to them. Many (but not all) subsequent marriages are models of consideration, trust, companionship, and devotion. Most women do not remarry unless they feel they can expect such a harmonious marriage, and most do not stay married unless such an ideal is achieved. Many stay single. This does not prevent them having lovers and having children, or marrying again at a later date if they are so inclined, but it seems to be better for children to have two parents, and rights in two sets of countries; most single women are either childless or past an age to have children.

Men who lose their promised wife may demand another promise. They are, however, free to take on another promise from other people or to marry a woman who is her own boss and who chooses to marry them. Many men have had the bitter experience of working for years to grow a girl, to make her brothers into young men, to work for her mother and other relations, only to have the girl grow into a woman and leave or, in a few instances, die. Some men have had this happen more than once, and this reason alone is enough to make a sensible man try to win the affections of his young wife.

Initially, promise marriages are based on the premise that the girl is being coerced. She has no choice in the matter. As girls grow into womanhood, gaining physical strength and knowledge, they gain the ability to make and enforce decisions about their marriages. Those who stay with their promised husbands do so because they choose to, and while there may be pressure on them to stay married so as not to disrupt reciprocities, wife-husband relations become far more symmetrical. Indeed, the greater the investment a man puts into his wife, the greater his incentive to retain her. A sensible man perceives his own self-interest in a symmetrical marriage.

Men can have more than one wife at a time, and at Yarralin a small number of men have two wives; an even smaller number have three. Co-wives are often thought of as sisters and are expected to behave as sisters, that is, as close loving friends. In Yarralin it was rarely the case that actual sisters were promised to the same man, for that would be to waste the potential for in-law ties. If co-wives are roughly the same age they seem to find the situation useful and companionable. Their workload is cut in half as they can split up the chores, and it seems to be easier for them to carry on affairs and thus to have a more varied and independent sex life. But if co-wives are of differing ages a hierarchical situation obtains. The old wife is 'boss' for the young wife and she expects the young wife to take over the bulk of the work. She can also act as a 'policeman', making sure that the young wife does not run away or do anything silly. Young wives may have to put in a number of years of servitude before they are free to leave. I found that not one young wife with a much older co-wife was happy with her lot, and, as far as I know, all of them planned to run away when they got the chance.

On the other hand, many older women resent their husband's taking a new young wife. A first wife may dissolve the marriage simply by moving out, and there is very little that the husband can do. Older women cannot be coerced. Alternatively, a woman may try to coerce her husband into giving up the idea. Stripped to the waist, crouched in a fighting posture, striking her fighting stick on the ground, and shouting abuse and aggrievement, an angry wife is an awesome sight. She may be successful; it depends ultimately on her husband. At the least, she will almost certainly succeed in terrifying the prospective promise.

Aboriginal settlements in this area are fairly few and far between. Settlements are centres from which people take care of many countries. Marriages which are contracted between nearby countries need not also involve a change of residence. Quite a few Yarralin people have opted for this strategy as it intensifies intra-community ties, strengthens community factions, satisfies the rules of exogamy, and assures that owners will remain close to their own country. Of the thirteen marriage promises contracted since 1972 for which I have sufficient data to be able to speak concisely, nine were intra-community (including Lingara as part of Yarralin) and four were extra-community promises. I have no indications that intra-community marriages are more or less stable than others.

In adults' efforts to control marriage, we can see two major forms of asymmetrical relationships: parents control of their children, and a wife's family's control of a son-in-law. We have seen control over daughters; young men, too, are controlled, but rarely by their own fathers. Yarralin people say that formerly young men were restricted in their access to women and in their access to camp. They associated primarily with men, and procured their own food; they were under food taboos and they were under strict supervision. They had options as to where they could live but no options as to the rules under which they would live. I am told that if they were extreme troublemakers they would soon run out of places to go. One old man, who had a grudge against young men because of the difficulties he was experiencing retaining his wife, described the situation:

> I been growing up blackfellow. I know what's the reason, what's the generation, all that sort of thing. Oh, they won't let you go, I tell you. Five years, or might be nine years, you might go, but blackfellow just watching you gottem one eye: 'Now, that's the troublemaker.' Oh, they watch every place where you want to come out. Might be people might be get away from here. 'Ah, so and so going to so and so.' Oh, they keep watching what time: 'Ah yeah, here he's come out.' Oh, they give him a good yard, play around, you know, this and that. And something like bone him or sing him [use sorcery] . . . [discussion of methods]
>
> They call to you to get up, and they talk to you. Oh, you'll feel sick in about two day, three day. Two days, three days, four days, you might die. You sick about three days, and you'll die. You'll die. That's the rule belong Aboriginal people.

More propitiously, if young men were circumspect, they might attract in-laws and so begin to live as young adults. These days young men hope to go into stock work soon after they have been through initiation. As they grow into their late teens or early twenties, whether they are working or are just drifting around, they begin trying to find a wife by attracting either a married or a single woman, or by finding a mother-in-law.

The second asymmetrical relationship is that of mother-in-law and other in-laws over sons-in-law. A son-in-law gives up his freedom of residence and goes to live with or near his wife's family, and works for her and her family. Women do not directly order their sons-in-law to do things because they do not speak to their sons-in-law. For all the avoidance belonging to this relationship, it is nevertheless a relationship of authority, often expressed most vigorously and abusively by the wife's grandmother (MM). Ultimate sanctions here seem to lie with the mother-in-law who has the power to curse her son-in-law. I do not know exactly what a mother-in-law's curse does, only that it is spoken of in whispers and said to be lethal.

When the son-in-law fulfils his obligations he 'goes free': he has the right to return to his own country and to take his wife with him. The son-in-law who chooses to remain is encouraged to stay. The actual authority involved is vastly diminished, and part of being gracious is to emphasise symmetry.

Getting out of it

Indiscreet affairs are usually initiated by young women who are seeking a divorce and by those men who are too young to be promised a wife and are hoping to persuade a woman to run off with them, thus by-passing the promise system and acquiring a wife more directly. Young men who succeed in persuading a woman to make an affair public by 'running away' (staying away from camp all night) must face the wrath of the woman's husband and his relations. At this time the formal rule is that the husband has the right to throw boomerangs at the lover and the lover has the right to defend himself but not to fight back. These are the rules, but feelings often run high and the 'fight' may become something of a free for all.

Yarralin people agree that prior to 1965 (approximately) retaliation against a young man who ran away with a young (married) woman was much more violent than it is now. Many men suggest that in the past the burden of injury fell more heavily on young men than on young women, particularly as they faced the anger of most or all of the men in the community. One man who had been a young fellow during that period, and who, like many others, had his share of scars documenting his escapades, said that a young man who returned to his community after having run away faced not only boomerangs but also spears. The husband and all of his male relations, as well as any men who selected themselves as strong upholders of Law, chased the young man out away from camp and threw their weapons with the express intention of shedding blood and breaking bones. In addition, mothers also had the right to beat their sons, and some of them did.

Young wives who run away are also subjected to physical violence. Taking account of all the violence engendered by marriage, it now appears that women suffer far more than men. Usually a husband does not beat his wife, since he wants her affection, not her resentment, but there are some men who think that physical power can prevail over personal will. None that I know of has been successful. Most aggrieved husbands ask one of their brothers to give the wife a hiding. Frequently it is the husband's female relations who are most quick to join in the fray. In the case of an old man with a young wife, his sons and daughters out of a previous wife or out of his sister's children will be the ones who express an outrage which is both the general outrage of the kin group (at the attempted disruption to their contract) and a personal outrage at an affront to someone they love. If the husband is younger, and his mother is still alive and active, she will express herself most vigorously. Daughters, sisters, and mothers rise up in their anger, wielding great fighting sticks. Afterwards they say that they were not satisfied until they had drawn blood. A runaway wife's own relations may also give her a hiding as they too have an interest in seeing the marriage preserved, and want to make it clear to the husband that they are committed to the relationship. Both men and women bear on their bodies the evidence of their attempts to wrest control of their marital arrangements from their elders.

Remember that people are trying to replace themselves in country. A man's sons are essential to him and he wants to keep them with him in his country. One strategy is to delay his sons' marriages for as long as possible so as to postpone the day when the son will go to another country as a son-in-law. Sons are generally treated indulgently. Men are frequently very tolerant of their own son's affairs, particularly their attempts to run away with a woman, for a woman who escapes out of a previous marriage is a wife for whom a man does not have to 'pay' with years of his life in another country.

The very behaviour that parents condemn in their daughters they condone in their sons. It is a situation in which everybody cannot possibly win. One night there was a good deal of shouting up at one end of camp, and in the morning Hobbles came over to explain to me that there had been an argument about a man beating his son. It's okay to bash a woman, Hobbles said, but not to bash a son: 'If you bash him, when he grows up he might not want to back you up or take your place.'

In order to terminate a marriage, a fight must take place between husband and wife. As Yarralin people explained to me, a man does not have the right to kill his wife, nor does a woman have the right to kill her husband. Refusing to remain married is an offence but not a capital offence. I witnessed one divorce at close range. In this instance the woman had run away from Wave Hill with a lover (the standard way of initiating divorce); they had come to Yarralin because they both had relations there. Her husband followed a few days later with a truck full of fearsome-looking relations. He had come to get her back.

The actual fight had *High Noon* overtones as the wife, her relations, and lover approached the centre of Yarralin from one end of camp and the outraged husband and his relations approached from the other end. I sat on an overturned forty-four gallon drum about thirty feet from where the fight took place. The husband told the wife to come back. She said 'No'. She didn't want to, she said, because she didn't like him any more. He closed in for a fistful of her hair, four or five boomerangs gripped in his other hand. One of her relations stepped forward and inserted herself between husband and wife. This was a vulnerable position and no person stayed there for long but someone was always between the two contestants and the message was clear: they did not want their relative killed, and were prepared to retaliate if anything happened to her. The husband broke several boomerangs over his wife's back, shouting at her all the time, but as she steadfastly refused to accompany him, his own relations began to give him advice. 'Leave her', they said. 'If she doesn't want you, let her go.' 'Plenty more women', they told him. And so he did let her go. He drove off in his truck making dire threats; his wife was now his ex-wife, free to do as she pleased.

The other way in which marriages are terminated is, of course, by death. When someone dies, Yarralin people are both grieved and angered. Grief and anger are the two sides to mourning, and much of the ritual surrounding death allows for the expression of these emotions.

When a woman's husband dies she immediately acquires the dangerous status of being married to a dead man. She does not speak with words but rather with hand signs because her dead husband might hear her voice and want to return. She is under suspicion of having failed to take proper care of her husband. So, too, are her husband's close relations, particularly his surviving brothers. The brothers and other relatives, along with the wife if there is no genuine suspicion, arm themselves with fighting sticks and boomerangs and visit every camp, crying aloud in their grief. This gives others the opportunity to express grief by crying with them, or to express anger by attacking them. In the one instance which I observed closely this visiting was a formality in that everybody believed that the deceased had been properly cared for. There was no fighting.

Shortly after the death of a married person, the surviving spouse's relatives make gifts of fabric to the family of the deceased. These gifts are intended for the mother and father, father's sisters and mother's brothers to acknowledge that these are the people who grew the person and had rights in the person. Later again, these people give back gifts of fabric to balance the equation and to mark the end of the period of mourning. The speech taboo is lifted some time later in a small ceremony in which the woman is rubbed with red ochre and given cloth to pass on to her relations. The woman's fathers or mother's fathers give the woman material and strike her lightly on the head, releasing her from the dangerous condition of being married to a dead body. The woman pays them with tea and bread, and after this she is free. According to Dora Jilpngarri:

> They rub with red ochre, that wash him out, finish, for that old man. Make tucker, make tea. They got to hit me. After, you can go married again if you want to. Might be two years, one year. No trouble now.

When a woman's husband dies, her husband's brothers continue to have some interest in her as a wife. If her first marriage was loving and considerate, she may want to marry one of the brothers; or, again, she may not. In general, men uphold the brothers' rights, and women uphold their right to choose. All Yarralin adults agree that brothers' rights are not compelling, and that widows who have fulfilled their obligations are free. Should a widow remarry outside of the circle of brothers, her new husband is expected to make some overtures of conciliation to the brothers who had an interest in her.

I have been told that the attitude of suspicion applies equally whether the deceased is male or female. In the two instances I have observed in which wives died, the surviving widowers were too grief-stricken to do anything but cry, and this was considered to be the appropriate behavior. One of these instances was complicated by the fact of murder and will be discussed shortly. My experience, while limited, suggests that the burden of grief-related violence falls most heavily on women. There are a number of reasons for this, and a case study will help to explore the disparity between the 'rules' and the complexities of life.

In 1986 a man in the prime of life dropped dead of a heart attack. He had been living away from his home community and country for a number of years, had remarried, and had died away from home. From a European point of view his death was yet another instance of the middle-aged death syndrome which afflicts Aboriginal people. Throughout the communities in which his death was felt as a close and personal loss, it was perceived to be the result of a very potent sorcery. It was an instantaneous death, and did not allow for any amends or attempts to heal social relations.

Initially, the death was too fresh and dangerous to be talked about openly; there were only whispers and denials of responsibility. I knew enough of the histories of the various families directly involved to form an opinion about who would be fingered as the sorcerer, and I waited for the name to be mentioned. As the days passed, people who were some distance from the families began to speak more openly of the event. They tentatively attributed the man's death to his wife, and pointed to the fact that her previous husband had also died. The fact that the earlier husband had died of injuries sustained by being run over by a truck while lying in the road did not alter the wife's responsibility, in their view. Most deaths have social causes; the immediate cause is only a means. I noted that the wife was from a distant community and had no local relatives to back her up, and as it became more possible to discuss the topic, I asked about the one person whom I knew to have a strong motive for killing the man. My questions were met with consternation, and I was gently told to keep quiet. The very few people with whom I felt able to raise the subject tactfully but firmly told me that they were not thinking about it. The firmness of their denial seemed to me to indicate that they were thinking about it, and that they did not like what they were thinking.

I took a truck load of people to the funeral. It was a distressingly intense ritual, filled with loud cries and self-violence, and punctuated by a sermon by a visiting missionary which struck me at the time as one of the most bizarre statements about death that I had ever heard. We women left the grave site while the men remained to deliberate on the cause of death. I sat under a tree back in camp with some Yarralin women who were concerned but not directly involved. One of the women held her young granddaughter on her lap and spoke to her softly, saying 'your uncle gone now'. She listed all the uncles the child had still alive, asking the child to repeat the names back to her. I sat and listened; along with the granddaughter I had an expressive lesson in kinship and continuity.

The camp bristled with tension as the women waited for the men's verdict. But before the men came back, the mothers and sisters of the dead man took matters into their own hands, savagely attacking his widow with clubs, iron pickets, wires, fists, feet and teeth. They had said they intended to kill her, but the missionary intervened, much to everyone else's relief, and the grieving women had to be satisfied with blood and broken bones. For weeks afterwards the dead man's mother sang a haunting lament for her son just as the sun went below the horizon in the evening.

In the aftermath, I was told that the men had decided that four people were responsible for the death. The wife was identified as one of them, and as she had received her 'punishment', she was in the clear. The other three I understood to be men, and I was told, in a roundabout way, that the man who had a strong motive was too dangerous to be named. Anyone who had such potent sorcery and would use it so cruelly would not hesitate to do so again.

In selecting the wife as a 'guilty' party, people chose a likely and relatively powerless culprit on whom they could vent their feelings and assure their dead relative of their desire to avenge his death, while waiting for more anonymous methods of sorcery to seek and kill the other killers, whoever they might be. There appears to be some displacement here, but there is also the fact that while men are extremely reluctant to shed women's blood, women have no such compunction. Some of the women who had beaten the wife told me of their extreme satisfaction at what they had done for their dead relative. There is also the fact that the widow fronted up at the funeral to get it all over with. Henceforth, her involvement with her dead husband was truly finished, and she was not under sentence of death by direct or indirect means.

Going home

Group strategies with regard to country are designed to maximise the opportunities of assuring a new generation to replace the older generation. Strategies are based on the expectation that not all efforts will be successful. Some people will be lost as effective owners, moving to other countries and staying there. Ideally, however, both men and women return to their own country.

The length of the husband's probationary period varies. If the wife's brothers are younger, the period lasts until the brothers are made into young men. If the brothers are older, then the length is dependent upon the girl's development. When she is fully matured physically she will be recognised as a wife rather than a promise. At the end of his period of brideservice the husband has the right to return to his own country taking his wife and children with him. He will then be able to resume his responsibilities in his own country, and will be able to raise the children in his own country. The importance of childhood in establishing intimacy with country means that both the husband and his relations and the wife and her relations have a strong interest in raising the children in their own (different) countries. The wife's relations may try delaying tactics, arguing that their daughter is too young to be taken away from her parents; that she should be with her mother when she has her first child; that they should receive a wife in return. But as far as I know, the formal requirements are that the wife be a grown woman, and that the brothers (or at least one of them) be made into young men.

Adults use their daughters and sisters' daughters as 'bait' to get sons-in-law into their own country. And although the husband is 'on probation', his in-laws are likely to treat him well; they say that they try to make him happy so that he will not be anxious to leave. As long as the husband is resident in his wife's country there is heavy pressure on a girl to stay with her husband and not run away.

Husbands, particularly older ones, are often anxious to return to their own country. They sometimes say that the wife's mothers (and fathers) 'spoil' her by allowing her too much freedom, and that the only way to make a marriage work is to take the wife away from her parents. I first heard this idea expressed when a man took his wife away from Yarralin at an age (sixteen) that her family considered too young. The wife had run away from her husband and he used this action as an excuse to remove her from Yarralin. I believe that the act of separating a wife from her family is an act fraught with bad feelings, for the wife's family wants to raise a new generation in their own country, while the husband and his group want the same thing. Since both groups cannot be satisfied, one group will suffer the loss of members in the present and may lose future opportunities to solidify ties with the new generation. In the few cases with which I am familiar, feelings about this loss were redirected toward the young wife herself. She was a pawn in the game all along, and, like many pawns, she bore the brunt of anger. On the other hand, the older people–husband and wife's relations–were able to maintain a measure of cordiality by shifting their ill-will onto the least powerful person in the whole situation.

Not all husbands are anxious to return to their country. Age is a significant factor here. As a general principle, the older the husband the more anxious he is to return. Younger husbands (thirty-five to forty-five years) have not yet achieved an age at which they are likely to have much authority in their own country. As in-laws in their wife's country they are treated graciously, whereas in their own country they may well be regarded as insignificant. And, of course, some husbands want their wives to be happy, both as a practical consideration and as a sympathetic regard for their well-being.

If the husband stays long enough, his wife will have marriageable daughters and she and her brother will want to promise these daughters and acquire sons-in-law there in their own country. In this case one strategy available to them is to relinquish some of their control over the daughters, so that the husband can promise his own daughters. That is, brother and sister offer the right to acquire a son-in-law in exchange for the continued presence of the sister's husband. This strategy has an appeal to a husband as he will the have a strong share in authority over the new sons-in-law. Alternatively, someone else in the local group may promise him another wife, thus extending his tenure in the area. Sons-in-law who choose to remain in their wife's country, living near their mother-in-law, are expected to provide their wife's relations with food, to drive them places (if a vehicle is available), and to take their part in community politics. On the other hand, once a son-in-law has fulfilled his obligations to his wife's relations and is free to leave, then it is clear that if he stays he does so by choice. The wife's relations try to treat these men well because they do not want to drive them away. Of the nine in-married men at Yarralin in 1981, three were pensioners and formed a political faction, three were unemployed, and three were employed, two as school assistants and one as a health worker. As there were only four paid jobs available for men at that time, it is clear that the distribution was not random.

A woman's loss of independence, like that of a man's is only temporary. A promised husband is usually much older than his wife, and he will not live forever. Some girls consider themselves lucky. They are promised to very old men; while their husband is alive they collect a pensioner's wife allowance from the Australian government and when he dies they collect a widow's pension. A young woman of, say, twenty, whose husband has died, is in an enviable position: she has fulfilled her obligations to her relations, she is free to make her own choices, and she has an independent income.

Not all husbands are so considerate as to die early in marriage. But then it is quite possible that a young wife may come to like, and even love, her husband. All girls resent being promised, as far as I know, but not all girls resent their husbands. By the time women are about thirty years old they are either single by choice or married to a man of their choice. At this point, and for the rest of their lives, women have far more choice of residence than do men.

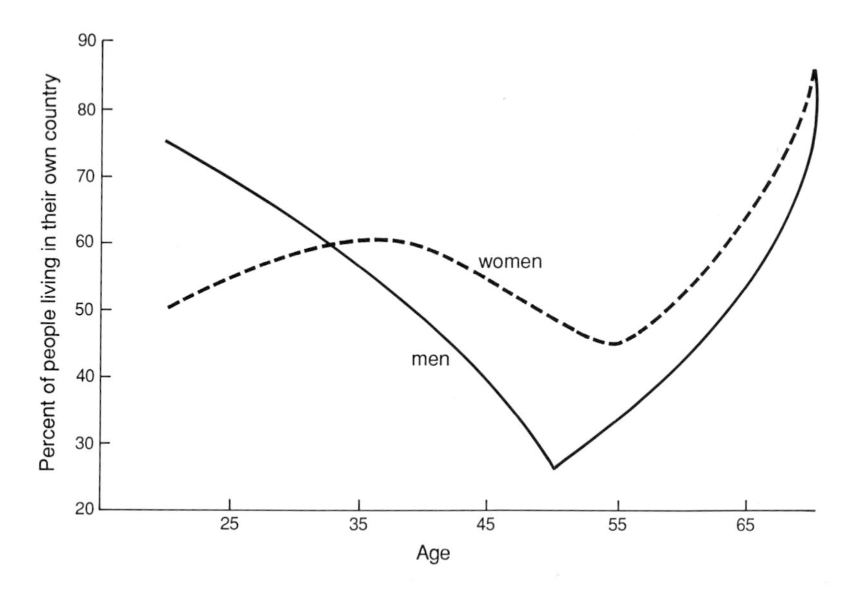

Figure 22 Ages and percentages of people living in their own country

Figure 22 shows the distribution of men and women in their 'own' (mother's or father's) country by age.

This chart shows the absence of men during the years when they are most likely to become husbands. It also shows that old men and women return to their own country at about equal rates. Because it is possible to caretake for several countries from a single residential base it is not always possible to specify whether people have returned to take care of their mother's or their father's country. Indeed, they may well be taking care of both.

Nancy's story

Nancy Kurungkikarri and I had many conversations about love, marriage, work, children, and the state of the world. She agreed to tape portions of her life history with me, turning the tape recorder off whenever she wanted to speak of intimate details or women's business. The tape was for the public, and she did her own editing as she went along. Here I reproduce sections of that tape, edited to focus more particularly on marriage. Local history, marital histories, European brutality, introduction to sexuality, birth and death are woven together in Nancy's words because they are her life experience.

A Ngaliwurru/ Wardaman woman, Nancy spent the early and late parts of her life in or near her father's country (Ngaliwurru). She was married to a European man for many years, and their travels took them away from her country. When I met her she had left her husband and had come back to live and die near her own country. She moved back and forth between Yarralin and Timber Creek, waiting for the land claim which might return to her some of her father's country. A chain smoker with an impish smile, lively eyes, and a devastatingly direct sense of humour, none of my photographs do justice to Nancy's vivid presence.

> My mother had three husbands. First one, but too cheeky he was. He's not this land, but nother land. On that Moolooloo side, that old fellow [his country; probably Wardaman]. And my mother didn't like to live with him. She was run away. Left him. That old fellow, my father's brother, she lived with him. And she had one daughter for old fellow, other old fellow, my father's brother. And he was same [cheeky] but he passed away. I don't know. I wasn't born yet. And after that she's come and married to our old fellow [father]. Old man Lisa's father [also Nancy's father]. She's married to him then. And this father, last father, had two girls, me and Lisa. And Japalukarri, this young fellow here.
>
> And this last father, our father, was too cheeky. And he had another girl [wife] then, come from this way, Wolayi side [northern Ngarinman] you know. From bush, you know. From bush side to go to station. Young girl he [she] was, I think. And my mother had had me. That young girl left my father.
>
> My mother couldn't find another bloke. She was there working single at Timber Creek. Keep me there . . . We was there. We was big girl a bit now, that time. And my father and my step-father had trouble in there. They ran away with the handcuffs.

Subsequent discussions clarified that her father and step-father had been arrested for cattle killing and brought to Timber Creek where they managed to break the chains and run away.

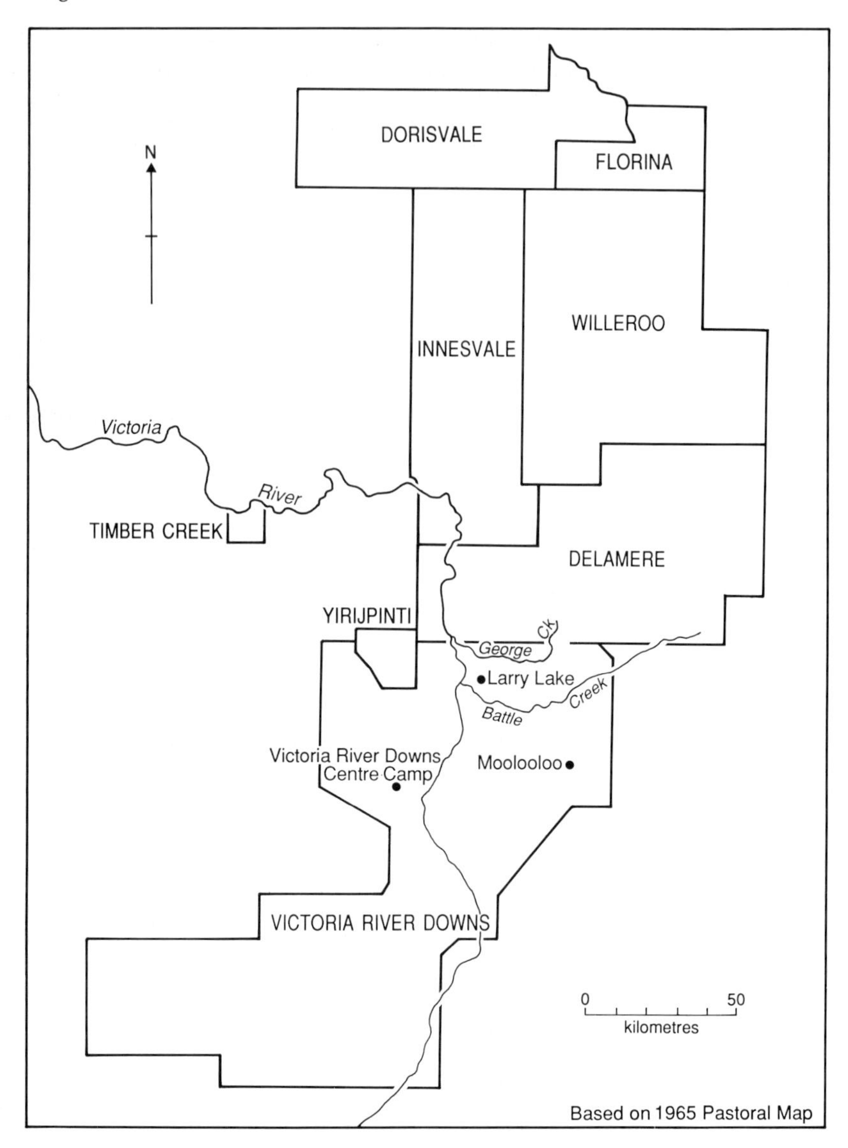

Map 6 Nancy's story

So they reckon. I don't know. I was only girl. And they run away from police station. And they cut em with the axe, something, tommyhawk, that handcuff. There was big trouble then. Run away, and my mother and my step-father went bush. And my old father. They was all right, mates together now.

They took me to bush. Living la gorge Yirijpinti now. We was there all the time. No man [European] been get through in that, you know, gorge. Too high that ground [cliffs]. And they used to think about for tucker. . . [discussion of all the different foods they used to eat in Yirijpinti country]. Till I been get big. My father took me to that country now, Yirijpinti. Till I been big girl. It was all right now. We went to Willeroo [station]. From Willeroo station and come back Delamere station. From Delamere station we was making to VRD, coming down from Battle Creek, ah, sorry, coming down from George's Creek to Larry Lake.

And that's where my father and my step-father been get caught there now over that trouble with they cut the handcuffs. Couple of copper there, what they used to hunting for trouble man ... [discussion of police and trackers]. What he had, prisoner. Prisoner you know. He tie em up longa tree, line up, six or seven boys. They going to gaol in chains. Give 'em a hiding before supper, before breakfast. With a big stick. Give em a hiding before they havem breakfast. They used to have breakfast after ... [discussion of trip to Timber Creek police station; the men were in chains and Nancy and her mother walked with them].

Soon as we get Timber Creek, he give em hiding again, [at the] gaol-house. And my other step-father, one who was married to my mother, he passed away right in the gaolhouse that time. He's dead [apparently beaten to death]. And my father went, they was finished there now, court, they went to Darwin [to gaol]. And one father was dead ... [further discussion of identities of police and of original 'wrong'-doing]. And starving there [at Timber Creek] for a while, for about one month we stopped there, Timber Creek. And go straight for VRD then ...

Come VRD. That be last. I never go back to Timber Creek again any-more. Took me out long way from here. My auntie took me. My mother working to Moolooloo then. She [the auntie; father's sister] took me to Florina [station], no Delamere, Willeroo, Florina, Dorisvale, back to VRD. Take me all over. My auntie used to do that ... [discussion of identity of her auntie, of the perils of walking around in those days, and of the foods they used to eat].

When I went, my auntie took me up from my mother. My mother was working Moolooloo, and my auntie took me right up to Dorisvale now. But that was all right. They never used to shoot them people, nothing, only when I was little girl all right, rough times. And I had promise from father and mother. Put me to one bloke. ... [discussion of identity of bloke]. When I was big girl really now, when I used to have thing [menarche]. I don't know [what age] because I wasn't in school.

Well, put me married to him then. My auntie was doing that. My father was in Darwin. I been get married. But his sister told him after. My auntie told him. 'Yeah. You right' [he said]. Well I didn't know I was to live with [that] man all the time. But he used to just chase nother bloke [woman] now. He used to chase another girl, chase nother girl front of my eye all the time. Because I couldn't fight. Too young. Well I didn't worry about, then. I didn't worry about him. I just walked away from him. That's all.

I come back here then. Other bloke [man] help me, pull me back to my mother. I never go back again [to her first husband]. I never go back there. Still here now. And after that, that bloke where he was help me, and he start to want to marry me now. I was just kangaroo married you know, not really. All right. Well, when I was live [with] that bloke now, other one, oh, he was good boy too. Good old man. He was all right. Cheeky bugger. He never used to let me go talk to any young girls, you know, mates. And he passed away. I had one boy for him. Yeah. I lost one boy. [Pause here, and some indistinct words, as she recollects the death of her only child.] And after that I find that bloke I tell you. White bloke now. I been married to him. Really married. Me and him been get married.

Later, in response to my questions, she spoke more about the experience of being promised.

You got a frighten for [you are frightened of] that man, what they give you married. You going to get scared: 'What he going to do with this thing [penis] here? What he got to do with this?'

> You know, all this, you frighten. They been give it report this man here, you see, all this [the women have told the husband that the girl is old enough]. Ah, when you get used to it, they take you away from mob. Aboriginal people do this. They take you away from people, you know. He might take you bush. And you get used to all that stuff [sex] because you got nobody to talk to you, you know. No mate, girls, there for you. He take you away. That's the way Aboriginal people do . . . [discussion of the laxity of today's youngsters].
>
> They used to have a meeting, when I was there anyway. Old people used to have a big meeting, you know. And they got that promise man there, [and] that girl.
>
> Right. I used to camp there, but I used to camp away from him, from his bed, you know. And my auntie, I always think about: 'What for you been give me this man?' You know. Mmmm. It's true.

Nancy also described in some detail how she tried to resist being a wife. In her discussion of sexuality she used a prevalent metaphor equating a penis with a spear and a wife with game.

> Auntie used to talk [to] me: 'You want to follow him now, get goanna, something, and bring him back for me?' 'No way. I'm not going with him. You want me to come back got a big spear [in my body]?'

9 *Freehold*

Dreaming actions created countries; no country, however, defined is subject to an outside social authority. I refer to this structural position as one of autonomy. Hobbles contrasted the current situation with life before Europeans came to the area:

> This land, he no got a lease [use-rights granted by a higher authority]. He's only the freehold. He's the freehold altogether. When that Captain Cook been come in stealing the freehold, people been free, sitting about on land belonging to him. Well, the same thing I want it. It's the freehold all over, people been havem.

Since invasion, no country-defined group in the Victoria River valley has been autonomous. All are constrained by an outside social authority. For the moment I want to explore relationships between countries as they are thought about, and as people try to maintain them in spite of conquest. I cannot sustain such an analysis for long; the purpose is to examine what 'ought to be' in order to understand more fully the kinds of constraints within which people now live.

Group testing

Assertions of group difference and group autonomy are emphatically group statements. They are phrased as the autonomy of country and the autonomy of ceremony lines, and they emerge most forcefully when people get together for young men's business.

When we went to Daguragu to make a little boy into a young man, the situation became extremely difficult. My classificatory brother, Jimija, was boss for this boy. He decided to run the *Wangka* line which belongs to him from his father. A group of *Wangka* people from Western Australia and the Northern Territory was already in Yarralin, having brought back a Yarralin boy and made him into a young man. After dancing all night, men and women together as it is done in *Wangka*, we piled into trucks and went to Daguragu, taking the Daguragu boy with us. The *Wangka* people came along to help Jimija,

Timber Creek men dancing *Wangka* at Yarralin, January 1984.

defining him as a countryman on the basis of their shared management of ceremony.

When we arrived in Daguragu we noted a certain amount of tension. As I understand the situation, there was an outbreak of violence which was unconnected to ceremony but which had divided people roughly along lines connected to the *Pantimi* (big river country) and *Yalaju* (desert) ceremonies. Into this situation came more *Pantimi* people and a sizeable group of *Wangka* people from salt water country (Kolig 1981 discusses the extension of ceremonial networks through increased access to vehicles).

On that first night there should have been dancing for a few hours.

Some Daguragu people said that as the little boy really belonged to that country and had ties going into the desert, they should dance *Pantimi* or *Yalaju* for him. That is, they wanted nothing to do with *Wangka*. Really, people said to me, they had no right to say this. Jimija was there working for his in-laws; they had contracted an alliance with a *Wangka* man, and *Wangka* they would get. I wondered, though, because Jimija also belongs to the *Pantimi* line from his mother. Were his in-laws really expecting *Wangka*? Jimija shrugged; they should be, he said.

The *Wangka* men said that their throats and feet were sore and they were tired; they asked the Yarralin boss for *Pantimi* to lead *Pantimi* just for the one night. He was outraged. He told them that if they wanted a rest they could have one. That was their business. But *Pantimi*, he said, is serious business: 'If you run that line you start at the beginning and carry it through. You don't just do it to give someone a spell.' Everyone's tempers were short from tiredness, from earlier violence, and from the arguments about ceremony. For that night someone else sang a bit of *Pantimi*, and the Yarralin boss, who was a regional boss by virtue of age, knowledge, and genealogies, declined to participate. About halfway through the dancing a different group came and tried to persuade him to sing, for it was not right to be singing this ceremony line with one of the key owners off in a huff. He refused.

The next day we went to the river to spend the day washing, painting, singing, and getting ourselves and the little boy ready for the evening. We danced *Wangka* during the day, and again the *Wangka* men appealed to others to take over the all night job as their feet were too tired. Many of the women became incensed at this abdication of responsibility. They said darkly and meaningfully that if the ceremony line was changed part way through, the little boy, and probably others, would die.

We brought the little boy into the ceremony ground dancing *Wangka*, and things seemed normal, but by night the hostilities were on again. The Yarralin boss still refused to sing *Pantimi*, as he would not allow it to be subservient to *Wangka*. The *Wangka* men were adamant that their feet were too sore. In the end, some men from the desert country, and some others who had ties to that area, decided to sing *Yalaju*. The *Wangka* men and the Yarralin boss for *Pantimi* all retired.

In the morning I had the feeling that those of us who were identified as *Wangka* and *Pantimi* people were in bad odour. A number of *Wangka* people left. Mirmir and I were jointly doing the sister's work for Jimija at his request; we drifted around for much of the day waiting for the local women to call us. When summoned, we went to the boy's mother's camp; the local women did a minimal portion, without our assistance, and then told us that we could leave. Thus deprived of our rightful work, we left.

The Yarralin *Pantimi* boss had been asking me to get him out of there almost since we had arrived. It was clear that he neither wanted

Mollie Nampijina (behind) and Jessie Wirrpa painting Maxie Horace before giving him back to the men during 'young men's business' for Maxie, January 1982.

Daisy Nguriya, Agnes Draper, and Kitty Tawil (right) toss Douglas (Big Mick's son); this is part of the work that women do in making little boys into young men, December 1981.

to diminish the autonomy of *Pantimi* by using it as a compromise, nor to become involved in antagonisms between *Wangka*, *Pantimi,* and *Yalaju.* Since my work was done, and as I was considerably distressed by the hostilities, my own exhaustion, and the occasional outbreaks of violence which were unconnected to ceremony but added an undercurrent of threat to the whole affair, I agreed to leave. I learned later that the ceremony had been completed using *Yalaju.*

Later some of the *Wangka* men explained to me that they had been too tired and that the Daguragu mob was too 'cheeky', that is, hostile. I understood that they were a small group of salt water people venturing into the fringes of the desert. They were surrounded by foreign languages, Dreamings, ceremony lines, and Law which were represented by a much larger group of people. I think that in the end their determination failed them. They were, I suspect, frightened by the aggression and violence which people to the north believe to be characteristic of desert people. Rather than press ahead in a situation which they felt to be weighted against them, they left, preserving their autonomy through strategic retreat rather than through assertive pushing.

The *Wangka* mob was 'testing'; the term is roughly equivalent to the American expression 'to run it up the flagpole'. In 1982 nobody at Daguragu was saluting. But in subsequent years they repeated their test with more success, and by 1984 they were joking and telling tall tales about how easily they could get to Daguragu.

Warfare

Personal and group autonomy are maintained competetively. Groups are potentially hostile, striving to attract people and retaliating against the loss of people. Both intergroup and interpersonal (adult) relationships are conceptualised as ideally symmetrical: personal and group strategies aim at defending the integrity of a unit against the depredations of others, while at the same time defining the boundaries of group in ritual and in daily life.

Yarralin people see both warfare and sorcery as forms of vengeance. The specific wrongs which require a 'payback' (balance) are loss of women, murder, and threats to autonomy phrased as the usurpation of rights (objects, songs, designs, and other items) which define groups as autonomous. These grievances are conceptualised as group concerns. The group that is attacked retaliates against the whole group of the person(s) who caused the trouble; it is not a question of tracking down the actual person(s) responsible, although this is seen as a satisfying enterprise, but rather of inflicting a loss in exchange for a loss.

I have far more specific information about sorcery than warfare, and while I am unable to make point to point comparisons, I believe it is best to regard sorcery as an alternative to direct killing through warfare. The same principles of group responsibility and the need to effect an end to the 'trouble' apply in both instances, although I believe that warfare may have involved larger groups than sorcery now does. Warner's (1969) study of Arnhem Land people, based on field work in the 1920s, offers considerable information on warfare. His statement that fighting 'prevents modifications in society that would possibly destroy it' (ibid:144) indicates both the need to fight and the need to contain hostilities.

My understanding of warfare derives from the post-invasion period which was a time of intense disruption. This is the period which Yarralin people's memories encompass; they agree about the fact that there were 'blackfellow wars' before this time but they have very little knowledge of the details of such wars or of methods for establishing peace. Big Mick Kankinang was born and raised in the bush. He died in 1990 at the age of 90, and the stories he heard from his father and other old people go back before invasion. He said that his father told him that before Europeans came into the region, Aborigines used to make peace in the context of ceremony. In Big Mick's words: '[They] used to come together for ceremony and cut it off, that war. That was good country then.'

Sorcery, a form of covert warfare, can be seen as a way of redressing wrongs at a distance, of redressing wrongs personally, of redressing wrongs where personal knowledge is insufficient, and of explaining the otherwise inexplicable.

The type of sorcery through which wrongs can be redressed at a distance is referred to as *munpa*. *Munpa* means a person whose life is flowing out of him or her, a person who is dying. It is the body, that which one shares with one's countrymen, that which has been nourished out of country, which can be interfered with. To do so is to make the victim *munpa*: a dying body rather than a living body. I was told that another way to accomplish *munpa* is to attack a person's Dreamings rather than go directly for the person. Dreamings are part of one's physical-spiritual being; an attack on a Dreaming is an attack on the life of the people belonging to that Dreaming. Yarralin people told me very little about this form of sorcery; my impression is that it is a rather circuitous way to accomplish something which can be, and usually is, accomplished more directly.

Munpa sorcery is relatively indiscriminate; people said that a 'song' or similar means of accomplishing sorcery at a distance, would go through a group of countrymen systematically, killing them one by one until an agreement could be reached whereby the grievance could be settled.

Let us suppose, as a hypothetical case compiled from several actual cases, that my group has a wife who has been promised to one of our old men, and that woman leaves him. My group has a legitimate grievance: a promise was made and one of our men worked to fulfil all the obligations owing to another group in order to establish his rights to the promised wife and to the children she might bear. If she leaves, we have the right to fight and also to take back one of our women who is married to the other group. Rather than tracking down the woman and fighting with her group, my people may send out a 'song' or other form of *munpa* to follow and kill the woman and her lover (if any). Alternatively, we might mark Dreamings, make objects, or point a specialised bone to accomplish the same purpose. Such an action has much to recommend it to us: the net result will be the death of the woman, her lover, and possibly some of their countrymen as well. This result can only be satisfying to us as we have lost our wife and her potential children whom we had hoped would become a new generation of owners for our country.

Yarralin people described a number of incidents which involved sorcery to avenge the loss of a wife, and in their evaluations it became clear that this type of action has one serious drawback. It is not a capital crime to leave one's husband, or for a man to run away with a woman, and death by sorcery following from a broken marriage is interpreted by the runaways' relations as an unwarranted attack. Both the woman's countrymen and those of her lover suffer an unwarranted loss and thus have their own legitimate grievances. Having been attacked, they will retaliate against the group which sent out the *munpa*. Each death is a loss which must be paid back. Like any form of warfare, this has the potential to escalate.

One earlier form of dispute resolution involved non-fatal spearing. The person who had 'made the wrong' would present himself to the injured parties. They had the right to spear him (the thigh seems to have been the favoured location). Afterwards, those who had done the spearing gave the wrong-doer a firestick as a sign that the trouble was finished. Once finished it was indeed over with; it was not to be considered again.

Other instances in which *munpa* may be used are those in which people come close to knowledge which is secret. Most of the instances I know of are of young women, more rarely young men, who were said to have disrupted men's business. Sorcery was not considered to be the most likely form of retaliation in these instances; Yarralin people said that the 'business' itself might kill intruders, or alternatively, that people from the Warlpiri language area to the south (who are said to have a Law for killing men and women who intrude) might hear of the matter and come and kill the person directly.

When one group attacks another by *munpa* they do not make it public: the point is to inflict a loss without being open about it. It may take years for *munpa* to accomplish a death, a fact which further serves to preserve anonymity. All the people with whom I discussed these matters had a grievance against another group and believed that others had grievances against them. When a person dies, the countrymen start discussing all the difficulties that may have caused grievances over the years, trying to determine who might have caused the death so that they will know where to inflict a loss in retaliation.

The concept of *munpa* is important, not only because it can be used to explain the otherwise inexplicable (why a certain person died), but also because it can provide an alternative explanation to the otherwise obvious. When Daly was a young man he killed another man with a boomerang. According to his account of the event, two men were fighting with his brother and he rushed to the defence, hurling a boomerang at one of the men and hitting him on the back of the neck. The man died. Daly said that he felt terrible about killing this man, who was one of the last of the 'bush blacks'; Daly had great respect for him and had had no intention of killing him. The final consensus on this event was that the dead man had been *munpa*. That is, someone (not Daly) had interfered with the life processes and the man was dying. It was unfortunate that it was Daly's hand that threw the fatal boomerang, but Daly could not be considered guilty of murder. He had only been the unwitting agent in a process that he had had nothing to do with.

Some Yarralin people said that this form of sorcery is no longer practised. Others were not so sure. Some felt that there were no local sorcerers, but that in other areas sorcery was still being practised. This latter concept demonstrates a point which anthropologists working in many parts of the world have discussed: the belief in the existence of cruel practices, and the attribution of these practices to people beyond one's own social sphere (Evans-Pritchard's 1937 study of witchcraft is a classic text in which many of the points made here are discussed). Regardless of current practices, the fact that it may take years to accomplish death by *munpa* means that this type of sorcery is still extant and every person in Yarralin has had contact with it.

Personal sorcery is essentially a face-to-face encounter. What distinguishes it from *munpa* is that the sorcerer secretly attacks his particular victim, either with fast-acting poison or surgery. The most commonly discussed type is said to be carried out by 'kidney fat men' who steal a person's kidney fat, leaving the person unmarked but dying. While the attacker remains unknown, death occurs rapidly, usually within a few days. Yarralin people say that they do not practise this type of sorcery although they believe that certain neighbouring people are adept at it; I heard many stories of people from other areas, principally to the north, who steal people's kidney fat, poison people, or otherwise accomplish death. Most Yarralin people had no explanation as to why these sorcerers kill people. Most suggested that they do it randomly, 'just for nothing'. But according to one in-married man whose father had been a 'kidney fat man', the old man never killed people 'just for nothing'. Rather, he was a hired killer, working for others who had specific reasons as to why they wanted a person killed. In addition, he said that his father had rubbed his hunting and fishing equipment with human kidney fat to improve his success in his regular subsistence activities.

In Yarralin this form of sorcery constitutes a free-floating information pool which may be drawn upon to explain otherwise inexplicable events without having to accuse any person or group in particular. One old man, who died just before I went to Yarralin, was said to have been killed by someone who stole his kidney fat for reasons which were, and remain, unknown.

The third type of sorcery is that which is used where there is insufficient knowledge. This is a form of direct payback for the loss of a person through death in those cases where the killer is not known. There are several methods of accomplishing this payback. The body of a dead person can be specially treated before it is buried, with the intention that the treatment will seek out the killer and kill him. One method people told me about is the insertion of a wire between the dead person's ribs. Another method involves Dreaming power. Near Wave Hill there is a dangerous site for the Dreaming snake Jurntakal, the embodiment of all poisonous snakes. If the clothes of a dead person are burned at that place, the snake rises up and goes travelling across the sky until he finds the killer and strikes him or her dead. In Kriol this snake is called 'Traffic' meaning that 'he only goes one way': he finds the correct killer and strikes him dead.

The value of this form of sorcery is that it is believed to be accurate and predictable. Using Traffic, people say, assures that the correct killer will be found. A death subsequent to the one for which Traffic was called upon will be attributed to Traffic, provided that the death occurs in a group which people are willing to believe might have killed someone. From the point of view of the group which summons 'Traffic', the results are unambiguous. But this is not necessarily the viewpoint taken by those who suffer the subsequent loss. They may well deny that the dead person ever killed anyone, deny the claim that Traffic killed the person, and instead seek, through Traffic or other means, to find and destroy the person who killed their countryman. Traffic is thus unambiguous in one context, but thoroughly ambiguous in another context. Events must be interpreted to become meaningful, and one group's satisfaction may well be another group's 'bullshit', as it is expressed in Aboriginal English.

A case of murder

Let us now look at a detailed example which will illustrate many of the principles developed in earlier chapters. The particular points I have in mind in analysing this murder case are:

- the flexibility of identities;
- the meta-rule of symmetry;
- the use of available information to define and redefine the meaning of events;
- the lines of responsibility for individual and group autonomy;
- the negotiation of events and identity, autonomy and dependence.

This murder took place towards the end of my 1980–2 research period. I was then conversant with all of the participants and with most of the background information necessary to follow the flow of discussions. I was able to understand enough of a range of languages to follow the issues, and I became involved in the negotiations in a fairly intense way. Everybody realised that a murder would have to involve European authorities and concepts of justice. Many people hoped that by having me write their words in my notebooks, the notebooks would become a sort of context-free data-base which might prove useful in dealing with Europeans. They also thought that I might be called to court as an outside witness. To this end, people took a great deal of time teaching me everything they thought I might need to know as an 'expert witness' and I was present at all the public negotiations about the event. In addition, some people took the opportunity to enter their private views into my notebooks as a back-up against the possibility that they might wish to make their private views public at some future point (this use of my notebooks was not unique to the murder case).

In this analysis I have assigned arbitrary non-local names to the key participants in order to safeguard their privacy. Since all the opinions expressed to me privately were also expressed publicly at one time or another, I treat the public expressions as public knowledge. One of the points I want to make through this case study concerns the negotiation of meaning. I will present the information as I first became aware of it, for the convolutions in the events are a large part of what makes the case worth discussing.

On the morning of 6 April, 1982, a message came from VRD on the clinic radio: a woman had been killed at VRD; the police had been called in and would arrive shortly. In Yarralin the consensus was that grog (alcohol) had had something to do with the murder. This was not an unreasonable assumption. Every violent death, and most serious accidents, that I heard about were connected with grog in one way or another. By that afternoon we had learned the details of who had been killed and who had done it. A genealogical sketch of the participants (figure 23) will help to clarify the relationships involved.

Murray is a senior man at Yarralin. The murdered woman was his daughter out of his brother. He felt the loss keenly and because his

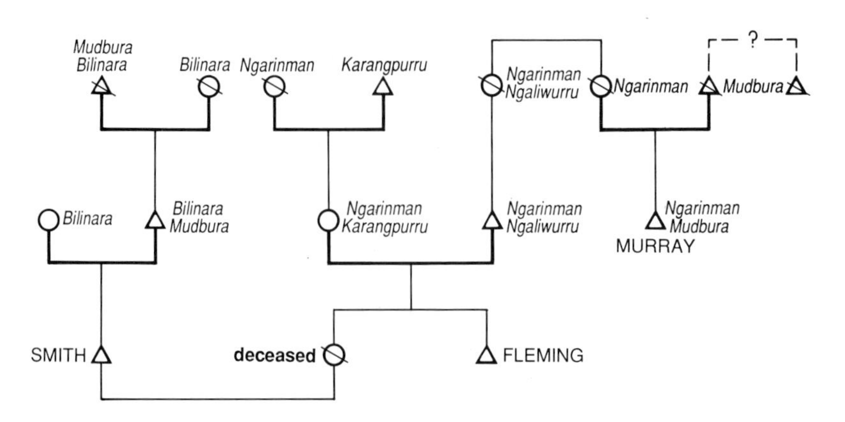

Figure 23 Simplified genealogical and language-identity sketch of the main participants in the murder case

brother was in Katherine he immediately took responsibility for the funeral arrangements and became the chief spokesman for the kin group which had suffered the loss.

As the news trickled through bit by bit, various people who were visiting Yarralin decided to cut short their visits. The murder was referred to as 'big trouble over at VRD' and many people who had no immediate connection to the people involved decided to dissociate themselves. People who usually resided elsewhere but were visiting Yarralin because it was 'their country', quickly reaffiliated themselves to more distant country and dispersed.

By evening of that day, discussions had begun as to where the body was to be buried. These discussions were pertinent because the disposition of the body would be one way of determining the country/identity of the dead woman and thus a way of defining the relationships between the protagonists and antagonists. Some people said that she should be buried at VRD because that was her *jawaji* (MF) country: Karangpurru. Others, including Murray, said that she should be buried at Yarralin because she was a Ngarinman person. In the end, the funeral was delayed for two weeks because the medical officers in Darwin were slow to return the body after the autopsy. This was a very painful two weeks because the sad and terrible business could not be finished until the body was buried. By that time, the identity of the deceased had been negotiated and she was buried at VRD out of consideration to her *jawaji* (MF) who lived there. I believe, although nobody said this openly, that it was a relief to have the body buried at VRD because it kept the locus of trouble away from Yarralin, and because it allowed for the possibility of future negotiations of identity should the need arise. That is, if Ngarinman people, for instance, later wanted to say that the murder did not concern them, they could point to the fact that the body was buried in Karangpurru country.

On the next day, 7 April, fairly detailed accounts of the murder began to circulate. Many people, myself included, showed a morbid curiousity about the murder, and the story was told and retold many times. Omitting many lurid details, the gist of the story was as follows: Smith (the husband of the deceased) had become drunk at the 'Old Hospital', an abandoned building where his family was staying for the wet season, and had beaten his wife there. He then carried her to the airstrip and left her there while he went back to the Old Hospital to get help; from there he took her back to the 'Centre Camp', which was the residential area for Karangpurru people and for others who were working at VRD. In one version of the story there were many people around and none of them offered to help the woman. Others added to this story, saying that when the couple got to the caravan where they were camping, Smith dumped her on a bed and turned the mattress over on top of her. She apparently died during the night.

Once the body had been taken to town for an autopsy, Murray took possession of the woman's clothes, which he intended to keep in case they were wanted for sorcery via Traffic. According to Murray, Smith and his countrymen had already started assembling the material (fabric) that constituted mortuary payments. In this case, material was collected by Smith, his mothers and his fathers, and was to be presented to the dead woman's fathers, mothers, mothers' brothers, and fathers' sisters. In traditional Aboriginal Law, as people explained it to me at this time, if a woman is murdered, her relations, particularly her fathers, mothers' brothers, and mothers' fathers have the right to fight and cripple or kill the murderer. The murderer does not have the right to defend himself, and his countrymen have no right to avenge his death. According to Hobbles:

> If he kill his wife, he got to go off away from the mob and stay away for two or three days. Paint himself up with white paint [clay] and come in to all that woman's relations. They can't give him fair go because he's the one who made the wrong. His blood just running for nothing. He's to blame because he made the wrong. They can just kill him dead.

The anger of a group which has lost a person is a justifiable anger which puts the murderer's group at a terrible disadvantage. They must lose a member, and lose him in a public way without the satisfaction of revenge. Rather than being an autonomous and assertive group they become supplicants who must plead and bargain for the life of their countryman. Their loss of autonomy is severe, and the other group correspondingly gains, holding the life of another human being at their mercy.

The Lingara mob had heard the news from the first, on their own clinic radio, but for a couple of days they stayed away from Yarralin and VRD. Since I was in Yarralin I do not know just what was said in Lingara; I only know that people there were discussing the details of the case and the identities of the people involved.

On 9 April, a group of people came from Lingara and had an informal meeting with Murray. One of the men, Nelson, said that the dead woman was his countryman: her mother's mother's country is in the same area as Nelson's father's country. On this basis, in particular, he defined the deceased as 'full Ngarinman'. He then proceeded to define all her husband's relations as Mudbura and to say that 'this the first time Ngarinman ever been to war with Mudbura'.

Now Smith's fathers are two brothers who are part Mudbura and part Bilinara; they have lived in, and taken care of, Bilinara country all their lives. As I understand Nelson's reasoning, he chose to define them as Mudbura for three reasons: first, he did not want a state of hostility between Ngarinman and Bilinara because his branch of Ngarinman people are closely related to Bilinara and there would have been too many people trying to mediate the dispute; second, if the antagonists were defined as Bilinara they might call upon other Bilinara people from other communities to back them up; such backing would have been from some extremely forceful people who have a long history of antagonism toward Ngarinman people; third, the antagonists have been taking care of Bilinara country for so long that their claims on their Mudbura countrymen would be quite weak; the western branch of the Mudbura, to which they belonged, had problems of their own at this time and would not have been likely to respond to appeals. In other words, Nelson wanted hostility. He defined the group held to be responsible for the death in a way that diminished their geographical/social identity and weakened their ties to others. At the same time, while not usurping Murray's rights as a father, Nelson effectively took over the position of chief spokesman. He weakened Murray's rights to a hostile stance because Murray himself is part Mudbura. In this move, Murray became a countryman of the very people he had the right to kill. Nelson is a master politician.

Murray neither accepted nor denied these definitions. He continued to advance himself as the person to fight the murderer, a definition of himself which nobody denied. The talk around Yarralin and Lingara became increasingly anti-Mudbura. There were stories of how Mudbura people were always drunk, and could not maintain a community; how they were unwanted everywhere, and were generally the troublemakers in any situation. One of my close 'brothers' said to me: 'You been see that, Debbie. Every time there's really trouble, that's Mudbura to blame.' I had actually never seen that, but then my brother was not asking me what I had seen.

It was very convenient for both Yarralin and Lingara people to define the trouble-makers as Mudbura. While many people had rights to Mudbura country, nobody in Yarralin was actively taking care of that country. After the first exodus of visitors, which included some undeniably Mudbura people, the remaining people could all conveniently claim to be other than Mudbura. Nelson's wife, for example, is an owner for Mudbura country from her father. But she and Nelson were quick to assert that she is 'really Nungali'–her mother's language area.

So the Mudbura became the common scapegoat for the hositilities. The only people in the local area identified as Mudbura were Smith and his relations. Everyone residing locally was something other than Mudbura. All the Mudbura people in the region chose to remain uninvolved.

The locus of grievance shifted from Yarralin to Lingara. For while Murray could, and did, maintain his posture as the aggrieved father, Nelson secured and maintained for Lingara the posture of the aggrieved group. Communities which function well, which are not divided by factionalism, can do these things–they can afford to be connected with trouble because members know each other to be reliable.

Over the next few days, people's concerns focused on three issues: first, repeated assertions of their own identity as something other than Mudbura; second, discussions of how the murderer should be treated; third, discussions of the responsibility of the dead woman's brother. The general consensus regarding the murderer was that one way or another he would not live long; it was known that Murray was prepared to use sorcery and people also considered it quite possible for the dead woman's spirit (*manngyin)* to kill Smith. After the initial anger there was a general attitude of mercy toward him. People felt that since he was going to die he might as well be allowed to remain in his own country, and that sending him to gaol only for him to come home and die was both unjust and pointless. Some others felt that he should be allowed a period of time in which to die and if he did not do so in that time then he should be sent to gaol. In all these discussions it was taken to be fact that Smith had murdered his wife and that he would have to die. For that, some people felt sorry for him, and blamed the grog as much as they blamed him.

There was a good deal of discussion about the dead woman's brother, Fleming. At first the general opinion was against him, as people said that he was wrong not to have saved his sister's life. This was part of the initial anger about the death. But later, as people's feelings settled somewhat, the tide of opinion turned in his favour. A close classificatory mother of Fleming told me that he had gone all over Centre Camp and the Old Hospital trying to get people to help him save his sister, but nobody would help. Eventually, it was agreed that Fleming would have saved his sister, but he had been surrounded by Mudbura people who were either too drunk or too cruel to help.

On 17 April the formal fight was held at Yarralin. The event communicated some of the definitions of the personnel involved and demonstrated intent. The people from VRD–all the so-called Mudbura–arrived in the afternoon. The women carried fighting sticks with which to defend themselves, if need be, against the aggrieved relations of the dead woman. The men were unarmed. Yarralin fairly bristled with spears and boomerangs. But by this time, eleven days after the murder, people were beginning to reassert ties of marriage and kinship which cut across boundaries of hostility. The signs of hostility were all present but the tense feelings of anger, grief, and murderous vengeance had diminished considerably.

Fleming was the first to face the boomerangs of his relations, who expressed their outrage that he had let his sister be killed. The man who threw the boomerangs was, at that time, a Lingara man and an excellent fighter. He threw skillfully and with great force. Fleming was allowed to defend himself with a shield; he was also skillful at dodging and was not hurt. After Fleming, Smith had to face the boomerangs. He was not allowed to defend himself. Murray threw these boomerangs, as was his right. Smith was not hurt, and that was the end of the fight.

The brief fight allayed many feelings. It showed that Lingara had taken over some responsibility for the grievance; it allowed Murray to express his anger; it satisfied people's feelings toward Fleming, who they had decided had not been negligent in any case. It did not constitute a payback to Smith and his kinsmen. In this regard the fight was gestural. It allowed the relations of the dead woman to express their right to kill Smith, but as physical punishment is controlled by the Australian judicial system, the real payback would come later, via 'Traffic', or some other extra-human agency.

Even more important, perhaps, was what went on before and after the fight. This was the first time that VRD people had visited Yarralin since the murder, and Yarralin/Lingara people had been avoiding VRD to a great extent. One of Smith's mothers is related to Hobbles' family. The group of mothers all came to Hobbles' camp to visit their relations. In reinforcing these ties of marriage and kinship, in coming prepared to fight but making a show of visiting their kinsmen, they effectively pointed out the arbitrary nature of the identities which had been assigned to them and they reasserted the value of cognatic networks over unilineal identities. After the fight they returned to Hobbles' camp and stayed for a little while. They were hardly a cheerful group but they were very relieved.

The funeral was held two days later. It turned out to be a hurried affair as Murray was to go to Katherine for annual regional meetings and was anxious to get started. The Lingara representatives had already gone to Katherine and were unable to attend the funeral. The men's portion of the funeral (digging the hole, carrying the coffin, sending the spirit away) was managed jointly by Murray and Smith's fathers. The women's portion (crying, presenting children to say goodbye to the spirit, cleaning up with green leaves) was managed jointly by the dead woman's mothers and by Smith's mothers. Smith himself was too distraught from grief to be able to do anything but cry, and that is all that is expected of a surviving spouse.

I, too, was going to the meetings in Katherine. As I settled down on my swag in the back of the cattle truck and tried to make myself comfortable for a long and arduous trip, I felt thankful that the 'big trouble at VRD' was finished. I had found it difficult and challenging to try to keep track of the changing identities, the various accounts of what 'should' be done in such situations, the many assertions of anger, and the repeated stories of the terrible Mudbura. In fact, I longed for things to get back to normal.

We had a few weeks of normalcy, but then the time came for Smith to go to Katherine for trial. This added a new element to the situation. Prior to this, people's concerns had been with their own involvement in the murder: their definition of themselves, their assertions of relationships, the expression of feelings appropriate to relationships, and so on. Now that much of the anger had subsided, the loss of the dead woman had become an accepted fact; people had done all that needed to be done to send her spirit away, to sort out the relationships of the survivors, and to try to resume life.

With the trial approaching, people began to be concerned about Smith's relationship to European authorities. Several Yarralin men, led by Nelson, decided that it would be a good idea for them to go to Katherine to give Aboriginal Legal Aid people their recommendations on the case in regard to traditional Law. Initially their concern was to keep Smith out of gaol because they thought he was going to die soon; it may also have been an opportunity for them to define themselves as 'Lawmen' in a European context. They were in a curious position in that as Ngarinman people they were relations of the deceased and thus in opposition to Smith, but as spokesmen vis-à-vis European Australians they were arguing for Smith and thus became his back-up men (*kanga*/countrymen). In order to communicate effectively to whites, the back-up men had to decide what their recommendations would be. So the whole issue was re-opened and, ultimately, redefined.

The one thing that everybody was agreed upon, initially, was that it would not be right for Smith to have to go to gaol. Some people felt that since he had killed his wife while he was drunk, he was not morally responsible for her death, although he was, of course, physically responsible. Others felt that since he was bound to die from 'Traffic', or some other means, it was unfair for him to have to be in gaol, just waiting for his death to catch up to him. And his own relations, of course, simply did not want to lose him.

The various opinions settled into one single question: did Smith kill his wife or not? In the earlier discussions, this had been the one 'fact' which was never in doubt. There were many conflicting stories about how he had killed her, but they all agreed that he had killed her. Earlier discussions had taken a time frame that was fairly narrow: Smith and his wife had been married for years, he had occasionally been drunk and beaten her; this time he had beaten her too much and she died. In the last week in May the time frame was expanded. People now began to discuss the general issue of women running away from their old husbands and the terrible ways that the injured relations can follow up the runaways and kill them. This was a general context for a specific event.

Years earlier (in the early 60s, I believe), the dead woman had been promised to a very old Mudbura man, who is long dead now. Her obligation to her own relations and to her promised husband and his relations was to stay with this old man and take care of him. Instead, once she was big enough, she ran away with Smith, a man who, by subsection, was her son-in-law. People stressed the wrong of leaving an old husband to whom one is promised, and the further wrong of marrying a man whom, above all others, one ought to avoid.

Of course, the dead woman was by no means the only woman to have done two wrong things. This, too, was stressed, but only by men. If her fate was to die, such would be the fate of other women who had done such wrong things. Women were not impressed with this interpretation; as I have said, it is not a capital crime to run away from an old husband. They went along with this version for a while, for this specific context.

Now that the context had been expanded to include actions on the part of the dead woman which are known to lead to death, the murder began to be presented as a possible case of *munpa* (sorcery). One man stated:

> The first wrong: that bloke [Smith] took him [her] away from that old man. Death got to come back to the woman and man who run away. That girl had that sick [possible *munpa*] for long time and she should have looked after that old man. Somebody got her. Somebody chuck spit, or got a song. That wrong [running away] now, they're sorry for their old people [the first husband].

According to participants in this discussion, all the relations for that old man are now deceased so it is impossible to know who might have made the woman *munpa*. The genealogies show a number of people who can quite reasonably be considered close kin of the old husband; I conclude that what people were after in this explanation was not an alternative murderer, but simply an alternative explanation.

The country that the old husband was an owner for is country which is also owned by Smith's fathers. It was inconceivable that they would have assisted in *munpa* designed to kill their own son and his wife. Murray is also an owner for that country and it was inconceivable that he would have assisted in *munpa* to kill his daughter. So if it was a case of *munpa*, it was sorcery instigated by person or persons unknown and unknowable. The only known thing about them was that it was not any of the participants in the case–antagonists or protagonists.

In order for the concept of *munpa* to be acceptable there had to be a reshuffling of identities. It was at this point that Nelson again entered the scene. He now proposed that since Smith's fathers and 'all that mob' were 'really Bilinara' and since Bilinara and Ngarinman are 'just like family', everybody should agree to back up Smith. It must have been *munpa*, he argued, that had killed Smith's wife; it could not have really been Smith's fault at all.

Smith and his relations were glad to accept this version of events for several reasons. First, it would mean that Smith would have the back-up of traditional Law explained by respected and uninvolved men, a fact which it was believed would carry weight in court. Second, Smith and all of his relations would be reclassified as Bilinara which was where they felt that they belonged, and which would make them allies with Ngarinman people, rather than enemies.

The relations of the dead woman were not entirely satisfied with this explanation, and they continued to maintain that Smith, too, would die. But at this time they were willing to leave this assertion ambiguous: either Smith would die from the same *munpa* that had killed his wife, or he would die from 'Traffic' set on him by his wife's family. The issue was left open, giving Murray and his relations the option of renegotiating the event later should they care to.

From Smith's point of view, he now had some hope, but he was hardly in the clear. He was now indebted to all those non-relatives who agreed to back him up, and he was under the shadow of his wife's relations. At any point they might decide that he had, actually, murdered his wife and they might decide to kill him. In one of his master strokes, Nelson said that since Lingara needed more men,

Smith could come and live there and they would vouch for his good behaviour.

We can now begin to see how chance deals out events which are negotiated and controlled by men of political perspicacity. The first event, the killing, was a wrong inflicted by a member of one group on a member of another group. One group had lost a person, unique, irreplaceable, and gone forever. The murdering group, so to speak, was at a terrible disadvantage for nobody could deny that this was wrong. At that point they were put in a position of only two options: either to accept the other group's definition of themselves and the event, or to make war. Warfare in the overt sense is out of the question these days because Australian society does not allow it. A surrogate warfare might have been possible using various methods of sorcery. The trouble with this option was that the murdering group had little hope of winning such a war. And, also, they had many kin ties to the other group–they did not want war. The identification of the dead woman as Ngarinman and the alliance of all those people who could call themselves Ngarinman, coupled with the identification of the murderer as Mudbura, and the dispersal of all those people who might call themselves Mudbura, left the murdering group diminished. They, and only they, belonged to the country to which they had been assigned by regional consensus. There was no one there to back them up.

Given the impracticality of this second option, they had to select the first–to accept the definition of themselves and the event. With time, this definition began to weaken. Nothing lasts forever in ordinary time. Women reasserted the family ties which move through countries and which create cross-cutting sets of obligations and responsibilities. The formal expressions of rights were completed, the dead body was laid to rest, the spirits sent on their way; it became possible to renegotiate the event.

In the second round of negotiations the murdering group was still at a disadvantage. They wanted to save Smith, they wanted a cessation of hostilities, and they wanted to be defined as Bilinara. The first two reasons are fairly obvious; the latter requires some explanation. They wanted to be Bilinara because it was the country in which they had grown up and which they had been taking care of for years. It was the only country for which they had comprehensive knowledge developed over years of experience; it was only country on the face of the earth where they fully belonged. The meaning of their lives, and their hopes for their own future and that of their children and grandchildren, were all at stake.

As I have said, countries are autonomous, as are the groups living in them. In this 'big trouble at VRD' one group had temporarily lost its autonomy, lost the ability to be self-defining in terms of country, allies, and relationships. They became supplicants for their own identity. The price was Smith. In exchange for being redefined as Bilinara they gave Smith to Lingara. And looking at the options realistically, they had no choice.

Smith himself had lost his personal freedom. In exchange for his life he offered the only thing he had of real value: himself. On 1 June, a plane was scheduled to land at Yarralin to take Smith and his back-up men to Katherine. Shortly before the plane came there was a public meeting in which the new version of the event was publicly stated and publicly agreed to. The story now went like this: many years ago Smith and his wife had run away from her old husband, breaking traditional Aboriginal Law. Someone unknown and unknowable followed them up with sorcery. As a result the wife died. She died at her husband's hand but he was not morally responsible for her death. Nelson put it neatly: 'We are all sorry for that thing [the death] but Smith's not the one.'

The older men all admonished Smith to tell in court exactly the same story that he had told the police. They said that he must not lie, but just trust the men who were there to back him up. The plane arrived and as my truck was working that day I drove Smith and his back-up men to the airstrip. We shook hands all around and the men left.

I thought that finally that was the end of the trouble, but I was wrong. Within the next few days two more versions of the event were put forward. One version was specific to women who were extremely dissatisfied with the proposition that women who run away from their old husbands will be killed. An alternative version, which was asserted in varying details by a number of women, went this way: Smith and his wife walked back to the caravan arm in arm and lay down in bed together. During the night she got up and went outside of the caravan and was found dead on the ground the next morning. Clearly, according to the women, she had been killed by a kidney-fat man or some other sorcerer. The unpleasant intimation that she had brought on her own death by running away from her old husband was thus neatly avoided while still exonerating Smith.

The other version was stated by an old man who had a great sense of historical accuracy and no love for the Bilinara. He told me that that sort of *munpa* has not been practised for decades and that the story was 'bullshit'. But he maintained, in a subtle way, that it was useful 'bullshit' when dealing with Europeans. He was alluding most delicately to one of the truly curious aspects to race relations in the area. From the Aboriginal point of view, European Australians will refuse to acknowledge plain and obvious facts: such as the facts that Aboriginal people have their own culture or that they need nourishing food. In contrast, they will readily accept the wildest and most fanciful or obscene stories of magic, sorcery, mysterious and cruel practices.

When Yarralin people developed the *munpa* version of events they did so out of a belief in its probable accuracy and the sincere desire for the negotiations such a version would entail; at the same time there was also a sensitive reading of European concepts of Aboriginal people. The *munpa* version was important, probably vital, even without national influence in the situation. But given that the context of murder also included Australian law and justice, the *munpa* version was probably the only one which would have had much impact in Australian courts of law. In the Northern Territory many European Australians have an attitude towards what they term 'tribal' that is a mixture of awe, arrogance, and avoidance. Their concept of 'tribal' includes sorcery, punishment of women, and any other customs which they firmly believe are not present in their own culture. So in defining the event as *munpa*, Yarralin people proposed the one story which their experience of Europeans had led them to believe would go unquestioned. My understanding of European Australians in the area is not that they necessarily believe these stories but that they treat such cases with avoidance. If anything could convince a judge that this case was best handled by Aborigines, the *munpa* story would do it.

I do not know precisely what the verdict was with Smith, but he was given the unusually short sentence of approximately two years in prison. After serving his sentence he spent the next year or so at Lingara. By 1985, he was spending more time back home with his family, and he had found a new wife.

A few years later when I was in Canberra, I received a telephone call from the Solicitor-General's office in Darwin asking if I would be willing to interpret at a trial, or if I could recommend someone to do so. A few questions and answers forced me to disqualify myself. Smith was again in gaol, accused of murdering his new wife.

10 *Testing*

Symmetry and balance among people, like balance among countries and species, can be lost in two directions. If one part overwhelms another, as in conquest, balance is lost. If one part self-destructs or diminishes drastically, balance is lost. Aggression and self-destruction threaten, in different but related ways, the relationships which sustain country and people. Testing is a process through which people attempt to sustain balance.

Mature adults expect that in their own country they will not be controlled by others. They will, of course, participate in the symmetrical exchanges which are integral to social life, and they attempt to sustain asymmetrical relationships in which they are the controlling person, but they expect that others will not be able to control them. I refer to this structural position as autonomy (Myers 1982a provides an excellent analysis of these issues as they are managed by Pintupi people). As we will see, asymmetrical dependence has become a fact of life for many adults and creates considerable social distress.

Interpersonal Testing

People have options and make choices. Interpersonal relationships must be regularly subjected to social verification. Called *testembad* in Kriol, this process is the substance of much of Yarralin life in general, and is the essence of political life. In daily life individuals test, communicate, and maintain their interpersonal relations through demanding: 'give me this', 'give me that', 'do this for me'. Demands are frequent, persistent, and imaginative. In my early months in Yarralin I was asked to do many things: 'give me sugar,' 'give me that dress', 'tell the President of America to send me one hundred drums of mange soap', 'give me your hair', and 'give me a lift to Alice Springs'. Initially, I found this quality of Yarralin life exceedingly abrasive. Once I learned to say 'no' I found I could live with the style, but it was only as

I began to understand what it was all about, and to sort out the different kinds of demands, that I ceased to feel irritated by it.

My first encounter with this style of testing was as an outsider. Outsiders are a free resource–one plucks them clean, giving back as little as possible. By definition outsiders are expected to have no lasting commitments or demands of their own. It 'just wastes' things to give them away in this context. Later, of course, I was classed as an insider. Things started coming back to me, not as unexpected gifts, but because I went and asked for them. I learned to go into somebody's camp, look in their cooking pot, and demand some turkey, wallaby, or whatever. This is how goods move around Yarralin: people move from camp to camp, visiting, chatting, playing cards, and demanding.

It is a sociable enterprise. If one were to sit in one's own camp, never visiting and only being visited, one would soon starve. It is not that Yarralin people are hard hearted. Children, sick people, old people, and dogs are cared for although not always in ways that Europeans recognise readily. Able adults are expected to take care of themselves. In fact, a person who does not demand is incomprehensible: why do they not assert themselves, why do they not initiate interactions, why do they not respond to demands by making their own demands?

There is only one style for demands, and it is always peremptory, but contexts differ. Demands made among close kin, countrymen and mates are an expression of need which can be made because these people are, by definition, interdependent; they do not test each other. One does not turn down ('knock back') close kin because it is understood that they would not ask if they did not need, and that, in any case, there will always be a return. Kin do not take advantage of each other (see Sahlins 1972 for the classic analysis of reciprocity).

My dear friend Jessie and I shared a great deal: store-bought food, game, money, work in ceremony, travel, stories, jokes. When I went for a visit in 1983 she asked me to bring her a rifle. I was happy to do this for I had long wanted to give her something out of the ordinary that would express, so I thought, my deep obligation for all that she had taught me. I gave her a lovely little Winchester single-shot .22 and I was a bit surprised when she asked me several times how much she owed me. I kept telling her that it was 'just for free'. Shortly before I left she gave me forty dollars and said that she was sorry she could not give me the full amount. I said again, 'but that rifle was just for free'. She pressed the money into my hand and replied, 'well this just for free, too'. One does not pluck clean ('run down') one's kin, countrymen or close mates.

On the other hand, people outside this circle of sharing are to be tested. A person's autonomy is asserted in demanding; it is defended in saying 'no', or again, in graciously sharing. People exchange things beyond this close circle all the time. There would be no social life if this were not so. The essence of this interpersonal testing, however, is to ask for things which one does not really need; to the extent that people are dependent on non-family for their needs, to that extent they suffer a loss of autonomy.

Demanding, fraught as it is with the potential for hurt feelings and loss, is the basis of a great deal of humour in Yarralin life. There is a rather personal humour in which people imitate other people's demands, mimicking their quirks and asking for silly or outrageous things. There is standardised joking having to do with giving promises, and with beating ('killing') uncles. And there is a form of humour that sends up the whole mode of demanding: 'give me a helicopter', 'give me two thousand dollars', or, if a person asks for tobacco, to say, 'this tobacco costs two hundred dollars'. I became much more at ease with the system of demanding when I learned to joke about it. And my jokes were always well received because in Yarralin people's experience Europeans take material possessions seriously. They had previously encountered few Europeans who joked about property.

Yarralin people assert that goods are not a scarce resource. 'Plenty more food', people say, or 'plenty more money'. As Doug Campbell put it: 'I can't worry about money. Money just paper. I can wipe my bum on it. One day I'll be six feet under, but that money still going round and round. That's not my worry.' These assertions are statements of autonomy. In many communities they obscure the fact that essential goods are indeed scarce, and that many people are dependent on others for their basic needs. The ideal of autonomy, vigorously defended, is far more an ideal than a lived reality in Yarralin and other relatively large communities.

Lingara is a small family community, in which people take care of each other because they are all countrymen or spouses with many overlapping and cross-cutting ties: relations among adults are symmetrical. Yarralin, being much larger, allows greater scope for dependence. For many people it is only in the bush, and often only in their own country, that they experience directly the freedom which is signalled in the phrase 'plenty more food'.

Bossmanship

It is to be understood that senior caretakers, male and female, are 'boss' in their own country, and are most thoroughly 'boss' in their father's country. As a formal position in community life, 'the boss' in my experience is male; I understand that this need not necessarily be the case, particuarly in small communities.

As I understand traditional Aboriginal society in this area, a person who disagreed with a decision, or who did not like the existing situation, had the right to go to another country. Likewise, people who belonged to country had the right to stay there. Remembering that country and kinsmen belong together, and that country is always occupied, at least in the sense that people are taking care to know what goes on in their country, then it is clear that while leaving is often expressed as geographical mobility, the options and constraints are, in fact, social. Authority consisted of reducing people's options, either by preventing them from leaving or by forcing them to leave. The most extreme punishment was death, which renders the question of options largely irrelevant.

For Yarralin people, to be a mature adult human being is to exercise freedom of choice. The heart of the matter is the relationship between person and country. The person who is deprived of mobility is deprived of the right to nurture and enhance themselves, their people, and their country; deprived of the opportunity to take the place where they are most thoroughly wanted and needed. The coercion which underwrites authority is the ability to interfere with this relationship. As we have seen, it can be legitimately interfered with, but only for a while, to accomplish certain ends. Interference is not yet institutionalised for groups or categories of people.

The potential of being autonomous is equally available to all adults, but one's identity as an autonomous person is always set in a context of group and country. This is a very neat paradox: to be part of a group requires that at some level one become interdependent, considering others as well as oneself. People are born with certain options; they learn and travel to increase options, but they never have total freedom in regard to options. They can shift identity by shifting place or shifting context but they can never be identity-free.

Mobility is expressive of autonomy; in literal terms it identifies travel. In Yarralin people's view, their most pressing need is for greater control over more land. Second only to land, and possibly even more pressing in the short term, is the perceived need for increased mobility. To own a vehicle means not having to ask others to take one fishing or hunting, or to bring firewood. It means being able to visit one's country and relatives according to one's own timetable. It thus means better health, improved capacity to caretake, and the opportunity not only to be autonomous, but to put others without vehicles into a dependent status. It is not surprising that a great deal of the factionalism in Yarralin centred on the control of vehicles.

Options enhance autonomy while constraints diminish it. Cognatic affiliations to country enhance people's options, giving them a freedom to shift contexts and loyalties. They also give a competitive edge to relationships between countries. Predation, a fact of life between species, is also metaphorically part of the relationships between countries. Cognatic affiliations both create competition and contain it by allowing for diffuse loyalties. Except where people come together from unusually great distances, competitive and potentially hostile relationships are cross-cut by the persons and groups whose interests are invested on both sides of the boundary.

Yarralin people's speech is fraught with ambiguities. The term *ngurra* (country), as we have seen, is used in numerous contexts, and country is an excellent example of ambiguity. One of the most frequent expressions I have encountered in Yarralin and other places is the question 'which one?'. It is spoken aggressively, being both a demand for a clearer context and an accusation of social ineptitude. The listener has failed to comprehend the speaker, therefore the speaker must have been at fault. Of course, the speaker need not accept the blame. A competent speaker will equally aggressively spell out the context, or alternatively, refuse to spell out the context, demonstrating in either case that the listener should have understood and that therefore the listener is at fault.

Communications about country, particularly political debates phrased in the context of country, become very confusing at times–not only for me, but for Yarralin people as well. My confusion initially stemmed from the fact that I did not understand the process of shifting contexts. Yarralin people's occasional confusion stems from the fact that sometimes they are not able to identify the context. Once I became conversant with contexts, modifiers, genealogies, and place-names, I found the process of playing contexts fascinating, occasionally frustrating, and always entertaining.

One way to define context is to offer the name of country. It is up to the listeners to deduce the context on the basis of the speaker's relationship to that country. For example, if the speaker's family area were Layit, and he said 'my country Layit' then it would be clear that family area was the intended context. But if he said 'my country Pukaka' (another family area within the geographical area) then it would be safe to conclude that geographical area was the context intended because that is the minimal context in which he could be considered to be an owner of Pukaka. This particular process can be carried out much farther but is generally used in fairly familiar contexts. There is little point in defining context of language area by reference to places that are so far afield that the listeners might never have heard of them. In such cases it might just be better to name the language. However, old men with great knowledge are more likely to display their knowledge in the most convoluted, rather than the most direct, fashion. In baffling their listeners they score political points.

Another method of defining context is to offer a parental relationship: 'my mother's country' or 'my father's country'. This does not necessarily define the context, it merely shifts to a different generation, requiring the listener to know genealogies as well as country. A combination of these methods can be particularly effective. A further refinement on this method is to put the context back to the grandparent generation. To define the context in terms of grandparent's countries requires even more specialised information on the part of the listener. This method is used to particular advantage by those old people who know other people's genealogies even better than the others know them.

Adult men and women see themselves as having their 'own will'; they are 'free' to come and go according to their own choices. That some of the coming and going is accomplished by staying in one place and changing one's identity within the various options available to one, is irrelevant to the way in which Yarralin people define autonomy. Many arguments in Yarralin during 1980–2, while set in the context of country, were about the control of motor vehicles: vehicles were held fixed while the country was shifted around. In arguments over who would hold the keys, and thus control, the community tractor, the issue was phrased in two parts. First, it was taken as given that: (a) the tractor belonged to the community, and (b) the person who was 'boss' for the community should be 'boss' for the tractor. Second, discussion focused on the question of who was 'boss', and this question was handled as the question 'in what country is the community located?'. I spent hours and hours in formal and casual meetings listening to discussion of this question, 'where are we?'. And for most of that period the question was not resolved.

In 1980–2 there were three aspiring bosses in Yarralin–all men. One of them reckoned he was boss for Yarralin because the place is in his mother's country; one reckoned that he was boss for Yarralin because the place is adjacent to his father's country. This second man emphasised a patrilineal model of bossmanship, asserting that the first man's maternal tie was of less value, boss-wise, than his paternal tie. The first man's assertion was that Yarralin was in a family area within the Ngarinman language area, and that the context of family area was the pertinent context. The second man did not dispute that identification, but argued that as there were no senior patrilineal owners for that area, bossmanship should pass to his country.

The third man undercut both these assertions, defining Yarralin as part of Ngaliwurru language area. This was a cunning argument, for although he himself had no direct claim to ownership, he was the senior man for adjacent Ngaliwurru countries through patrilineal ties. By extending his responsiblities he could claim to be boss for Yarralin, particularly if he could convince people that neither of the other two claims had substance.

Then there was a fourth contender although, in the case of this man, 'peacemaker' is the more correct term. When the situation became too chaotic to be operable, people would agree to let this fourth man act as boss for a while. He was an in-marrying man whose wife had ties to the area; he himself had no claim of ownership.

There was, then, this mode of asserting ownership through genealogical ties to country. There was also another mode. One man argued back to the origins of Yarralin: 'I took all these people on strike, I brought them back, I got all this land, all these houses, all these motor vehicles. You all got to listen to me now.' This mode of argument was taken up by other contestants and there were great arguments about the origins of Yarralin, who had done what, had said what to whom, had been promised what by whom.

Finally, there was a third mode, not so much of asserting bossmanship, as of denying it. In this mode, nobody had any ties to Yarralin at all. A contending boss, presenting his arguments about ownership, would see his listeners drift away and hear them mutter to each other: 'No matter. It's not my country. It's nothing to do with me.' The unchallenged contestant would be left with no listeners, and this was one of the most effective brakes of all. Mobility triumphed, if only in the short run.

The politics of country is a dangerous game in this sense: the man who is left standing alone, deserted by all, may be dictator, tyrant and emperor, metaphorically, of his country. But in that moment he has failed his country utterly. For the ultimate responsibility in life is not to become a big boss. It is to take care of one's country and provide a future generation to take over the area.

The situation at Yarralin as I document it here, is not likely to be the situation that will be remembered one hundred years from now. And that is probably a good thing. I saw one man become, in a moment, both emperor and fool. It was one of the times when I was glad that I understood something of the Aboriginal sense of time, for the only real consolation was to know that one day it would all be changed. But at that time, this man, as complex, brilliant, and generous as any person present, stood politically naked. He had tested and he had failed. All the people there cast their eyes away; to give him space, I thought. But country does not blink.

In these complex arguments about country men test their knowledge against that of others. They test who can show the closest relationship to country by knowing the most about it. Using the context of country, they test social-political boundaries. If they say that they own such-and-such a place, who is there to recognise the name, identify the context, produce the genealogical evidence, and refute the contention? The older one becomes, the fewer opponents one has. This is an old man's game, a game of intelligence, passion, and mental swiftness.

In the last analysis it is the old women who oppose the old men, not as contestants but as arbiters. They offer a running commentary on the proceedings. 'True God,' they may say. Or again, 'bullshit!' They may listen intently, or they may get up and go fishing. They do not compete politically and thus they cannot be politically opposed; their judgements are thought to hold good because Yarralin people believe that women do not test but rather only assert the truth as they understand it. Their understanding is thought to be reliable because it is received wisdom which has not been subjected to manipulation.

What such debates actually accomplish is a more convoluted issue. Fred Myers (1982b:79–114) has shown with admirable clarity and compassion that very few decisions made in many public meetings are actually binding on anyone. In part this is because of the overall powerlessness of Aboriginal people in Australian society. Many of the most important decisions affecting their lives are made elsewhere by bureaucrats and politicians. In part, too, it is attributable to people's sense of autonomy. To alter one's own choices in favour of those of another is to imply that one is dependent. Many people attended

Yarralin meetings in which issues were passionately debated using a great range of contexts. Many participated, speaking, agreeing, supporting, or denying. And at the end they went away and did whatever it was they were planning to do in the first place.

The most important consideration, however, is that these debates sustain and continue to achieve symmetry for just as long as the issue remains unresolved. As long as there is no winner there can be no losers. While bossmanship was debated, no one person or group could become too powerful. Winning is what is to be most intensely avoided, not necessarily by the contestants, but by all the others whose lives would be affected by such an outcome. The fact that there were three contestants produced a stability exactly opposite to what Von Neumann's game theory predicts (Bateson 1973:209–10), precisely because the goal was not to win but to prevent others from winning. People actively promoted this process by shifting factions, shifting identities, and shifting contexts, sometimes with overwhelming speed and agility, so that no one could win.

I often found this political process frustrating because to me it seemed like stagnation. There were many times when Yarralin people too were frustrated, but that was a cost they were willing to bear. What I understood as stalemate, they understood as balance: no one person or group could control others effectively as long as nobody won. As long as the identity of the place was ambiguous many people could legitimately say that they were there not as dependants but as people with rights; and so they had a dual interest, promoting both their right to be there and their right not to be bossed.

It did matter, in the long run, who became boss for Yarralin. The successful contender achieved his position through two factors. One of the contenders threatened to become too powerful and was forced to withdraw. His departure left a gap in the balance which another man filled with the assistance of European Australians. Once he became a conduit for European goods, services, and decisions, he was able to gain control of context, defining the country as a family area in which he was the only senior male with rights to bossmanship. Others were significantly disenfranchised. We can see here the very beginnings of what could become locally institutionalised disadvantage–relationships which construct dependence as a fact of life for whole groups or categories of people through time.

For most adults outside of their own country, life offers more or less autonomy depending on the extent to which the power of the boss is unchecked and therefore asymmetrical. The repercussions of asymmetry are extensive, and can be understood through the example of alcohol ('grog') at Yarralin. Since its establishment in 1973, Yarralin people had wanted a dry community and had been quite successful in effecting control without European assistance. In 1981 they convinced the Liquor Commissioner that it would be appropriate to declare Yarralin a dry area. This law gave State support when dealing with wrong-doers; those who broke the law were subject not only to community sanctions, but also to the Australian judicial system. A dry community, however, really only exists where there is a will. If people tolerate those who break the law, then there is no dry community. As the man who came to be the sole boss was tolerant of alcohol, Yarralin became less and less dry. Other people did not want to enforce the law against the wishes of the boss. In 1988 many residents described Yarralin as a violent and unhappy place.

The socially recognised response to unpleasantness is to move, and where this is possible it checks the would-be boss. Frequently, however, the decision is difficult. Conquest and sedentarisation have imposed constraints on everybody regardless of age and locale. Every person has the right to be in more than one place; all Yarralin people have some choice of community; but very few communities offer better opportunites. The small places that are peaceful are family concerns, oriented toward a minimal unit and occupied by the families who belong there (see Loveday 1982 for an analysis of the outstation or homelands movement). In such places others, whose ties are less intense, are at a political disadvantage. Other larger communities are rarely peaceful; they offer little improvement. Many people remain at Yarralin because it is still the best community for their purposes: large enough to have a school, a store, and a clinic, and close enough to their countries to allow them to take care and to have some voice, however faint, in political life.

When bossmanship debates develop it is primarily because there are more people than can be accommodated within the kin/country nexus and there are not enough other options available to people. As long as debates are stalemates communities do not run efficiently, but they remain within a moral order. Rules can be bent and even broken as long as the underlying relationships are sustained. That which is to be sustained is balance; symmetrical blocking is the means. Like the moon, one 'wins' by disabling the opposition. And as is the case with over-predation, 'winning' may lead to irretrievable loss.

Free Will

Freedom is understood with respect to country as 'freehold'. To be personally free is to have one's 'own will', one's 'own mind', and to act upon that will. With respect to the process of disengaging from asymmetrical relationships upon completion of obligations, it is 'to go free'. Women who have been widowed and subsequently released from the mortuary taboos 'go free'. Men who complete their obligations to their wife's family 'go free'; often these men and women go home to their own country, but they need not actually move in order to go free.

Asymmetrical relationships, as we have seen, depend on controlling other people's lives and choices. Within their own country seniors have authority over juniors. This authority structure has led some anthropologists to characterise Aboriginal societies as gerontocracies:

the rule of the old (cf F. Rose 1968; 1987). Fred Myers (1986) has analysed this relationship extensively and elegantly in his ethnography of Pintupi people, and much of what he says is equally true for Yarralin people. The senior-junior relationship is usually set in the minimal context of country. It is primarily within a group of countrymen that seniors have authority over juniors, although in the case of runaways seniors may act upon their perceived group interest and this is understood to be legitimate.

The central concept is that of dependence: juniors are dependent on seniors for knowledge and protection; sons-in-law on mothers-in-law and others for a wife; young men and women on their mothers, uncles, and fathers for the care which gave them life and growth. As dependants they are indebted, and the way in which indebtedness is socially expressed is through a diminution of personal autonomy either with regard to residential choice, self-definition in relation to country, or in the more daily contexts of work.

Most young people in Yarralin respect the knowledge of their elders while at the same time resenting the restrictions that are placed on them. They know that they do not know the country well, that their skills are inferior, that there is much knowledge both public and secret which they have yet to learn. 'Mistakes' are punishable; death is still a possibility, effected by extra-human rather than human agency. To leave one's seniors is, metaphorically, to go into the unknown where one is dependent on the goodwill of others to protect one from dangerous places and events.

To have dependants is to have care and responsibility: mothers, fathers, uncles, aunties and grandparents protect and nourish their children, feeding them, affiliating them to country, giving them knowledge. These asymmetrical relationships are seen by Yarralin people as part of becoming autonomous. Juniors need the protection and nurturance of seniors if they are to grow up and take over as caretakers.

Ideally, both symmetrical and asymmetrical relationships are nurturant; they build and maintain 'healthy' (*punyu*) people and country. People exercise authority in ways that country does not but the implicit threat is the same: people who fail in their obligations face death. If people do not take care of the country, the country will not take care of them. This is not a question of revenge or anger, it is simply a self-evident fact of life. People who do not obey their seniors risk endangering their own lives, the lives of their relations, and ultimately the life of their country. No one in Yarralin expects anyone to like being the controlled person in an asymmetrical relationship, but as these are necessary, adults expect people to co-operate. More often than not they are disappointed.

Formerly, old people had more authority to limit options than they do now. The process by which Australian governments (local, state, and federal) have taken over the power and authority functions previously held by local Aboriginal groups, and diminished the options of all Aboriginal people, is well documented throughout the literature (see, for example, Rowley 1981). Of most immediate concern to Yarralin adults is the matter that today young people can leave their elders in a complete way by turning to European society. Women can marry European men (the reverse is virtually non-existent) thereby escaping the reciprocities, and hazards, involved in Aboriginal marriages. Equally, they can search for an Aboriginal man with whom they can share the kind of marriage they desire, and if this is not agreeable to their relatives, they can live somewhere else. Young people can go to other cattle stations and to towns where they can work or hang around. They can collect wages or unemployment benefits and live on their own outside of their own countries, in situations which make them independent of their elders.

In 1964, Aborigines in the Northern Territory were granted freedom of movement (Rowley 1972:14); as this date coincides closely with the dates Yarralin people gave me for the time at which old men stopped being so violent to young men, it is likely that it was this freedom of movement which initiated the change. When young people had a chance to escape from the control of their elders, many of them took it.

Young people can and do escape the control of their elders by getting into a truck, car, or plane and leaving, and old people may punish young people in ways that cause severe bodily harm. But this is not the whole picture. For an Aboriginal person in the Northern Territory, life away from one's kinsmen, one's country and one's familiar style of life can be lonely, degrading, and even dangerous. Unless they become addicted to alcohol or other items available in town, most young people return to their own family. Old people can make things hard for young people when they come back, but when all is said and done, old people worry about losing their young to town life. They do not want to be so hard as to drive away the next generation. This poses a problem which Yarralin adults worry about almost all the time, finding no clear-cut answers. Loving their children, their country, and their way of life, they do not want to lose any of them. Yet to preserve the country and culture requires that the young be obedient, that they put up with a loss of autonomy. Many young people leave because they chafe at the restrictions placed on them, and not all of them return. Old people say that they are not as 'heavy' as they used to be. They have had to opt for lenience in order to keep their young.

Free will is not the same as self-will. Yarralin people use a number of terms in talking about self-will or irresponsibility, the most common of which is 'wild'. It carries connotations of wilfulness, lack of control, lack of care, being anti-social, or, in some instances, being ignorant. Human beings who are 'wild' are not *punyu*: they act irresponsibly, endangering themselves and others. Young people are expected to be a bit wild but they are not expected to remain that way. Rather, they must learn to exercise their will responsibly.

Several particularly vital messages concerning the constraints to wildness are contained in dingo and dog life. Throughout the continent dingos have been accommodated within Aboriginal myth and practice. While never domesticated as a species, individual dingos have become companions, hunting assistants, warm bedfellows on cold nights, and watchdogs (Meggitt 1965; Gould 1969; Hamilton 1972; White 1972; Breckwoldt 1988). Yarralin people frequently make a distinction between camp dog (*walaku*) and bush dingo (*ngurakin*). These days camp dogs are mongrel hybrids of dingo and many non-dingo varieties. Formerly, however, there was only the one species, and the distinction between camp and bush had to do primarily with domestication. Camp dogs were usually acquired when people raided dingo lairs during the season (signalled by the position of certain stars) when pups were newly weaned. The evidence suggests that dingos did not breed well under conditions of domestication, and that Aborigines relied on a continuing supply of bush pups (Meggitt 1965). Dingos were inclined to revert to the bush, and Yarralin people own songs which can be sung to encourage dogs to stay with their owners. Young dogs were taken on by specific owners, were socialised to the requirements of living in human society and became valued companions. Those which failed to adjust, which became dangerous and would not leave, were destroyed by a poison derived from an orchid (*Cymbidium canaliculatum*). Today it is not so difficult to retain dogs, for the hybrids are not inclined to revert to the bush, and they breed more successfully in camp than dingos would have done. Indeed, hybrids apear to be far more dependent than bush-derived dingos ever were.

One set of messages is found in the contrast between dingo and domesticated or camp dog. Camp dogs are dependants. They are like children in that adults give them skin identities, personal names, food, and shelter. Where humans travel, dogs travel too. Like children, they are fed and cared for but unlike children, they do not grow up to be responsible adults. In contrast, dingo represents the other end of a dependent-wild continuum. He hunts his own food, makes his own camp, finds his own shelter, and follows his own law. One contrast that Yarralin people draw relates to food. According to Big Mick: 'dingo only himself, only from Dreaming. Him been go longa bush for rown [his own] feed, rown beef: raw one, no fire, that's bush dingo.'

Putting this quote into a more complete context, it is clear that dingo does not distribute food, nor does he manage resources, collect, prepare, and store vegetable foods, or cook food. Put succinctly, dingo is much like male human beings, for in Yarralin it is women who gather, prepare, and store vegetable foods, who cook and distribute foods of all kinds. Dingo can be understood as an answer to an unasked question: what would human society be like if there were no women? The answer is that it would not be human. Camp dog lives with humans, and is a recipient of human culture without being a participant. From a human perspective, he is the complete dependant. Dingo lives apart from humans, does not share in human culture, and is wild. To be human, then, is to be neither totally dependant nor totally wild. Human culture requires that we engage with each other; the ideal is symmetrical interdependence.

Young males start out as dependants–like camp dogs. Formerly when they were made into young men they were pushed out of camp and expected to lead their own lives, ranging the bush; these days they are expected to work and travel, and to maintain a low profile around camp. They become much like dingos, stalking food and sexual partners. Through marriage, young men are brought back into the human/camp domain. A man's obligation to the earth is to take care of his country, and to affiliate to himself a son who will later affiliate his son to take over that place. Men come into camp as sons-in-law: they bargain away some of their autonomy in order to gain a wife and thus to acquire rights in people to whom they will transmit their rights in country.

One dingo message, then, is that males must enter into asymmetrical relationships in order to become fully adult. As young men, their proper place is the bush and they can be seen as 'wild' (asocial, lacking knowledge and responsibility) in the sense that they are outside human culture. They come back to camp because, in order to take their rightful place, they must marry and find children. To be human is to participate in human culture as it is managed by women.

If men are dingos it is easy to jump to the conclusion that women are camp dogs. I have occasionally heard this kind of analogy made by white men in the Northern Territory, but I find no basis for it in Yarralin life. The dog metaphor which most suits women is that of the original Dreaming dingo. It was this dingo who made people human in the first place, who gave us our characteristic human shape, human brain, and human culture. In ordinary time, this is what women do, giving birth to male and female human beings. It is women sitting in the camps, giving birth and cooking food, allocating food and people, who make human life specifically and uniquely human.

There is another set of messages which is particularly relevant to female autonomy. This is the *mungamunga* (wild women of the bush) set. I believe that the *mungamunga* are telling us that women cannot be totally wild any more than can men. The *mungamunga* have no ties to country. They go where they please, do not marry, and seek out sexual affairs with ordinary men. They do not bear children. If the cost of being 'wild' is to be childless, it seems logical to suggest that the cost of bearing children is a loss of autonomy. I suspect that mothers everywhere would recognise a certain rueful truth to this assertion. For Yarralin women the issue is particularly keen, not so much because of the responsibilities involved in raising children but because children tie them to their husband and to his choices. Remember that women who choose to leave their husbands may be forced to leave their dependent children. Many are torn between the desire for their own freedom and their love of their children; their desire to sustain the close ties between themselves and their country, and their desire to nurture their youngsters.

A woman's primary obligation in life, like that of a man, is to take her rightful place: to maintain the care of country which she shares with her brother, to find and nurture a new generation of owners, to teach the public and secret knowledge which sustains country and people. To do this, women, too, must participate in asymmetrical relationships. Uncles, mothers, and fathers bargain away some of a girl's options, but in the end women, too, become fully adult.

Men and women must learn how to exercise their will responsibly. Formerly, those who could not adapt to human society were, like the dogs who remain vicious even when they are cared for by humans, done away with. Yarralin and other adults look back to the pre-invasion period as a time when the Law was harder than it is now, and as a time when anti-social behaviour was more reliably controlled (Williams 1987 provides an excellent analysis of Law and social change). Jimmy Manngayarri offered an example in the context of people marrying indiscriminately. He said that before invasion a man who consistently showed himself incapable of respecting rules would have been killed, probably by his own family. The responsibility for doing so would be phrased as Dreaming Law. In those days, because the wrong-doer was one of their own, the family had the responsibility of trying to straighten him (or her) out. Others, of course, might wish to accomplish his death, but if they took direct action they might well be overstepping the limits of authority and inviting retaliation. Responsible action within the kin/country nexus also included this grievous obligation: that people kill their own if that was the only way to assert control. Jimmy explained:

> When he go other way [marrying wrongly], that broke the Law. They could kill for that. He should go straight way married. If you go wrong, [you're] balls-up for kid. [You] Don't know which way [your] family. If you do it right, you know where you got to put your kid [how to arrange subsequent marriages]. [When you go wrong] You make a big mess. [The relations would say] 'Not me, but Law say you broke that Law.' . . . Your own family can kill you. [They would say:] 'Dirty trick. He's rubbish one.' They put him away.

The ideal that asymmetrical relationships are nurturant is one side of a set of understandings about dependence and authority. Authority is backed up by the fact that old people do know more than young people about how to protect and damage others. Dependence is real, and it raises the fear that old people might refuse to nurture. Often people express this as a fear that old people might become disgusted and resort to sorcery. One man, speaking from the position of old people, explained to me that he and others were getting sick and tired of young women's and men's disobedience:

> If they chuck away old people, where they going to find a Law? Uncle talk: 'You go longa old people, stay with him, work for him. Don't go mad

> way, wrong way. You got to get the Law from old people' . . . They make a wrong now, this time. That's what we been tell this mob here. Every young boy, when he get away from school, he should know two Laws. He been chuck it away both sides. Pick up nother man['s] woman, sick [sorcery] coming up behind [him] from old people. Drink grog, make a fight, this arguing, anything. Might be man pick up a little sick, kill him dead, home.

There is a profound ambivalence to relationships in which those who can help you can also hurt you. It is compounded by the availability of anonymous sorcery and by human duplicity. Another old man explained:

> White man rule, he can put you in the gaol, and might be three years or four years gaolhouse. No more blackfellow, I tell you. Blackfellow got more, more brain. He want to try and kill you, they'll kill you. Yes. They'll kill you. They'll catch up you any time. You broke that Law belong to blackfellow, you'll be there. He'll laugh you [joke with you]. Yeah. He'll laugh you. But you don't know his feeling inside . . . You might see him, yes, all right. He'll give you good word, but nothing [he doesn't mean it]. You can't see his heart there inside, and brain there inside. He can't tell you. He's still gotta get you. Not only him, but everyone watching him. Old people got more power. Old people got more power than young people. What young people got? Nothing! Nothing on his brain!

Adults are well aware that their obligation is to secure a new generation of owners, not to destroy it. People have by no means recovered from the demographic catastrophe brought about in the first fifty or sixty years of invasion. A group of adults who fear that they may be on a trajectory towards oblivion do not willingly hasten the process, unless they have been driven to the limit.

Self-destruction

One of the men with whom I was very close had lived at Yarralin, his wife's country, since its inception. He had come, he said, to give them a hand. In 1981 he was given a promise: a young girl from that country. Shortly afterwards his old wife left him, supported in her move by her daughters. His young wife took no notice of him, refusing to cook for him or to sleep at his camp. She declined to spend time with him, and regularly (virtually daily) 'ran away' to her mother and grandmother. By 1986 my friend was losing heart. The Yarralin dream of a self-sufficient and Lawful community, to which he had devoted years away from his own country, had not become a reality. His family was dispersed; the young woman who should have taken care of him wanted nothing to do with him. Several times he threatened to hurt himself, hoping to induce his in-laws to exert greater control over their daughter. One evening he threatened himself with a knife, and the next afternoon, knife in hand, he went alone to the river. People raised the alarm, and groups of men went searching for him.

I could not help search because my friend had gone into the men's area. To soothe my feelings I went to one of my older 'brothers' and told him that I was worried. Usually he joked with me. This time, he said 'pull up a chair, sister'. No one at Yarralin would profess to know what is going on in another person's mind, but my brother explained that when a man's wife will not stay with him, he starts to worry. In this case, the wife would not sit down in the shade with him or do anything for him. My friend could not stay at home, but had to go and take meals with his in-laws because he had no one to cook for him. My brother explained that when things like that happen a man might think, 'Well, that mother and father, they don't like me' and he might go off and do something to himself. That would make trouble come back to the wife and her parents and would re-pay them for the lack of concern they had shown for him.

Later that evening my friend was back in camp and I was able to tell him that I was terribly concerned. He said that he had not been worried about his wife so much as about his culture, and that he had gone off quietly to visit and talk with the old [dead] people. Songs, he said, are a language for talking to the dead who hear and understand, and feel close. He was worried about the ceremony lines he runs: they came up from stones in the beginning times, and they have kept on going. Old people taught young people; young people learned, and grew old, and taught new young people. Now, he said, young people were not learning. Once the old and middle-aged people are gone, the songs will be gone; once gone, they are lost forever.

My friend borrowed some Christian terminology, although he was vehemently opposed to the missionaries, saying: 'This is the last days now. Everything's getting lost now.' He faced a barren future, both in life and in death, for he expected to go to his own country as a dead body, there to live with ever diminishing contact with the living. He said that he did not intend to kill himself, because that would not help. What he intended, as I understand it, was to make threats which would arouse others to his own awareness of how badly wrong things were.

Violence inflicted against one's self is not a new phenomenon. It is a structured and predictable part of funerals, a 'traditional' way of expressing sorrow. It is also a way of expressing regret over one's own wrong-doing. In funerals it incites kinsmen to care for and to protect each other, and may be intended to elicit the same response from the dead body. In wrong-doing it shows sincerity of regret and may forestall worse punishment from others by moving them to compassion. Like the dingo's gesture in dying, threats of self-violence are a demand for others to repair damaged relationships.

Actual self-violence may also be a form of retaliation. Humbert Tommy was the last man of the last generation of men who had never given in to the fact of conquest. Although he spent time on the stations, he was primarily a 'bush blackfellow'. Many younger men lived with him periodically, learning bush skills, secret-ceremonial knowledge, and developing the roots which would sustain them during subsequent decades of hard work for whitefellows. Towards the end of his life (1965), ceremonial events which he tried to organise fell apart because younger men wanted to escape the rigours of the Law. Cattle station Europeans treated him like a child and, he believed, were robbing him. Well-meaning white doctors wanted to take him away and treat him for leprosy. Seeing little hope for the future, and wanting to die in his own country, he shot himself in the head. Daly Pulkara, one of the men who had lived with Humbert Tommy in the bush, told me about it:

> Something, doctor or sister [nurse], might be doctor really, that's what I believe. I been working that place [Humbert River station] then, and I said: 'Here's a doctor come out here, and I should have Humbert Tommy in here' . . . I can tell you now, he had a worry thing. Humbert Tommy had a worry thing for his way. This doctor said: 'I'm still [going to] take him.' And Humbert Tommy said: 'I'm going to try myself.' His rown worry, you see. 'You believe mine, or if you don't believe mine, I'll believe myself. I'll kill myself too.' You know, 'you'll get me around another way'. See. That's what him been reckon.
>
> And I asked them: 'What happened to Humbert Tommy? What worries him?' He had a lot of worries for Aboriginal way too . . . And Humbert Tommy got worry this time, till he could have everything organised right way, if he lived. He should have given him about might be two or three weeks, like that.
>
> DR: Oh, the doctor wanted to take him straight away?
>
> DP: Yeah. Doctor wanted to take him straight away. And he beat that doctor that way [by killing himself] . . .
> 'You know him grandpa Humbert Tommy? He shot himself.' *Kartiya* [whitefellows] told me that too. I just sit down real quiet.

When human life is valued as Yarralin people say it ought to be, self-violence is a cause for massive concern. It is acutely distressing, to say the least, that there have been people who, driven by the powerful sense that everything is going wrong, kill themselves. This is an act of defiance as much as an act of despair, and in Humbert Tommy's case was directed to two groups. Aimed against white Australians it indicated a final seizing of control over his own life. Aimed against his own people, it was a last desperate effort to force others to right wrongs.

Another form of destruction is that of self-will gone wild. The person who is always making trouble, who refuses to take responsibility for him or herself, and who disregards or even mocks the rights of others, makes other people feel helpless. Legally they cannot kill such people; few would want to. People who are not wild want and need other people; they want them obedient when they are young, and self-controlled when they are adult. The wild person may be driven out of one community after another, but their wilfullness leads others to prefer not to antagonise them, for there is no telling what they may do. The very fact of their uncontrolled aggression inspires fear.

Almost invariably the people who are wild are people who drink to excess. Wildness is not confined to drunken behaviour; rather, people who are drunk and wild frequently also are violent and unpredictable when sober. Self-controlled Yarralin people, and others throughout the region, tolerate their behaviour, saying that drunk people are not in possession of their senses. They forgive them, one might say, in the belief that they know not what they do.

What they do, so predictably that it is difficult to believe that they are completely unaware, is beat up those less powerful than themselves (see Brady and Palmer 1984:38–65 for an analysis of this issue). Men beat women, particularly young women; women beat and often neglect children. If other individuals try to intervene, they are turned on and attacked. In any given situation most people do not intervene because, unless it is their own close relative, they have no right to do so. From my Yarralin perspective it often seemed that drinkers sought out those contexts in which their behaviour would be most noticeable and those people who had the greatest obligations to control them. When there are both drunk and sober people present, it sometimes seems, as Bateson (1973:280–308) suggests in his analysis of alcoholism, that the drinker is in a double-bind which commits him or her to testing constantly the boundaries of self-will and the limits of authorised response. Drinkers seem to be trapped in a failure to establish a sustainable intersubjectivity. Not infrequently they impose a double-bind on those around them: their violent behaviour requires intervention; intervention in the form of restraint maddens them; to be ignored or unrestrained stimulates them to greater violence. Everybody loses.

Wildness promotes powerlessness. This is so in part because people are reluctant to intervene and therefore find themselves in situations over which they have very little control. This is so, most distressingly, in that those who are wild do not fulfil their family responsibilities. They repeatedly fail to nurture, to teach, and to protect their own relatives. In threatening others they generate feelings of powerlessness beyond their own circle of kin. In failing to nurture, they produce their own generation of deprived people.

All of my long-term periods at Yarralin have been before grog came to be a regular part of daily life. When Yarralin was a dry community drinkers had to live elsewhere. They came home to visit family and country, and for the most part they came and stayed sober. Some people, indeed, used Yarralin as a place to dry out and regain their health. My restricted contact with drinkers limits my understanding of specific cases. From what young people have told me, I find their hostility and despair directed primarily toward their own kin. They know that in turning against their family they violate one of the first and most basic tenets: that country and people take care of their own. What they assert is that they have not been taken care of. Their statements suggest that their elders are engaging in a form of self-devouring predation. In these cases young people's lives, bodies, and wills have been controlled by others for others' purposes, and they have not been protected, defended, and nurtured in return. Through violence young people turn outwards, testing, in a manner that is guaranteed to fail, whether others really do care about them (cf. Bateson 1973:293).

Annie

Intensely aware of the fragility of human endeavour, older people look to the young to take over when they are gone, and they worry. They worry, and they blame. The problems they perceive in breaking the continuity which has sustained them are problems which they assert are the fault of the young. They are, I believe, perpetuating a strategy which may once have worked but does so no longer. Perhaps without realising it, they avoid confrontations among equals and avoid the contradictions inherent in community life by forcing the young into increasingly asymmetrical relationships. All adults are meant to be autonomous, yet many are dependent. Confrontations, when they occur, ought to be between equals, but frequently, when balance is lost, they are not.

Adults sometimes push the blame, the anger, and the responsibility onto their relatively powerless dependants. In sustaining their own symmetry in one context, they generate increasingly harmful asymmetry in another context, failing properly to nurture. And they resist acknowledging that the changes which are taking place are producing an unprecedented misery among some of the young.

One cold night in 1988, while camping in the bush, drunken fighting broke out and went on for hours. From where I lay, 200 metres away, I could hear the blows inflicted on human bodies. The cries were unbearable. Unable even to think of sleeping, I finally got up and walked around, hoping to ease my mind by moving my body. A little figure, as light as a butterfly, appeared out of the dark and threw herself into my arms saying, 'Debbie Rose, Debbie Rose, save me'. This little girl, whom I will call Annie, was about thirteen years old. She was on school holiday, had left her mother to visit relatives, and had become caught up in the drinking and fighting. She said that her father's brother had been demanding to have sex with her, that her father's brother's wife had fought with her rather than with the husband, that other women had taken the woman's side, and that no one had taken her side. Her voice trembled as she said, 'A father's not supposed to chase his daughter, Debbie, isn't that right?'. 'Very right,' I said, 'in your law and in mine'. For that night she slept with me, and in the morning she decided to go back to her relatives.

The next day several of the participants explained to me that there had been a bit of trouble the previous night, and that it had all been Annie's fault. I thought of the adults who had purchased the alcohol and brought it away from the pub; of the adults who had consumed it; of the desperate derangement which is involved in physical, psychological and sexual abuse. I knew that Annie was not the only young person to have been victimised, both as the target of abuse and as the scapegoat to allow others to avoid responsibility. Thinks like this do not happen often, as far as I know, and they are most emphatically not unique to Aboriginal societies. The problem is that they do happen and that they are denied.

A good deal has been written about substance abuse among Aboriginal people; on a global scale the topic has generated a vast literature. Most sociological studies do not address the physical causes of disease, probably because these are not yet well understood (Goodwin 1988). Focusing on social and cultural causes and prospects, they tend also to avoid the question of spiritual damage and the power of spiritual recovery; these matters are difficult for an outsider to assess, and are not granted legitimacy within a 'scientific' discourse. Particularly in the domain of public policy there often appears to be a facile linking of cause and effect. If distress is thought to lead people to substance abuse, and if distress is caused by dislocation, inadequate housing and other facilities–limited education, unemployment and the like–then to redress these problems will be to solve the problem of substance abuse.

Such a prognosis ignores the well-known fact that addictive disease is not constrained by economic, class, ethnic, or religious status. There are almost certainly physical causes which no amount of goods and services will affect. More important is the fact that housing, education, the right to work, and the right to religious freedom are basic human rights which the Australian government is pledged to provide for people whether they are sick or well. To say that land rights or any other government policy will stop the spread of addictive disease is to place the sufferers in an intolerable double-bind. It is to say that their recovery is beyond their own control; that they must wait for others to find the political will to provide for them before they can begin to repair the damage. Such distorted thinking only serves to reproduce disease by circumscribing the possibilities for recovery.

I do not speak here as an advocate for policy or programs, nor do I speak to condemn those who suffer. We are not responsible for our diseases, but we are, each of us, responsible for our recovery. Recovery begins with the conscious decision to stop denying that there is a problem (cf. Bateson ibid:283–4; Goodwin 1988:198). This is precisely the step that most direct and indirect victims of disease find extraordinarily difficult. It is the step that many sober Yarralin adults are unwilling to take. In blaming the young, and denying the problems among adults, older people avoid confronting and taking responsibility for the antagonisms and contradictions in community life. Without ever intending to, they perpetuate disease.

Intergenerational antagonisms are not new. What is overwhelmingly evident is that they are intensifying. When old people dismiss the distress of the young they preserve a symmetry which may often be illusory. For many, these illusions are important to their place in community life, but the final cost is damage and death.

I once sat in on a good natured argument between a few old women and a group of young women. The old ones were berating the young ones for not being more obedient, and the young cheekily defended their freedom. Drawing on missionary terminology, they spoke of a 'new sun rising' and a 'new generation' of people who neither needed nor wanted to be controlled by their elders. One of the old women responded to these statements by saying in the driest possible voice but with an amused gleam in her eye: 'Fuck the new generation.'

We all laughed. But in the end, this is not a joke.

Most of my self-selected teachers have been older than me. They speak about and through the culture which has enabled them to survive with their dignity intact. Decades of cruelty and injustice have not subverted their sense of their own worth as individuals and as links in networks which exist in both space and time. The values of nurturance, dependence and autonomy are alive and well in their minds, hearts and families, if not always in their communities. The Dream countries which situate their lives in a moral order are sometimes relatively inaccessible and most are in a state of decline, but they are known and cared for. Culture, values, spiritual awareness: these are the essential means through which people all over the world heal themselves of the wounds of addictive disease.

My old friend was not mistaken in thinking that his culture may not survive. In his calmer moments he asserted that the threats are not only grog and the recalcitrance of the young. These are local problems which are amenable to local management, however difficult, even painful, this may be. The broader problem, in his and others' view, is the destruction of country, plants, animals, Dreamings, soils, water systems, and people over which Yarralin people are mostly powerless. Damage, wastage, and destruction on this scale are the result of a systematised process of conquest which he and others spent considerable energy in analysing and trying to curtail.

11 *Jacky Jacky*

'Jacky Jacky' is the standardised and stereotypical European name for an Aboriginal male. As the Aboriginal song writer Dougie Young expresses it:

> I'm tall, dark, and mean, and every place I've been
> The white man calls me Jack.

With a delightful sense of irony, Jimmy Manngayarri explained that the first white man ever was called Jacky Jacky Pantamara. Jimmy's story borrows European ideas of evolution; he said that Jacky Jacky 'bred up' from monkeys. At first he had 'no tools', only the shanghai, sling, and bow and arrow. Jacky Jacky established London; from there he went to America where the Union people taught him to make machinery. Returning to London, he made the rifles with which he invaded Australia.

Yarralin people have developed many stories to account for European invasion, to try to understand the European mind, and to explain the holocaust without accepting the ideologies which either deny that it happened or assert that it was inevitable and that somehow Aboriginal people are at fault. A few like Jimmy accept a partial European understanding of the origins of at least some human beings. Others take human origins to be universal. When Hobbles told me about the track of the Nanganarri women, for example, he said that people used to think that the women stopped when they reached the salt water, but now they know that the women travelled all over the world because women everywhere give birth. Similarly, Old Tim said that all human beings come out of dogs. The belief that white people come from white dogs while Aborigines come from dingos does not negate the basic relationship between dogs and humans. While Yarralin people understand their particular culture to be localised, they also understand the essential conditions of life to be universal.

The stories to which we will be attending now in some detail are of a type which is not unique. In their focus on European goods and people they have sometimes been linked to the 'cargo cults' of Melanesia (cf Petri and Petri-Oderman 1988; Glowczewski 1983), but while goods–wages, food, transport–are often involved in the stories, the point is to examine kinds of actions. Burridge (1960), in his perceptive analysis of Melanesian cargo movements, indicates that stories like these constitute both an explanation of wrong and an offer to right wrongs. They include the search for the 'moral other' along with the identification of immoral others.

Among the most prominent in north Australia are the Captain Cook stories which are told throughout the Victoria River District and the Kimberley (Kolig 1980; Rose 1984), as well as in Queensland (Kennedy 1985). In Arnhem Land stories about Captain Cook have a somewhat different significance, although they too deal with invasion and its consequences (Mackinolty and Wainburranga 1988; see also Maddock 1988). Identifying Cook as the persona of conquest, the quintessential immoral European, Yarralin people's stories are complemented by those which deal with the search for moral others–'the Union mob', and 'the Big American Boss'.

Yarralin people say that white people have 'treated them like a dog'. They mean, of course, the way whites treat their own dogs. In Yarralin people's thinking, it is whites who are cruel both to dogs and to people. They say that prisoners were chained up like dogs, that people were shot or hunted away like dogs. They point out that whites used to kill old or sick people who were no longer useful as workers in the same way that they kill old and sick dogs. White people fed Aboriginal workers with scraps: stale bread and stinking beef.

The comparisons of the ways Europeans have treated Aborigines (and in some instances still do) and the way they treat dogs are all too horrifyingly true. At least in the early decades of contact, the dogs probably came off better. But the comparison also points to the loss of autonomy which Aboriginal people suffered at the hands of whites. They lost control of their country and Dreaming places, of their own labour, of their ability to carry out many basic moral actions such as renewing cycles of growth through setting fires and burning the country. Much of their subsistence has been lost through changes to the land, and they have lost their freedom of being in country. They have become dependants.

It does not require a great deal of imagination to understand that the experience has been a terrible one. Part of the horror of it has been in the monumental losses, and they are continuing. Part, too, was in the total reversal of what Aboriginal people take to be Law. I have suggested four meta-rules: balance, response, symmetry and autonomy. Captain Cook denied all of them. Yarralin people ask why the white people did not ask them about the country so that they could have told them that it was already occupied. Or, if whites were determined to make war, why they did not give Aborigines rifles so that the fight would be equal. They ask why Europeans fail to respond to all that has been offered, and why they refuse to think about what has happened and what they are still doing.

Ever since Victoria River Aborigines first encountered Europeans they have debated the question: what manner of being is this? As in many parts of Aboriginal Australia, first encounters were often interpreted as meetings with deceased relatives. In his provocative study of religious adaptation in south east Australia, Swain (1990) suggests that in classifying foreigners as relatives, Aboriginal people sought to bring them within a moral order. His analysis is equally perceptive with respect to the Victoria River valley. Big Mick said that his father told him about the first foreigners to come through. This first group was called the 'Marinbala' mob (the term may possibly derive from 'Marines'; Marines were stationed much further to the north at Port Essington). They came on foot and, according to Big Mick's account of his father's account, they spoke both Ngaliwurru and English. Ngaliwurru people sang out to them, saying: 'We here, countrymen'. The whitefellows gave Aborigines flour and salt beef: 'Flour, they reckoned "white paint"; salt beef, they reckoned "devil" and chuck it away.' This event occurred near the place where Gregory made a camp on the Victoria River and the account may refer to those early contacts.

It does not seem to have taken long for Aborigines to have recognised that these foreigners were humans, but humans of a particularly 'wild' and lawless kind. Wild is sometimes equated with the Kriol term 'myall' which denotes ignorance. The term developed in the context of black-white antagonisms and may derive from 'male', reflecting Europeans' early access to Aboriginal women and their contempt for, and fear of, Aboriginal males. The truly wild person, however, is not simply ignorant. He or she is also one who consistently demolishes the moral boundary between self and other. The wild person conceives of social relationships as a matter of disabling and winning.

Hobbles enjoyed turning the words and actions of invaders against them with an irony so subtle that it risks being misunderstood by a non-local audience. In one of his narratives he points out how wild (wilful and anti-social) Captain Cook was:

> And Captain Cook reckon, story belong Captain Cook: 'He's [Aborigines] the wild now. He's the myall. He's the wild one all right.'
>
> He's the wild one, he's the myall all right, but he's owning the land. He's owning the land. That's our land. Captain Cook should have give him a fair go.
>
> Captain Cook been ought to sit down for a while, you know, till him can come, my people, and tellem Captain Cook slowly: 'Hello, g'day.' All this story. Our people, when they frighten. And that Aboriginal, till him been let go, he might be come back again next time and tell him. When him been get up, go way, walking away, frighten, he [Captain Cook] start to knockem. Shootem. Get rid of him. That's [what] Captain Cook reckoned. And he's [Captain Cook] the *really* wild one. He's the wild one, all right . . . Them people might be walking around myall and myall, but he [Captain Cook] didn't know where that people been run away, and

where the place. Because Captain Cook couldn't know the country. That's where my people been raised. Only my people.

In Hobbles' long narratives concerning Captain Cook (see Rose 1984) he makes it perfectly evident that Captain Cook could not plead ignorance; he was offered all the evidence he needed to know that he was encountering human beings. He saw people doing specifically human things: cooking and distributing food, for instance. He saw them living in their own country, and they told him that it was their own. They also told him with words and with spears that they did not want him. Rather than listen and take notice, he pursued his own relentless course of destruction.

In these long narratives that course is mapped geographically as well as socially. Captain Cook started in Sydney where he met Aboriginal people, queried them about the country, shot them, and landed his people and animals. From there he travelled by ship north along the coast, around Cape York, and around Arnhem Land to Darwin (map 1), repeating his actions at every stop. From Darwin he travelled south, exploring a number of rivers and finally reaching the Victoria River, which he sailed up as far as Wave Hill station. His travels up the Victoria River are remarkably similar to those of the explorer Gregory. At Wave Hill he landed, repeating the same actions and stating what came to be known locally as Captain Cook's law: the ways in which land was to be stolen, Aboriginal people killed or captured, foreign animals introduced, and the whole of the process denied.

Hobbles refers to Captain Cook's 'law'. I understand him to be using the term two ways: as a set of rules, and as a structure of relationships that persists through time. And here is the rub. In Hobbles' view, and he is by no means alone in this, while predation is part of the structure of the moral universe, annihilation is not. How is it that rules which depend on destruction are reproduced through time so that they take on the qualities of an enduring law? How can annihilation persist? More locally, the question is: can conquest be located within a moral universe?

Logically there are only a few strategies for dealing with this question: capitulation, resistance, and accommodation. Capitulation is the strategy offered by the missionaries: a reframing of the understanding of the cosmos to include a concept of evil. A few Yarralin poeple have opted for this strategy, and the cost is high. Missionary cosmology not only expands but inverts indigenous cosmology (see also Swain 1988). Defining Aboriginal culture as a primary locus of evil, missionaries teach that this world has no enduring value; that the self (one's personal salvation) is to be valued above others; that time is the unfolding of an external will (God's) upon an estranged and wicked world; that time is leading toward ultimate confrontation and the final destruction of this world (see Rose 1985; 1988). An Aboriginal missionary once preached a sermon in which he exhorted people:

'Praise God. Don't be on the losing side. Come in on the winning side.' Tempting words, it seems, for a conquered people.

In the 1980s, most Yarralin people rejected this strategy. Some rejected it out of hand; others considered it closely. One man, who joined the missionaries for a while and then went back to his own culture, explained to me that he had thought about things for a long time before finally deciding that what he wanted out of life was the continuity of his own culture. Just as his father had upheld the Law, had put him through ceremony, taught him esoteric knowledge, trained him in the responsibilities of adulthood, so he, too, wanted to do the same for his son. If he had remained a Christian (in this particular sense of joining the missionaries), his country would have ended up with no one to take care of it, his father's and grandfather's lives would have been for nothing, and his son would have no place in the world. This man seemed uncertain about the fate of his own soul. He thought that perhaps he would join the devil in the fiery pit, but he asserted that the continuity of Aboriginal life on earth was worth that risk.

The strategy of resistance was Hobbles' forte. A strong story teller with a tremendously inquiring mind and a gift for political analysis, he told many versions of the Captain Cook saga. These resistance stories explain how certain things came to be while yet sustaining the essential moral structure of the cosmos. All are based in the fundamental problematic of invasion and Law; all rest on the proposition that Captain Cook is an outlaw, morally speaking. Many refer to two of Captain Cook's successors: Gilruth, Administrator of the Northern Territory from 1912 to 1919, and Dr Cecil Cook, Protector of Aborigines in the Northern Territory for over a decade beginning in 1927. Sometimes Hobbles taped stories for an audience; other times we conversed, trying ideas out on each other.

Many of the stories detail a process whereby conquest led to control which allowed the means for conquest to be continually reproduced. Working with a labour theory of value, Hobbles explained that once the land was appropriated ('stolen'), Aboriginal people's labour and land was used by Europeans to 'make themselves strong', and Captain Cook and his henchmen denied that stolen land and labour were the basis of their strength. His analysis is on a par with, but far more eloquent than, Karl Marx's analysis showing that the relations of production are reproduced in the interests of those who control the means and forces of production, and those who control mystify their position, representing relations of production as serving the interest of the whole, rather than simply the interests of the controllers.

> You been bring that law. My Law only one. Your law keep changing. I know you keep changing now lotta law. You and Gilruth. That's another headquarters longa Darwin. That's the Gilruth. You, Captain Cook, you the one been bringing in now lotta man. Why didn't you give me fair go for my people. Why didn't you give it me fair go for my people? Should have askem about the story. Same thing, I might go on another place, I

must askem. I might stay for couple of days, you know. That's for the mefellow, Aboriginal people. But you the Captain Cook. I know you been stealing country belong to mefellow. Australia. What we call Australia, that's for Aboriginal people. But him been take it away. You been take that land, you been take the mineral, take the gold, everything. Take it up to this big England. And make all that thing, and make your big Parliament too.

Nother thing. Captain Cook coming back big boss now. Bringing nother lot government belong you. Still you been bring your book, and follow your book, Captain Cook. We know you government. When you been bring it over to Sydeny, there people been work it up. Government been work it up. You reckon: 'white man's country.' No. This not the white man's country. This Aboriginal country.

Hobbles took the primary cause as given: arrogance and greed. Yarralin people are not unacquainted with these human qualities; they are probably universally human. Greed and other human frailties are facts of life; the problem is how they come to be 'laws' by which humans live. The most comprehensive stories are the ones that integrate a number of factors into a political economy. Hobbles contended that arrogance and greed, perpetuated through the cruel use of technology became a driving force which led Europeans to expand and devour the earth and the people who stood in the way. As they destroyed, so they needed more, and conquered land and labour became the fuel for further conquest.

Hobbles and other story tellers are concerned to show that invasion is not a process of the past which is now finished. Rather, they go to considerable effort to explain that the process is on-going and is continuing to destroy people and land. The other integral point, which is rarely stated explicitly, is that conquest is based on desire and on the illusion of winners and losers. One wins by disabling not only the opposition but the very life systems in which the opposition is embedded. This is a fatal error, for there are no other life systems. As Riley Young said (chapter 3), 'I know government say he can change him rule. But he'll never get out of this ground'.

As in other areas of life, when the the cost of winning is disablement, everybody loses. Many of the stories dwell on the sorrow, the losses, the injustices suffered by Aboriginal people. The style is one we have already encountered in Daly's account of the moon. The intent is twofold: to elicit compassion for the victims, and, correspondingly, to heap blame upon the perpetrator. More abstractly, the intent is to demonstrate the quality of wrong–that it is not simply a series of wrongful events but, rather, is a failure of intersubjectivity which damages life-sustaining relationships and which must, therefore, eventually rebound.

In this context, Hobbles and others used the term 'Europeans' in a very loose way; the Japanese, who bombed north Australia during the Second World War, and any other conquering peoples are said to be of the same quality as Europeans.

Both logically and experientially, theories of conquest which attempt to sustain a moral order entail another cast of characters: the moral others who oppose cruelty and injustice. Logically this is so because Dreaming Law is everywhere; everywhere localised and culturally distinct, it is also everywhere the same. Where there is wrong there must also be those who oppose it. Experientially this is so because Yarralin people have encountered Europeans who clearly were appalled at what was happening and tried to change things. Usually such Europeans are classed under the generic term the 'Union mob', and as trade unions have been sporadically trying to achieve basic wages and rights for Aboriginal workers since about 1920, and as in Australia militant trade unionism developed in the rural sector (Ward 1966:212), this classification is an accurate rendering of Australian social history, although Yarralin people often attribute a stronger sense of justice to unions than may actually be the case.

In Yarralin people's stories, those who work for Aboriginal rights are usually labelled the 'Union mob'; they are identified as people who showed some desire to engage with Aborigines as fellow human beings, a form of intersubjectivity most clearly signalled in the term 'mate' (see Ward 1966; Altman 1987). Their opponents are people such as Gilruth and Dr Cook. Both opponents are well chosen. Gilruth was the Administrator who came into total conflict with trade unionists in Darwin and was forced to leave town through what is termed 'The Darwin Rebellion' (*ADB* vol. 9:18). Dr Cook was Protector of Aborigines (Northern Territory) at a time (1929) when the Bleakley Report recommended a very modified system of wages; the recommendations were never accepted.

Captain Cook and his cronies have their place of origin: England. The Union mob is often associated with another place of origin: the Unites States of America. Some stories construct the plot as a battle between government (Captain Cook, Gilruth, Dr Cook) and the Unions (including Americans and social activists like Frank Hardy). Fred Rose (1965: 90–1) suggests that the inclusion of Americans may result from the Second World War when American troops were stationed in Australia. Aborigines saw that black Americans were treated equitably. Understandably, black American soldiers perceived racial tension and discrimination against them (Potts and Potts 1985:48), but from an Aboriginal perspective the over-riding view may have been that of equality. Without denying the validity of this point, it seems to me that America's (often undeserved) reputation for justice predates the Second World War in the Victoria River District, although from the present vantage point it is difficult to be certain.

Old Tim and others have told the story of Mr Graham who was manager of VRD (1919–1926) at a time when there was some agitation for wages. According to the story, the 'government' gave Graham poisoned grog (liquor) which he drank. With his death, discussion of wages was finished. The longing for equal treatment, however, survived. As Old Tim said:

> But we been looking at American bloke, American Union. Looking at, looking at, looking at, looking at: Ohhhhhh Christ, we been want to. That Union been want to come get money and all that. They can teach the word longa this country. Proper word. We been want to get pay like six hundred, seven hundred, like that. I think they got the Union [in] America. But nothing [here]. We never been get a word.

Many stories deal with Aboriginal people's attempts to make contact with Union people so that they could let them know what was happening. In Hobbles' view, the laws restricting freedom of movement were attempts to enforce two kinds of silences: first, Aborigines were to be limited in their contact with other Aborigines, and thus able to gain only a limited perspective on their own situations, and unable to organise themselves for resistance. Word of mouth overcame this obstacle to some degree. Second, Aborigines were to be allowed very little contact with Europeans who might be able to help them, and information about Aboriginal workers was to be suppressed.

One of the most powerful representations of moral Europeans is a figure known as the Big American Boss. Most stories of the Big American Boss have him coming through the Victoria River District to VRD or to Wave Hill station. In a series of allegorical events, the Boss learns how social relationships are structured on stations. He goes to dinner, for example, and sees the white men sitting down at the table while the Aboriginal men take their food out to the woodheap. He states his surprise, saying that he had thought that here in the Northern Territory black and white sat down to table together. He is gently told that this is not the case. Other events teach him that wages are not equal, and that he is actually standing on Aboriginal land. Having been taught, he reciprocates, showing Aborigines how to use a western saddle (Australian cattlemen use a saddle adapted from the English type), how to ride a bucking bronco, and how to use a lasso. Then he leaves, promising that America recognises Aboriginal rights to land and will back up the struggle for land and freedom. Hobbles' account of the final exchange between the Big American Boss and Tommy Vincent Lingiyarri (later to become leader of the pastoral strikes) tells of the relationships:

> 'You know all these Australian people really bad men. We don't know Northern Territory. We only hear Australian people take it away longa you. You want it back?'
>
> 'Course.'
>
> 'You want help?'
>
> 'If you can give me help.'
>
> They shake hands.
>
> 'I'll help you. You keep going. Union strike [will] tellem Vestey mob finish. Don't you worry. Any day I might [be] hearing what you do now. You been fight for your land [before, and] you lost your land. Right we'll fix it up. Thank you, old Tommy Vincent. I'll really work for you. I'm behind you. Goodbye Tommy Vincent.'

Stories concerning American involvement are sometimes told as a hidden history; some speakers are concerned that if the Australian government knew that Aborigines had such powerful allies it might try to make things even harder for Aborigines. Because some stories are not fully for the public, and some story tellers worry about publicity, I cannot discuss these matters further. The point is clear, however: Aborigines need powerful allies in order to redress the wrongs that have been perpetrated against them, and they believe that some Americans are willing to become those powerful allies. It is evident to me that my American identity facilitated my accommodation as a person who wanted to learn, and entailed an expectation that I would want to help. The fact that Jack Doolan, an identified 'good guy' and an ALP politican, supported my research also indicated that, as people sometimes told me, the government (nationality unspecified) had sent me to 'help' them. When Yarralin people spoke of the audience for whom their stories were intended, they spoke most consistently of Americans and white Australians. Americans, they felt, really wanted to know; Australians needed to know and understand.

Passionate cries for equality and justice and deep calls for alliances with powerful others who can help are heard all over the world, often directed toward America, with its ideals of liberty and justice for all. American foreign and domestic policies have rarely deserved such faith, but that is another story.

Another way of dealing with the dilemma of conquest, closely linked to resistance, is that of accommodation. Most, probably all, Yarralin people accept that change has occurred; they look to ways in which the future can be structured so that the oppression of the past is not reproduced. Jimmy Manngayarri told of how it ought to have been. In explaining the wrong, Jimmy uses the expression 'fifty', indicating accommodation through equal exchange.

> Why he never say: 'Oh, come on mate, you and me live together. You and me living together, mates together. You and me can work for the country all the same then. I might want to go down to Sydney, down to country where you been born, well twofellow fifty on country. You can go this way down to England, and back from there, you fifty.'
>
> But you never been do that. You been like to clean the people out from him rown country. *Ngumpin* never been go and kill you there longa England! He never make a big war longa you there, finish you there! NO! You been do the wrong thing *mijelb* [yourself]. Finish off *ngumpin*. Like that now, no good that one game. Well you been make [it] very hard. You should have been kindfellow to give it back people country when you been shoot [them]. But you still, you still follow that thing all the time. You still follow. Well, we can't follow that thing same way what you do.

Jimmy's story points to a final inevitable problem. If people are to remain within their own moral universe, they cannot fight destruction with a more powerful destruction. As Turner (1987: 101) says, in the confederative mode 'under threat of annihilation by another, potential victims, each to maintain themselves intact, are moved toward accommodation, even toward accommodation with the threat itself'.

The only moral response is to continue to offer accommodation. And it is precisely this response which makes it easy for Europeans to ignore Aboriginal people's words, actions, lives, and deaths. When Hobbles told me that he had decided to stop attending meetings with European bureaucrats, he said that for years he had 'sweetened' himself up just like tea, trying to make himself and others understood, and 'nothing been come back. Just nothing'.

Silence, the lack of response, sometimes leads to bitterness and a terrible sense of futility. Daly said that his ancestors had not wanted to end up like crushed vermin:

> *Kartiya* [whitefellows] reckon Ngarinman too cheeky. They didn't do cheeky for nothing. They been go together anyway, *kartiya* and *ngumpin* [blackfellows]: 'Can't killem me like a squashed snake, anyway.' Like that now. Hobbles know about it. You can see it when you read a paper too, longa that beginning newspaper [written history]. What *kartiya* been do longa *ngumpin* . . . [discussion of written history] Him been just start up here, shooting *ngumpin.* And *ngumpin* come, talk: 'Well, we not a squashed snake. We gotta fight for our selves.'

Later he said: 'Even me, I'm not a squashed snake.' But he did not sound convinced. From the depths of despair, European indifference takes on the characteristics of a continuing policy of annihilation, and many Aboriginal people in Australia share this perception. I am not certain that there is such a policy, but as the ramifications of indifference and denial are achieving a slow and painful attrition which amounts to the same thing, the point is somewhat arbitrary.

At times Hobbles spoke with great impatience, trying to tell Europeans that Captain Cook is dead. Like many of his messages, this too risks being lost. Australians already know that Captain Cook is dead, just as they know that he did not travel in the Northern Territory. Hobbles' statements were founded in the distinction between Dreaming and ordinary. That which is Dreaming endures, while that which is ordinary does not. Captain Cook is not Dreaming; laws of destruction cannot last for ever, in this or any other time. Europeans keep him alive by continuing to promote his law:

> That's why Captain Cook been clean up, bring man, bring book longa this country. Book, start up a law. Captain Cook not been telling any Union mob. Take this land, take away mineral, take away country, call it all Australia. Union should know this country. Union come up before Captain Cook. They say this land belongs Aboriginal people. Captain Cook been stealing this boundary . . .
>
> This land belong we mob, Aboriginal people. We right person on the land. That law belong to you finished from Captain Cook's time. That law finished right out. Because he won't listen to Aboriginal people, Aboriginal government. Because you wanna come see Aboriginal people in the NT? You come and see we, Australian government . . . You start coming over Aboriginal people just like your boss, all the way, but that time been gone for you long time ago. Finished . . .
>
> Because people from your mob, Captain Cook dead and [you should] stop with that thing [law]. You still got that book from Captain Cook. You can't give me that building. You can't give me that big lump money. You

> know Captain Cook been passed away now. People here got no bit of money, got no better clothes.

Hobbles always holds out a hand, not only in alliance, but also in mateship:

> Now I'm talking again, over. Right now–till we can have a friend, friend together now. I'm speaking on now. We're friends together because we own Australia every one of them no matter who white and black. We come together join in whether we can you know–take it *mijelb* [ourselves] love *mijelb* one another [each other]. And cross-ways marriage, no matter what kind of marriage, we can have them because we own Australia today every one of them. That be all right. Make it more better out of the, out of that big trouble. You know before, Captain Cook been making lot of cruel you know.
>
> Now these days, these days we'll be friendly, we'll be love *mijelb* [each other], we'll be mates. That be better, better for make that trouble. Now we'll be come join in, no matter who: white and black or yellow, as far as there.

Hobbles says that we all own Australia now. What he does not say, because for him it is so obvious, is that Europeans have already taken most of the country and ought therefore to be more equitable. They ought, in fact, to allow more opportunites for Aborigines to control land. His suggestion that Aborigines should have more land (under Australian national land tenure systems) offers Europeans a form of accommodation. In more extensive narratives Hobbles says that the years during which people worked on cattle stations, offering their labour to pastoralists (Danayari in Rose 1984), ought to be understood as an attempt at accommodation to which Europeans have yet to respond.

He suggests, too, that there could be more marriages. Hobbles' concern, which comes out more clearly in longer narratives, is that marriage, like land relationships, has been abused by Europeans. He notes two points in particular. The first is the fact that white men marrried or consorted with black women and that black men had few opportunities to reciprocate. There has long been a scarcity of white women in the Victoria River District, but more importantly, cultural constructions of race, enforced by social barriers, work against this type of marriage. The second is that mixed-descent children were taken away from their families. In Hobbles' view, the most oppressive wrong in taking children away was that they were kept from their culture. The whole point of marriage as a system of accommodation is that a new generation shares in the locative identity of both parents; European practices of sexual exploitation and policies of assimilation effectively disabled this system. Hobbles asserts that marriage, descent, and land ownership can be tied together in ways that give everyone a fair go.

Hobbles has offered a set of profound gifts to a non-Aboriginal audience: an acceptance of the conditions of the past as the basis from which we will build our future; some means of transforming the wrongs of the past into more equitable relationships. Flesh and blood, earth and water are offered as media through which Aboriginal and European Australians can be truly at home together in this continent. Hobbles may not have realised that beyond his overt statements he was also offering other gifts; his narratives point to a theory and practice of otherness, of generating structures which empower, rather than diminish, people. He offers the means by which nobody loses, and all life is sustained.

These gifts, like the meaning of his stories, are not always immediately obvious. For me, the most profound gift is also, at times, overwhelming. European ideologies of conquest assert that conquest is finished, and that it was the product of so many compelling and inescapable causes that it was inevitable. Ideologies throw the ball back to Aborigines, metaphorically, telling them that they cannot live in the past, and will just have to adapt to the new order.

Hobbles and others disentangle the mystifying ideologies of conquest, showing that at every moment there is an act of will. They say that it is Europeans who are living in the past, still following a law that has no future. And they ask that others make choices, exercising their will as an act of consideration for the fact that we all live, and die, together. The challenge can be overwhelming because it throws open to us the limits of our own power within structures that oppress. Hobbles asked:

> But I think that time was finished now for the Captain Cook. And belong to Gilruth, that time been gone. It's finished now . . . And right up to Gurindji now we remember for you twofellow Captain Cook and Gilruth. I know. We're going to get a lot of people now. All over Australia. Australia, it's belong to Aboriginal. But you been little mistake. Why didn't you look after London and big England? He's bigger than Australia. That's your country. Why didn't you stop your government, Captain Cook?

Captain Cook, the living man (1728–1779), was the son of a Scottish labourer and a Yorkshire woman. He attended a village school, was apprenticed to a shopkeeper, and later became apprenticed to a shipper. He fought for England in north America, and continued to educate himself while at sea. His rise to the position of Captain, and his appointment as leader of an expedition to the South Seas were triumphs of extraordinary ability (*ADB* vol. 1:243) over the structure of the English class system. He could no more have stopped the British exploration and colonisation of Australia than he could have perceived how he would be construed by Aboriginal people. Sometimes when I listened to Hobbles I thought to myself, 'You don't know how powerless we are'. When I said this to him he pulled me up, always reminding me that structures and processes are not inevitable, and that the people who resist them are not alone.

Not every person is as humanitarian as Hobbles, but all the Aboriginal people with whom I have discussed these matters, from the

Kimberley through the Victoria River District agree that Captain Cook's law is a law of madness. It is based in and effected through destruction, and people cannot go on destroying for ever. Failing to understand their place in the world, and the interconnectedness of life, Captain Cook's successors continue to visit destruction on the systems that support them. From a Yarralin perspective it is so obvious that this cannot continue indefinitely that offers to re-form the future are understood to be in everyone's self-interest. As indigenous knowledge and rights are rejected through overt refusal and through the spongy obscurity of indifference, so European structures of law appear to continue to generate madness. Only wild and mad people fail consistently to act in their own interest, and at some point madness and wildness become indistinguishable.

Beyond the overt attempts to accommodate through offering, there is an accommodation which is even more profound. Some Yarralin people have taken the additional step of placing some European Australians and some of their values within Dreaming Law. The direct opposite of capitulation, this response depends on opening indigenous cosmology to Europeans. Hobbles' statement that the Union people were here before Captain Cook hints at this process. The key figure selected by some Victoria River people as truly belonging in Dreaming is an Australian national hero: Ned Kelly.

Kelly was the son of Irish immigrants; his family was among the thousands who came to Australia in the last century hoping to make new lives for themselves, only to find that the class structure and religious and ethnic prejudices of England had been reproduced in the Antipodes. As poor Irish Catholics, the Kellys and their cohorts bore the misery generated by a society that was increasingly skewed to favour those who had already established positions of privilege. John Molony's (1980) beautiful biography of Ned Kelly tells the story of how an intelligent and charismatic young man was persecuted and hunted beyond the limits of social justice. The family was dispersed, and some of them were killed. Trapped, wounded, and captured, Ned Kelly was hanged in 1880 at the age of twenty-five, his dreams of armed rebellion squashed by the powerful members of a society that had never given him that most Australian of opportunites: a fair go. Kelly became the hero for Australian working people. Ballads (many composed before his death and some very recently), melodramas, films, and art tell the story of his life. Ned Kelly continues to spur the Australian imagination, although for some people he is no hero at all. Outlaw and (for some) outcast, Ned Kelly still speaks of resistance, and the story still threatens those who benefit from oppression.

I once asked Big Mick if he could explain the term '*miki*' to me. It had come up in a discussion of dead bodies, and I was having difficulty understanding it. Darrell Lewis and I privately referred to Big Mick as 'the old man who knows everything', and it came as no surprise when he smiled and started in on a story. This is his reply, slightly anglicised here:

Miki? Early day people might be see him. This world been salt water before, every way, every land. This world been covered up. All the salt water every way. Two men came down from sky. Ned Kelly and Angelo [angels]. Come down, get a boat, travel round that sea, salt water. Can't findem any bank. Those fellows travelling. This leaf been fall down. 'Hello! Green leaf here!' Twofellow still travelling la boat. They hit a high ridge. 'Hello! Pull up here.' Put em anchor. Go down [out of the boat] and stand up. 'What me and you gotta do?' 'We'll have to do something.' They been makem river, and salt water been go right back. That's for Ned Kelly and Angelo. Dry now, every way. Twofellow just walking now. Some bush blackfellow been go longa business [doing ceremony]. They come down. 'Hello! Some blackfellows there!' Blackfellows been talk, 'What's this fellow here?'. The blackfellows understand English. Twofellow travelling now, longa dry land. Walking. Go longa Wyndham.

Wyndham people [Europeans] look those two whitefellows: 'Oh, really different men. Different to we. We'll have to get em policemen.' Four policemen been come. Had a bit of a row longa twofellow. Twofellow get a gun and shoot four policemen la Wyndham. And travel back, go back this way.

Captain Cook been come down to Mandora [beach, in Darwin], gotta boat. From England they been come. Captain Cook come longa this land, longa Sydney Harbour. Good country him been look. Captain Cook shot and broke a leg for one fellow belonging to that country Sydney Harbour. Get a boat and going back again. Bring longa this country now horse and cattle. Captain Cook got a revolver. Photo [rock art] there all around Daguragu, he's holding a revolver. Where that breed up bullock and horse, that's where the Ned Kelly going back to England. Ned Kelly by himself now, he lose his mate. Ned Kelly got his throat cut. They bury him. Leave him. Sun go down, little bit dark now, he left this world. BOOOOOOOMMMMM! Go longa top. This world shaking. All the white men been shaking. They all been frightened!

This *miki* been working for blackfellows, making gutters [to drain off the salt water]. Right la Crawford Knob there, some blackfellows there, that *miki* been come out there. He's not here now. He's finished from that salt water time. Him blackfellow, first blackfellow. That Dreaming been come up, and that blackfellow got Law now. That *miki* been finished altogether.

For Big Mick and others, Ned Kelly is Dreaming (see also Middleton 1977:121–2). More than that, he is allocated a creative position in Dreaming. No matter how many Captain Cooks, police, and settlers come later, it is unmistakably the case that Ned was here first, actively making the Australian continent. Furthermore, Ned Kelly encountered Aborigines, and his encounters did not result in death or dispossession. In that, he was quite unlike Captain Cook. European people, here located in Wyndham, recognised that Ned Kelly was different–and they condemned him for it. Judging him to be dangerously different, they called out the police. Ned, being Ned, shot the police. In doing so, he aligned himself with the moral position of those who were being dispossessed.

The inclusion of Captain Cook in this story sets up a dynamic tension between those who come to harm people and country, and those whose coming is beneficial. Ned Kelly was opposed to what Captain Cook and his mob were doing to Australia. He went to

White man, rock art, Wardaman country. (D. Lewis)

England–the place of origin of alien animals, alien laws, and intruders. There he was killed, and there, apparently, he rose up to the sky. The stories do not explain why Ned Kelly went to England. I think this sequence is meant to indicate that England is being brought into the same universe of moral principles as Australia.

Dreaming stories in which the same events are repeated across the landscape assure that Law applies to all people, not as an external imposition, but as the indigenous moral structure of the cosmos. Ned Kelly is located in the Victoria River valley at the very beginning; his law is there. And English people cannot claim that Ned Kelly has nothing to do with them. He died and rose again right there in England; his morality applies to them as much as it does to Australians.

Big Mick told this story with a geat deal of expressive evocation of the emotions involved, and part of it is a subtle joke. Big Mick said, in subsequent discussions, that when Ned Kelly rose up to the sky, there was such a great shaking of the earth that all the buildings in Darwin trembled and all the Europeans cowered in fear and wondered what was happening. He found this to be very funny. As I understand the joke, it is based on the Aboriginal perception that Europeans typically fail to recognise the significance of events, because they fail to understand the past. Rather than being frightened, they should have known exactly what was happening, for it is all part of Europeans' own Dreaming.

Ned Kelly is here conflated with Jesus, offering an exposition of the potential for liberation which both characters may be understood to exemplify. Like Jesus, Ned Kelly stood up for the rights of the oppressed, and stood against that officialdom which enforced the power of the ruling classes.

In the final page of his biography, Molony considers the possibility that Ned Kelly, myth and man, has something to say about Aboriginal land rights:

> The seasons of a century have come and gone and some men speak again of rights to the land, of resisting those who rape its heritage, and of raising a republic of the free. To many, such ones are visionaries, dreaming like prophets of an Australia still to be born. The legend that is Kelly stands with them. Ned shared their vision, dreamt their dream and, with them, loved the native land. (Molony 1980:257)

Yarralin people would agree.

For white Australians, Ned Kelly the historical person is dead. Yarralin people have resurrected him twice over–both in the story and by locating him in Dreaming. For them, Ned Kelly is still and always alive. In addition, they have given birth to an indigenous Ned Kelly: he belongs to the continent because he helped make it.

Unlike many white Australians, Aboriginal people in the Victoria River District have not found Ned Kelly to be ambiguous. They have analysed his actions and defined him as purely moral. Through Ned

Kelly an equitable social order, which includes Europeans, is established as an enduring principle of life. Captain Cook was an invader who had no place here, and as Yarralin people assert, he is dead now. Ned Kelly is a whitefellow and he is indigenous; he is the Dreaming answer to invasion and injustice.

These stories are directed toward Australians, but they offer a global message. In defining justice as Law, they also assert its universality. One need not agree with the particular conflations in order to assent to the general proposition that all cultures, human and others, are capable of recognising that life is good and that destruction is to be resisted. Yarralin people's desire to engage equitably with others is offered in gifts of understanding. As Daly said,

> We been listen to story. You, you whitefellow, [you] can listen to story too. I tell you: nothing can forget about that Law.

12 *Life Time*

Yarralin story tellers offer gifts, explaining how people can construct the future so that the earth remains a home for life. Like all stories, theirs are culturally embedded. It is essential now to look more closely at that embeddedness: to understand both the concrete expressions and the abstract propositions.

Dreaming and ordinary

For Yarralin people, time is not an entity in itself existing, or happening, outside of us. Rather, time is a quality of life. Given that life is complex, the manifestations of time, too, are complex. Yarralin people do not offer definitions of different kinds of time, per se. They define different kinds of entities and events with reference to the two categories Dreaming and ordinary, and I have applied this distinction to time. Here I am concerned with ordinary life in its temporal context.

Ordinary time, the temporal quality manifested in ordinary life, is sequential and bounded. This is time as it is experienced by the individual and I think that this is how individuals are thought to experience life in ordinary contexts. One's own life has a beginning and an end. Between these two points one's life has a sequential flow.

Temporal co-ordinates can be fixed through social events: when so and so was made into a young man; when Big Sunday (an important ceremony) was held at such and such a place. Space is a significant feature in mapping the passage of time, and people's lives are ordered by reference to where they have been–where they have lived and worked, where they have walked, and what country they have learned.

Ordinary time is a quality of life which might best be characterised as change. People grow old, and die, and are finished. Events occur and never recur in the same way. To live in ordinary time is to face death; to know that one will lose the people one loves, and that one will be lost as a human being. Yarralin people express some of this sense of uniqueness and loss by sweeping away the tracks of a dead person: those particular tracks will never again be made.

Following Yarralin people's usage, we can distinguish Dreaming life from ordinary life. One way of expressing this distinction is temporal: Dreaming precedes ordinary. Ordinary life belongs to the present in which we now live. It is characterised by temporal sequence, and is marked by beginnings and endings. Within what I call ordinary there are rhythmic patterns that recur. Seasons are one such rhythm: hot weather, followed by rains, followed by cold weather, followed by hot weather. In addition, these rhythmic patterns are also marked by regular, significant events which erase the particular, leaving only the pattern. Rain washes away the marks of the actions of people, plants, and animals from the face of the earth; human and animal tracks are washed out, plants die. The earth remains.

On a different scale, the same is true of individuals. In ordinary time what I refer to rather loosely as information does not accumulate indiscriminately; not only is visual evidence of action washed out, but the individuals who made the signs are also washed away. Information is 'a difference that makes a difference' (Bateson 1979:242). Differences that do not make a difference are noise. We will examine this proposition more closely (chapter 13); for the moment I focus on contrasts between that which is ephemeral and that which endures.

That which is Dreaming does not die, does not get washed out, but has the potential to exist forever. Yarralin people emphasise the importance of continuity and endurance; Riley Young spoke of these matters with reference to his Dreamings:

> That thing been never get away. He's still there. Blackfellow there, he's still there. Nother man taking over. Nother bloke taking over for him. From his father, to the father, from the son, all that sort of . . . [discussion of who would take over for him if he were to die before he had children] If I get son and daughter, well they might take over behind. Or if him dead, well he might get over to nother man. See? Might be somebody else son will take over. That kind of Law.
>
> We're living on Law, you know. Takem, takem, by nother, by nother. That kind of Law. White man got [it] you can; I don't know what you want to do write [it on] paper every day. How you teach him, your son? We tell him this kind, that kind. That [your] kind [paper], rain come out, you might have him wet, or might have him on the table, big wind come up, he chuck it away somewhere else. What you got to talk about? Why? Where that thing [paper; knowledge] gone?
>
> You see, my thing, you never take him out. He's there for years and years. People been die, and still him there. And nother bloke take over. Nother man die, he's still there in the ground. From beginning. When him from beginning.

Dreaming life is different from ordinary life in that that which exists as Dreaming endures. There is also something we might reasonably call a temporal distinction between Dreaming and ordinary. Most senior Yarralin people trace their genealogies back about three generations to their grandparents, and there it stops. Grandparents, for most people, came straight from Dreaming. As usual, Old Tim Yilngayarri showed some variation on this general proposition, while yet expressing it most eloquently. He said that his mother 'been come out from ground, underneath, from the ground inside, been come out'.

The point at which Dreaming became ordinary, then, is only about one hundred years ago. The change from Dreaming to ordinary is uneven. This is so in the sense that it is always relative to the speaker. The end point in our given span is 'now'–hence it is constantly changing. The beginning point is about one hundred years before 'now'. And at any given point that which is known and remembered is conceptualised as being ordinary. This is ordinary time: the one hundred year present, the time of change, of human strategies and negotiations. In Yarralin people's beliefs, underlying relationships came out of Dreaming and thus are not negotiable. Dreaming precedes us, and we are not it.

The distinction is uneven also in the sense that Dreaming penetrates all kinds of life, co-existing with ordinary. Ned Kelly, Captain Cook, and England were all there. It makes sense to speak of a temporal disjunction because things have changed. But it is equally important to remember that Dreaming is a quality of life and is therefore not temporally constrained.

The relationship between Dreaming and ordinary can be conceptualised in two ways. If we were to locate ourselves, hypothetically, in Dreaming, we would see a great sea of endurance, on the edges of which are the sands of ordinary time. Their origins are in Dreaming but their existence is ephemeral. If, by contrast, we locate ourselves in ordinary time and look toward the past, we see a period of about one hundred years: a present ordinary time marked by changes which do not endure, by sequence which can be accurately described in temporal terms, and by the obliteration of the ephemeral. Dreaming can be conceptualised as a great wave which follows along behind us obliterating the debris of our existence and illuminating, as a synchronous set of events, those things which endure.

When we start talking about Dreaming, synchrony becomes a salient feature. Dreamings all exist all the time, so to speak. Stanner (1979b:24) refers to Dreaming as 'everywhen': a delightfully accurate term. Synchrony is not always as easy to comprehend concretely as it is abstractly. Big Mick's story of Ned Kelly clearly exemplifies the conflating of temporality involved in producing synchrony: when Ned Kelly rose after being killed, all the buildings in Darwin shook and all the Europeans cowered in fear.

Both Dreaming and ordinary exist in real, named, localised space. Both are grounded in the earth, and both ultimately derive their life from the earth. Ordinary time, which individuals experience as days and nights, dry seasons and wet seasons, youth, middle age, and old age, is a period in which our Western concepts of time have a certain explanatory power. Dreaming, in contrast, is marked most powerfully by synchrony, and it, too, is located in real named space.

In ordinary life there is a temporal dimension to the concepts before and after which is contingent on the locus 'now'. As Ricoeur (1985:16) says, 'the now is constituted by the very transition and transaction between expectation, memory, and attention'. For Yarralin people, 'now' as a temporal locus is differentiated from past and future along a number of lines, most of which indicate people's attempts to construct continuity between before and after. Thus, for example, we here now, meaning we here in this shared present, are differentiated from early days people by the fact that they preceded us and made the conditions of our existence possible. In relation to them, we are the 'behind mob'–those who come after. From our perspective, they are the old or olden time people, the first people. Sequence and succession are the salient features. The future is the domain of those who come after us. They are sometimes referred to as the new mob, or simply as those 'behind to we': those who come after. It is our job to assure that those who come behind us are taught the Law and have a place and responsibilities to take over from us. More profoundly, although increasingly less successfully, Yarralin people seek to assure that the behind mob will inherit what their own forebears delivered: a world in balance and the knowledge of how to keep it so.

In Dreaming, the only temporal co-ordinates from which one could define a before or after are major disjunctions. Salt water covered the earth before it pulled back into oceans; Dreamings walked in the shape of humans before they became fixed with respect to place, size, and shape. Within the period demarcated by these disjunctions, synchrony prevails. However, there is sequence defined by movement through real geographical space. In Yarralin most (not all) Dreamings travelled from west to east. Sequentially, before means west, after means east. Before and after are contrasts which are contingent in part on the spatial locus of the speaker and in part on the spatial identity of the speaker. When, in Yarralin, people speak of Dreamings which are 'before', they usually refer to all those sites west of Yarralin or west of their own responsibilities, while the Dreamings which are 'after' are all those sites east of Yarralin or east of their own responsibilities. The geography remains fixed, as are the tracks; they are in the ground. Only we who are on top move about.

Dreaming geography gains complexity in ritual. When the songs are sung the Dreamings are made mobile, and frequently in discussing ritual responsibilities people speak of carrying the Dreamings. One mob of countrymen carry the Dreamings through their country and hand them over to the next mob who carry them through and hand them over. In men's business these handover points are the *jamaran* discussed earlier. In women's business the Dreamings are more likely to go underground and come up somewhere else in a different country.

Some of the great travelling Dreamings can, I believe, be understood also as being their own track. The snake Jurntakal, for instance, is sometimes spoken of as if he were lying across the continent. Different groups sing different parts of the body. I only know of this concept in relation to men's business, and it may be that the concepts are more metaphorical than I understand.

In Dreaming we find that events are organised spatially and morally. Spatially, they are kept separate. As Hobbles said, they 'never been mix up'. Dreaming men and women travelled separately. The great creative beings like the black-headed python and the emu never interfered with each other's progress through country. Each kept to her own track, naming and creating her own languages, places, and people as she went along.

The moral content of Dreamings is redundant. Key events are played out place after place after place. Moon and dingo argued everywhere, hyperbolically speaking; the result is that all people die, and all die by their own spatially-defined Law. Dreaming women gave birth to human beings, and the Law of birth also occurs everywhere. No group of women is dependent on another country for its unborn children.

Other key events have to do with social-geographical boundaries. Such events are open ended; they attract and accommodate specificity. Events may be conflated with the key event if they share the same content. Those in the present will, if they are determined to be memorable, be packed away into Dreaming by being conflated with Dreaming events. The result is a Dreaming past in which events are organised by content and by space but not predominantly by temporal sequence.

The process of packing the present away into the past is one which is difficult to discern and even more difficult to discuss. Such processes take place over a time span which is longer than the individual life, and no one person experiences all of it. Some specific examples are encoded in secret business and are thus not open to public discussion. This is true of women's business, and I think it may also be the case for men's.

Then again, Yarralin people's words seem to deny the possibility of Dreaming change: the Law is in the ground; it never changes. Anthropologists used to characterise Aboriginal religions as conservative and unchanging in part because of these sorts of statements, but it is now well understood that most Aboriginal religions are extraordinarily open to accommodating new events and ideas (see Rose and Swain 1988). Some of this misunderstanding has to do with the difference between qualitative and quantitative change. According to my understanding, any number of permutations, additions, and accommodations are possible as long as the underlying principles are not challenged.

The concept of conservatism, often based on the hypothesis that Dreaming refers to a distant past to which the present is designed rigidly to conform, may also derive from an unyielding distinction between mythic and historical time. Eliade, for example, promotes this distinction, but also states quite clearly (1959:68) that sacred time is not eternally bounded: 'it is a primordial mythical time made present'. Stanner's term 'everywhen' signals an even more serious deconstruction of putative boundaries between Dreaming and ordinary (time, life, space). Glowczewski (1988b:10), drawing on her work with Warlpiri people, puts the case most succinctly, stating that 'the Dreaming appeared to me not like a mythical time of reference but as a parallel space-time, a permanency in movement, with which the Warlpiri have a relation of feedback'.

Aboriginal cultures are oral cultures; people did not develop writing. Quite possibly people have maintained orality precisely so that the present, rather than accumulating, can be selectively packed away or forgotten (cf. Michaels 1988). The gliding possum (*Petaurus breviceps*) was playing the didjeridu in the coastal area to the north of Yarralin. She and the blanket lizard (frill-necked lizard; *Chlamydosaurus kingii*) decided to travel south, playing the didjeridu all the way. At each stop they found that when they played to the north they were heard, but when they played to the south they sounded faint. When they got to a hill near Daguragu they found that they had 'no wind' (breath) left at all. Unable to play, they turned back and went home. The gliding possum and the blanket lizard were testing social, cultural, and geographical boundaries, taking salt water culture–*Wangka* and didjeridu–down to the desert fringe. Their test was unsuccessful. More recently, living people have made this same test (chapter 9). In fifty or one hundred years it is possible that the story of their successful test will have been accommodated within Dreaming Law as a relationship between salt water and desert fringe countries.

We can understand this process of collapsing temporality most readily in stories which involve Europeans because here we have other reference points from which to gauge the process. A number of characters in European mythology are located in Big Mick's story about *miki*–God, Noah, and Jesus are all implicitly located in the person of Ned Kelly. All these figures from European culture are collapsed into the one; specificities are put aside and the overwhelming similarites are packed into the one event which is spatially located.

Putting it away

Old people, particularly those who are exceptionally competent, have the power to define the past and thus to determine the options of the present and, to some degree, of the future. We have seen that in the life and death game of taking care of country, of living in the present, the past is a powerful tool, for relationships to country are the product of past actions. Every person's actions are known; actions and events are information which must be evaluated over time. When we look at politics and testing we see that the present is the time of complex negotiations of the relationships between individuals, groups, and country. As events approach the limits of the present, marching back to Dreaming, they become less complex, less negotiable, more fixed.

The same is true of people. Temporally, one's life progresses back toward the Dreaming. As generations are washed away, ordinary time is collapsed into Dreaming. When a baby is 'cooked' it is brought up from the ground, and learns to walk around on the top. People's lives expand in terms of spatially defined knowledge over many years. But towards the end, people refocus their attention on the country in which they wish to die. The whole of life, one might say, is a great circle from the earth, around the top, and back to the earth, and personal autonomy is expressed in deciding where one is to finish. From my point of view, the grandparents who had only one country, who came straight from Dreaming, determined the conditions of life for their descendants in making a final decision about themselves.

Human life must be reduced as it becomes the past precisely because it is too complex. We have seen that marriage creates ties across boundaries of difference, and the cognatic system allows for options and flexibility. We have seen that boundaries are necessary to defining personal and group autonomy. If generations upon generations of past marriages were remembered, and if ties to country continued to be reckoned cognatically, it would be impossible to draw meaningful social boundaries. Like a drop of ink in a glass of water, the mix would become undifferentiated; everyone would belong everywhere. Collapsing the past into Dreaming allows boundaries to be both fixed and negotiable.

Lines of men maintain boundaries by defining them in fixed ways. Every country is identified by and with its localised Dreamings. People come and go but the identity of country remains the same. These Dreamings, *kuning*, are transmitted from a man to his son and his sister's son, but only his son has the obligation further to transmit that set of *kuning*. Lines of men, constructed out of fathers and sons, hold people in place through time.

If we look at the processes of women's reproduction we see a mirror image of the patrilineal perspective. Women give birth to their own and their brothers' physical and spiritual being which is also the physical and spiritual being of their own mother's country. Women are believed to have the power to do this without men. They are the ultimate maintainers of boundary, reproducing only their own country. Women's secret business is transmitted along matrilines, strengthening the ties between matrilines and country. From a matrilineal perspective, lines of women uphold country unambiguously. It is men, leaving their sisters and sisters' children to get wives and children of their own, who muddle the boundaries.

There is no hierarchy of process; it is necessary both to maintain and to demolish boundaries. If they become lost, the ability to define one's self clearly in relation to country is lost. If they become rigid, what is lost is flexibility and the ability to maintain autonomy through mobility. When we look at the past from the vantage point of the

Russell (Daly's brother's son) crawls through the legs of the men who have made him into a young man, January 1982. (D. Lewis)

present we see a cognatic system collapsing into single lines. Grandparents came from the ground; they have only one country identity. The intermediate point between the present and the past is the point controlled by the old people who remember.

Cognatic systems, then, are collapsed through time. It does not matter in the long run whether a portion of a cognatic system collapses into the mother's or father's country. In Yarralin thinking, there is an accepted basis for each. Matrilineal models of reproduction depend upon the concept of shared physical and spiritual being which is transmitted from mother to child via milk. Both brother and sister share this body and this milk. Sisters carry their mother's country as their own milk. Brothers, as I understand these metaphors, carry their mother's milk as semen.

Publicly, at least, men cannot have a physical share in the making of their children. If they did, the physical basis to the matriline would be obliterated. Boundaries would be demolished by genetics. Rather, men transmit their rights through ceremony. The unilineal relationships constructed by and through men are separate from those constructed by and through women.

In the ritual context of young men's business, men allocate to themselves the ability to give birth, making little boys into young men. When the new young man is reintroduced to his mothers and other relatives he crawls through the legs of the men who have made him into a man. I believe that they are expressing their role as the persons who have 'given birth' to a man. The use of blood in men's rituals heightens the understanding that birth is an organising metaphor in the ritual construction of patrilines. When young men are later made into 'full' or 'proper' men, it is again men who do this job. As this is secret business, I can only say that it involves death and rebirth.

I think that the metaphor of birth establishes a physical relationship between a man and his sons, just as women's processes of birth (involving secret knowledge and ritual) establish a physical relationship. Spiritual and physical being are not separate categories. Rather, spiritual identity and awareness are manifested through physical being; if there is no body, then there is no 'spirit'. Conversely, there is no 'spirit' without body. Matrilines are born of women; patrilines are born of men; both are culturally produced.

Keeping it going

People are like trees, Old Jimmy said; they must be grounded. Dreaming trees speak to issues of space and time, and to women and men separately. Dreamings who are trees are fixed in place. As Daly asserted through his own distressing experience, they are alive and conscious and must be protected. Yarralin people use plant metaphors frequently in talking about change, relatedness and continuity (cf. Merlan 1982), as do people in Papua New Guinea and south east Asia (Gell 1975; Fox 1971). Trees provide a model of asexual reproduction, and thus are particularly salient markers of unilineal descent lines.

Old Tim spoke of tree deaths associated with the deaths of men who were responsible for the country in which those trees grew. People expect that a new tree will grow to take the place of the dead tree. The growth of a new Dreaming tree is linked to the growth of new members of the patriline who will replace the old members. For men trees address the essential male problematic: the construction of patrilines. Male individuals are born of women; their first ties are to their mother's country. Many are born in their mother's country, and they have every right to stay there. Only later, when boys are made into young men, are they produced as links in lines of men. Hobbles seemed to speak to this issue when he contrasted cattle and people, saying that a calf drinks its mother's milk and stays with its mother.

Some Dreaming trees are specifically male and overtly salient to the process of male reproduction. Lingara is the Dreaming site for an edible grass seed (*Fimbristylis oxystachya*) which was once, before it became rare, an important food resource. The Lingara Dreaming tree has been dead for some years. It stood there, straight and grey, waiting, Daly said, until Riley Young who is the patrilineal owner of the place, should have a son. When he did, people began to look for the new tree which will take over from the old dead one.

A billabong near Lingara is a Dreaming place for the *karu*, or

Wallaby Janpakarri watches, while Morgan Fraser Yaringjangpar cuts bark to be used as *jirri*, June 1984.

children, who travelled in great long tracks and are the responsibility of men. The *karu* might be best understood to be uninitiated males of any age. At this particular billabong they stopped and 'played about', spilling their semen all over the place. All of the trees which grow around the billabong are identified as *karu*; one very large dead tree is the 'old man' or 'boss' *karu*. When we visited this place men frequently stopped to gather white clay from a deposit near the old man and to scrape some of the inner bark from the trees. They took these substances home to grind into fine powders called *jirri*, intending to use them to attract women. Men's *jirri*, according to men, will entice a woman to leave her own country and to find many children for her husband and his country. When men said that they had obtained their wives by *jirri*, the women laughed at them, saying that they had married of their own will. In addition to strong will, women have their own *jirri* for attracting men so that they will leave their country and stay with a woman forever.

Other Dreaming trees are identified as female and are associated with women. Female Dreaming trees are managed exclusively by women. In some (not all) instances, female Dreaming trees and their surrounding area are forbidden to men. Some trees are associated with birth, being sites from which women get babies. I have not, however, found the issue of replacement of identical substance over time to be an issue for women. Birth is a process which women control unambiguously. More powerfully, Dreaming trees speak to the female problematic of producing lines of women that are spatially fixed.

Yarralin people's Law favours the rights of husbands over the rights of wives in making residential choices. The problem for women is to replace themselves in space; to build a group of several generations of women who are related by matrilineal ties. Trees, by virtue of being rooted in place, attract elaboration as metaphors of fixity.

Dreaming trees speak to problems of continuity of identical substance in space and time. For men, the problem is time; for women it is space. Husband and wife are potentially hostile in that they strive to replace themselves with the same people in the same time but in different places. On the other hand, brothers' and sisters' interests are often identical. In the end, neither men nor women, siblings nor spouses, prevail absolutely. If there were winners there would also be losers, and that is not what these responsibilities are all about.

Bringing it out

Dreaming is a bounded period in which things happened that endure. Dreaming also continues to happen, if not forever, at least for as long as there are ordinary beings who make it happen. Every species indicates the interweaving of different kinds of being. Turtle, for example, originally walked the earth like a person, and where it changed over to turtle it may still be seen as a stone. People can strike this

Hobbles, Daly, and Stan Davey (then working for the Aboriginal Sacred Sites Protection Authority) at a turtle Dreaming site; Hobbles struck the stone while Daly called placenames, September 1982.

stone with green leaves, causing turtles to proliferate. Yarralin people say that when they strike a Dreaming they 'kill' [strike or hit] or 'humbug' [irritate] the Dreaming. The action is intended to stimulate the Dreaming much as a person who is struck or irritated responds. Action triggers a response. Yarralin people see their relationship to Dreamings as one of knowledgeable management: when Hobbles struck the turtle Dreaming, Daly called names of nearby waterholes, indicating places where turtles would increase.

Turtles are subject to laws of ordinary time: they lay eggs, they hatch and grow old, they die. But turtles are also subject to Dreaming Law: turtles always lay eggs which hatch into more turtles. Individuals come and go; species persist. Unless a disaster occurs, there will always be turtles.

In their own Dreaming period, Dreaming beings were living, mobile actors, creating Laws of existence. At the end, most things changed over to species and to places, both of which endure and contain their life power. As places (stones, trees, hills, and other features), they have become immobile sources of life for ordinary beings. I believe that Yarralin people can be understood to be saying that Dreaming action is the achievement of difference which is ordered and balanced. As ordinary beings, humans (as well as turtles) have the job of maintaining order and balance: to follow the Law.

We could cut short this rather convoluted analysis by saying that the Dreamings are simply a way of talking about whole species. We could suppose that the difference is between species and individual, rather than between different kinds of life. We would have to qualify these statements by noting that each country is autonomous, and that in a fundamental sense the concept of species may be less salient than the concept of located life. But in making such a short cut we would miss the essential feature of all life: that every individual participates in processes that have Dreaming origins and are meant to endure.

An individual human being is a participant in processes characterised by different kinds of life. Our living and our reproduction as individuals and as groups are part of Dreaming Law. Our two spirits indicate our participation in different kinds of life. *Manngyin* is the unique, the changing, the irreplaceable. *Yimaruk* is the continuity of life. *Manngyin* never returns, while *Yimaruk* can never be lost. *Yimaruk* thus binds us to Dreaming in the sense that having been created it cannot be washed out, destroyed, obliterated. It does not bind us to our own particular species, but rather changes from one to another. Cutting across boundaries of species and time, it ties us into the whole process of life: a process which, barring disaster, is everlasting. Through us and all others, Dreaming lives.

Birth brings Dreaming into the present. Each birth is a microcosmic recapitulation of the origins of the cosmos; and each birth regenerates women's Law and being. So, too, does ceremony. During young men's business, when people follow the *Pantimi* line, men sing the travels of the Dreaming women, naming places and events along the track. Women dance the Dreamings. They do not act out events; rather, they move from west to east making tracks which are identical (except in size) to the tracks the Dreaming women made. Through singing and dancing, therefore, the travels of the Dreaming women happen again. Yarralin people say that they dance and sing the Dreaming through country.

Initiation is the process whereby a little boy is changed into a young man. This change is, I believe, analogous to changes which Dreaming beings made: in order for it to happen it must be made in Dreaming. Human beings re-mobilise Dreamings, applying Dreaming change to an ordinary being bounded by ordinary time. During this event boys are first introduced to the Dreamings of their father's country. Comparable to women's events in which Dreamings are shown in ritual, this is the real stuff of belonging, having to do with building a relationship through the very essence of being: in ritual a person's roots are made manifest.

Dreaming is brought into contact with ordinary time; a context is created in which the temporal disjunction is altered. This bringing together is an extravagant play of contexts. Singing and dancing are, in this context, Dreaming: through ordinary people in ordinary time Dreamings travel again. Each song verse and accompanying dance is punctuated with a running commentary of verbal and physical jokes which refer specifically to events and people situated in ordinary time. Many of the jokes draw heavily on western concepts of time which are treated as sources of humour.

One set of jokes concerns the question: 'What time is it?'. Responses to the question take the form of elaborate jokes which mock European concerns with time. Various people call out for a wrist watch; they query whether it has been wound or whether the batteries are fresh. More people call for a torch so that the watch can be seen. The person who calls out the time will be criticised for not being able to tell time, and other people look at the same watch and call out different times, while others offer time at random, or make up times (28 o'clock). Joking goes back and forth until a time is agreed upon. Perhaps an hour later the same process is repeated and the agreed time may be half an hour earlier than the first time, or three hours later. The important thing is not to tell the time, but to punctuate Dreaming with ordinary.

Other jokes concern sexual affairs, suggesting unlikely combinations of individuals. Still others focus on the mother's brother/sister's daughter relationship; uncles incite their nieces by making sexual remarks ('swearing them'), and nieces respond by belting ('killing') their uncles. There are tall tale jokes which develop competitive and wildly extravagant uses of metaphor; and there are richly perceptive whitefellow jokes.

The essence of paradox is that boundaries are only meaningful in context. In ceremony paradoxical play becomes an art form, and boundaries are demolished, constructed, and above all asserted to be arbitrary. This is deep play (see Geertz 1973). In ceremony the immobile Dreamings walk the earth. Dead bodies hear the songs and feel happy. Human beings are transformed and relationships established. These human changes endure because they are fixed in a context which both is and is not ordinary. Dreaming past, human now, creation, endurance, obliteration–all are brought together and the boundaries which keep things apart are played into definition.

Closing it off

Human time, seen from the viewpoint of individual experience, is marked by a beginning and an end. In a larger context, these beginnings and endings recur. The cycles of women's skins and the alternating generations of men's skins is one structure through which social categories repeat over time. People's personal names are set into this pattern. There are names appropriate to each skin, so that names recur over time. Individuals come and go while the relationships between categories of people, and between people and country persist.

Human beings are set into oscillating cycles. In addition to subsections, there is, for example, an oscillation between night and day. From the individual viewpoint, night and day succeed each other through ordinary time. In a larger context there is just an oscillation. Night and day are not so much events as they are contexts. Day is the context of licit, the use of country, and the juggling of sets and boundaries relating to country. Night is the context of the illicit, the re-creation of relationships between Dreaming, country, and people, and the juggling of these sets of boundaries. Those things which one wants entered into public memory are organised in the day: caretaking, marriages, divorces, funerals, political debate. Those things which one does not want entered into public memory (sexual affairs, for instance) and those things which are already defined as public memory (*Pantimi*, for example) are organised for night. If one could stand outside of life one would see oscillating contexts through which the whole of life is lived.

The seasons, too, can be understood as oscillating contexts. From an individual's viewpoint these are sequential. In the larger frame there is only the wet and the dry, each creating the necessity of the other. The process of 'washing out' is a fundamental feature of human life, marking the termination of an individual time span. In cycles, the washing process takes on further significance. The rain washes the earth and in so doing makes her young and 'clean' again, erasing the marks of ordinary time. Washing, then, interferes with ordinary time by preventing the accumulation of past events. This is important because information is temporally and spatially dispersed, because understanding is built up through time and space, and because events are free-floating until they have either been forgotten or subjected to closure (chapter 13).

In human time the end of one's life is irreversible. In a broader frame, washing and cleansing allow for new cycles. Flood stories seem to speak of much larger cycles of obliteration, enacting on a vast scale that which happens every year: the noise is taken away.

Ordinary life is characterised by birth and death, expansion and contraction. We walk this earth as living and conscious beings, and earth too is alive and conscious. What this means, to us and to others, is the essence of responsible life.

Dreaming 'everywhen' is also now. Our lives are part of an oscillation which has preceded and will succeed us. This sense of cosmic vastness can lead to a sense of our own insignificance (cf. Ricoeur 1985). So too can the lurking suspicion that our lives are simply noise. Yarralin people rarely, if ever, understand human life in this way. The end point of sequential time is now. All that preceded us and all that comes after depend on us. What we do matters so powerfully that to evade our responsibilities is to call down chaos.

13 *This Earth*

The first satellite photos of 'spaceship Earth' launched a radical shift in perspective: an 'external' view that might provide us humans with the sense of shared place and purpose we so frequently seem to lack. James Lovelock has formulated the most challenging scientific analysis of this perspective: the Gaia hypothesis. Against all probability Gaia is a living organism: a 'complex entity involving the Earth's biosphere, atmosphere, oceans, and soil; the totality constituting a feedback or cybernetic system which seeks an optimal physical and chemical environment for life' (Lovelock 1979:11).

Yet, as Peter Bishop explains in his beautiful essay 'The Shadows of the Holistic Earth', with the emergence of the Whole Earth image inspired by satellite photos comes both hope and despair:

> The ecological imagination embraces fears of fragmentation, chaos, of imprisonment within the web of life, with a loss of human identity . . . Certainly the image of holistic Earth points to the urgent need for imaginative vessels to hold, cook and digest the fantasies of our time. But fragments also heal. The questions posed by a global imagining are in themselves shattering. (1986:68–9)

Lovelock notes that his understanding of Gaia as a living organism is not new. When Yarralin people speak of mother Earth they speak to a similar understanding. They are the inheritors of a theory and practice of participating in living systems. They understand these systems scientifically, through observations and hypotheses developed and tested through time. They also understand them metaphysically. Dreaming Law tells the story, often obliquely, frequently in bits that people have to put together for themselves. Dreaming and ecology intersect constantly, providing a rich understanding of universal and local life.

In saying that life is good, Yarralin people are asserting that every kind of living thing has its own place, its own origins, its own right to exist. They place no species at the centre of creation. Their understanding contrasts forcibly with human-centred cosmologies and with the nihilism of despair.

In a human-centred cosmos non-human life is thought to serve, or to be susceptible of being made to serve, human interests. A human-centred concept of the cosmos poses spiritual and moral challenges of a particular order: If humans are at the centre of creation, why is life so hard? Why do we suffer, and why do we die? Christians have grappled with these questions for almost two millennia, not making much progress, but generating many extravagant answers. Elaine Pagels (1988) examines these issues as they were debated during the first four centuries AD. She notes that in the fourth century Julian argued that the facts of suffering and death do not mean:

> That we participate in guilt–neither Adam's guilt nor our own. That we suffer and die shows only that we are, by nature (and indeed Julian would add, by divine intent), mortal beings, simply one living species among others. (ibid:144)

In contrast, Augustine's view, which came to prevail among many Christians, was that we are convicted to suffer for sins we did not commit. In his view, free will is impotent. Augustine thus sets humans at odds with the conditions of their lives, naming the 'disease' only to pronounce that there is no cure. Julian, by contrast, asserts that 'free will provides the possibility of moral action' (ibid:148).

The essentially secular world views which now dominate Western thought cannot escape these questions. With a few exceptions, they deny a spiritual understanding; they have 'killed Nature', replacing a female and organic conceptualisation with one that is mechanical and dead (Merchant 1980). If Augustine's views lead to one kind of human nightmare, that of original sin, and perhaps the deeper fear that God must be evil, secular world views lead to others which oscillate between domination and despair. To live in the late twentieth century, for all of us, is to know the fear of ultimate destruction. For many of us it is to walk warily along a knife-edge on one side of which lies the arrogance which leads to destruction, and on the other side the nihilism which equally leads to destruction.

Centralised or incorporative ways of organising relationships are familiar to most Westerners and many other people throughout the world. According to David Turner (1987:99–106), things (groups, individals, ideas) defined as being different are brought together in sets of relationships which achieve a unity; parts are subsumed within a common code or organisation. Like others, he refers to this mode as monism: a system that recognises one ultimate principle. Many scholars have analysed this kind of system (Wilden 1980 is particularly insightful). Edward Said (1979:188) puts the case forcefully: 'Monocentrism denies plurality, it totalises structure, it sees profit where there is waste . . . Monocentrism is practised when we mistake one idea as the only idea . . .'

An alternative to monocentrism is the model of an acentred

system. Deleuze and Guattari (1981) provide an excellent discussion of this type of system in an article entitled 'Rhizome'. They state that an acentred society 'rejects any centralizing, unifying automaton as "an asocial intrusion"' (ibid:61). Their analysis leads us to a position profoundly removed from notions of centralisation, hierarchy, privilege, and external frames of reference. 'Local initiatives', they contend, 'are coordinated independently of central instance' (ibid:69). This is a model–a view from the outside which can only be hypothetical; I believe that it is an accurate model of the Yarralin people's world view. However, the view from the inside is one of a multi-centred world in which each centre is structurally equivalent, and linked, to every other centre.

Systems at work

Yarralin people tell us that the earth is alive and constantly giving life, the mother of us all. The fact of one mother makes us all kin of a sort, as Riley Young made clear in one of his most eloquent statements:

> Blackfellow never change him . . . We been borning [in] this country. We been grow up [in] this country. We been walkabout this country. We know all this country all over . . . Blackfellow been born top of that ground, and blackfellow–blackfellow blood [in the ground] . . . This ground is mother. This gound, she's my mother. She's mother for everybody. We born top of this ground. This [is] our mother. That's why we worry about this ground.

In Dreaming ecology there is a political economy of intersubjectivity embedded in a system that has no centre. The essential points are:

- the system is self-contained and self-regulating;
- parts are interconnected;
- it is not necessary for every part to be in constant communcation with every other part because information from each part stimulates actions which are themselves information for other parts;
- the system has the potential to get out of balance and to be brought back into balance;
- there is no hierarchy, no central agency.

Everything comes out of the earth by Dreaming; everything knows itself, its place, its relationships to other portions of the cosmos. Every living thing has, and knows, its own Law. The result is a set of interrelated parts which is always in a state of flux. When the cosmos is *punyu* it is homeostatic. Like political debates at Yarralin, the system works best when nothing happens that can be marked as significant change. The system works, as a system, because its parts are conscious, because they communicate, because they act and react, and because they adhere, as a matter of self-interest and free will, to the same set of understandings.

The process can be seen in the seasonal cycle. The relationship between sun (often identified with femaleness) and rain (often identified with maleness) can be set out diagrammatically: if A (sun) then B (rain); if B then A. In ordinary time we experience sequence: A→B→A, but in Dreaming the relationship is simply A⟷B. Sun and rain, and by association, female and male, exemplify the fundamental feature of symmetrical complementarity. We can see here all four meta-rules which I have suggested underly this concept of system. Sun and rain are autonomous, each having its own Law. They respond to each other's actions. In opposing each other they sustain each other; they are balanced, being of an order to oppose each other. Their opposition is antagonistic in that while one is abroad the other is eclipsed, yet this is an antagonism in which if one were to 'win' by annihilating the other all of life would be lost.

Each 'part' is both part of the total system and a system in itself. The most significant point to this concept of systems within systems is that there is no hierarchy: the same meta-rules apply to all. Jimmy's repetitive statement (chapter 3) emphasises that their Law does not vary: 'We follow one law. Number one Law. No more two Law, no more three Law, no more four Law, no more five Law. No! Only number one! One Law! Number one. That's the way.' When Hobbles and so many others spoke of government always changing its law they spoke to this: that Europeans have constructed relationships such that different types of beings, and different categories of people, live under different laws, and the laws are altered to suit the 'winners'.

There is a cultural relativism in these concepts that is pervasive and elegant: all parts of the system have their own world view. That one's own view may be most important to one's own life, does not mean that the world is focussed on humans as a species or on one country and Dreamings over and above others. An essential part of human culture is to know that other Dreamings and other parts have their own views. Once one understands, one can learn the system from any point. The trick is to know what one is encountering.

Every part is cross-cut by others. Matrilineal identities (*ngurlu*), for example, tie people into different nodes. People who share a *ngurlu* are part of a category which includes that species. Emu people share their flesh with emus. If an emu person dies, other people are reluctant to shoot emus because this group has suffered a loss. In this way a specifically human or country viewpoint is enlarged; the enlargement is never uniform for every identity is cross-cut by others.

In the Christian religion it is said that not even a sparrow dies without God knowing about it. In the Yarralin view, not a bird dies but that sooner or later the whole world knows of it. True, we do not, all of us, know of every enhancement and loss to every group. I exaggerate somewhat. But autonomous units are cross-cut by others. Individuals have their own personal angle of perception, their matrilineal identity (*ngurlu*) angle, and their various country angles which tie them into other species and to the workings of the world. When a

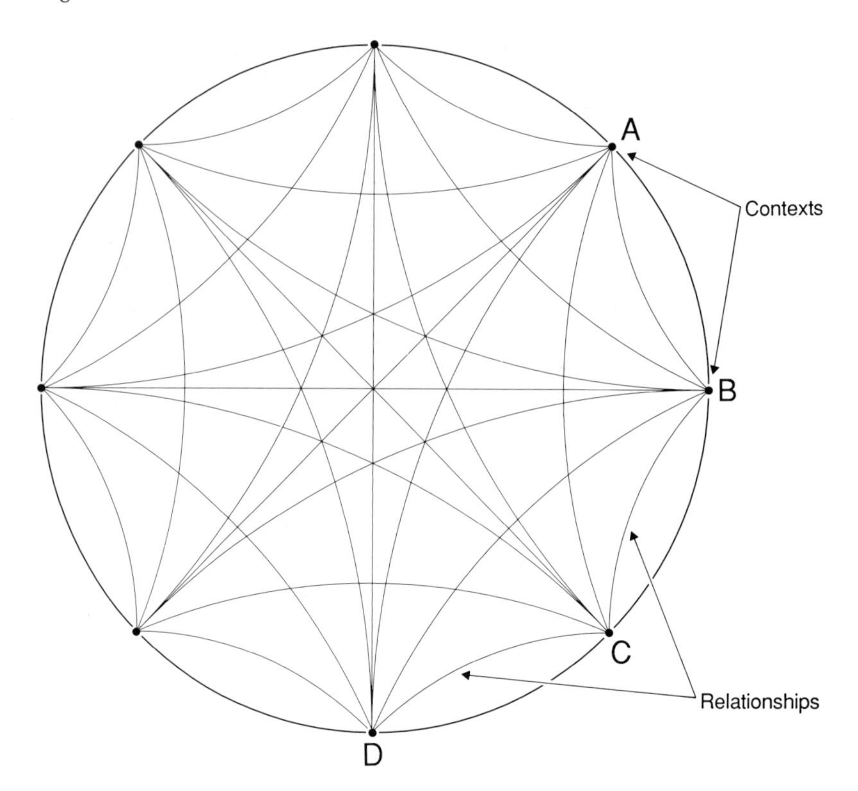

Figure 24 Relationships and contexts

catfish dies, catfish people take note; as catfish people are involved, so other people too must take note.

An angle of perception is a boundary, and boundaries are both necessary and arbitrary. Necessity lies in the fact that there are no relationships unless there are parts, and without relationships there is only uniformity or chaos. Arbitrariness lies in the fact that since all parts are ultimately interconnected, the particular boundary drawn at a given point is only one of many possible boundaries.

Each line in figure 24 is both a boundary and a relationship. Each node (A, B, C, etc) is both a context and an angle of vision, another centre. The view of the system changes from centre to centre. To be wise, as I understand it, is to know this: that there is only viewpoint. Our particular human angle defines our world as it is because it is we who are looking. Perception distorts, but wisdom lies in knowing that distortion is not understanding.

A country and its people can be bounded in such a way that it can be seen as a closed system. In doing this we see the intimate relationships between people and country: the food of the country grows people, and people return life in protecting the country, enhancing its fertility, and giving part of their dead body back to country. The flesh of humans flows into country just as surely as the food that flows from country gives us flesh, and Dreamings, themselves autonomous beings, are there in country. The viewpoint of country is like the viewpoint of any other part: it is unique, self-centred, and interconnected to other like units which are also unique and self-centred.

Earth is spatially bounded into social/geographical units each with its own Law. Law is replicated, so that while each adheres to its own, all adhere to the same. Each unit is **both** different **and** the same. Boundaries are maintained by being pressed against. This is the meta-rule of response: to be is to act; to act is to communicate; to communicate is to test and to respond. The process of testing and responding affirms relationships. Both expansion and contraction are seen as potentially destructive. Principles of symmetry and response assure that as any part tests the limits of its context by pressing others, it is balanced by a return pressure. Boundaries are preserved through testing, with the ultimate aim that nothing happen.

That the process of testing has the potential to generate hostilities is a fact of life, just as it is a fact that one way in which parts depend on each other is that they eat each other. The music of the spheres is not sweet harmony; it is made up of assertive, and potentially hostile, statements of self. When Yarralin people are deeply grieved or deeply affronted, they rise up in anger, saying that only blood will satisfy them. The emotionally satisfying response to one's own loss is to inflict a loss. Balance is not only an abstract meta-rule; it is the content of emotional life expressed in daily exchanges, politics, ceremonies, in life and in death.

The other side of self-assertion is co-operation. Context is never absolute; boundaries cross-cut each other, and can be drawn broadly or narrowly. The boundary between men and women, for example, is also a relationship. It involves the co-operative management of human life, but it is also competetive. Like boundaries between countries, gender differences are cross-cut by ties of kinship and marriage. One of the most significant ties is that between brother and sister. These two share the same body, country, and Dreamings; they share the same viewpoint, and a threat to one is a threat to the other. Another highly significant tie is that between husband and wife, who are, by definition, different. Yet their tie is deep, often because of their emotional commitment, but minimally because they share rights to a new generation of people.

Groups compete for people, attempting to affiliate as many people as possible to their country. Women try to involve their husbands in their own choices, while husbands try to involve their wives in their own choices. In any residential group, composed, as it must be, of people with differing affiliations, there is always the tension of competition. This is the texture of daily life: a muted, but very real, rivalry for people and for contexts. Competition is punctuated by a delightful sense of humor. It is cross-cut by many different ties of kinship and marriage, country and Dreamings; it can be banished by shifts of context. Nevertheless, tension is a fundamental feature of Yarralin life. The purpose is not to dominate but to sustain, and a great deal of social life is directed toward this end.

From one point of perception, my own Western-educated angle, the Yarralin cosmos once appeared to be dualistic. Like many researchers (cf. Stanner 1979b:31–2), I have come to believe that notions of dualism are misleading in this context. The rainbow, for example, certainly seems phallic as it rises up out of the deep reaches of the waterholes and hurls its 'spit' at the dry land. On the other hand, it gives birth to various creatures, and is spoken of as having breasts. It is not unique in this respect, although most examples that I know of are secret. Neither exclusively male nor female, the rainbow is complete.

There are many contexts in which gender is a difference that makes a difference. People die, or are said to die, from failing to respect this boundary. On the other hand, people told me that old men and old women learn much of each other's secret business. I do not know much about this; I myself am not old enough to ask. My understanding is that in these exchanges old people do not lose their gender identity; rather they become complete.

As a total system the cosmos accommodates both male and female, and in accommodating both denies the priority or singularity of either. This quality carries through to various beings within the system such as the rainbow snake. It carries through various social domains such as the maintenance and cross-cutting of boundaries. It carries through to human beings: all people share in the same burdens and privileges of being human.

Everything in the cosmos is potentially whole. I want to be clear; I am not saying that wholeness is a context which integrates a dualistic cosmos. I am saying that wholeness is a fundamental quality–so fundamental that it characterises the separate parts of the system, including human society and human individuals. To be a person, in the end, is to be simply that–neither singularly male nor female, but wholly human. We are dealing with a most basic assertion that everything is, at the same time, a singularity, a multiplicity, and a whole.

Yarralin people play with boundaries, contexts, and identities; they play with almost any intellectual proposition which can be played with. But they do not challenge fundamental order. Dreaming strings are networks of being and of value; each node is a matrix, and the people and other living things at any given place see themselves as the centre. For them it is. But they also know, and assent to the fact, that each centre is one among many and that none dominates.

Stanner expressed with great elegance his understanding of the Aboriginal concern for balance:

> I do not wish to create an impression of a social life without egotism, without vitality, without cross-purposes, or without conflict. Indeed, there is plenty of all, as there is of malice, enmity, bad faith, and violence . . . But this essential humanity exists, and runs its course, within a system whose first principle is the preservation of balance. And, arching over it all, is the *logos* of The Dreaming . . . Equilibrium ennobled is 'abidingness'. (Stanner 1979b:40)

Knowing

Country is alive with information for those who have learned to understand. Throughout the world information is spatially dispersed and locally controlled. Events, rather than calendrical time, provide information: the world talks about itself all the time. Crocodiles (*Crocodylus johnstoni*), for instance, only lay their eggs at one time of year. Yarralin people know that it is time to hunt for crocodile eggs when the black march flies start biting. These annoying flies carry a message: 'the march flies are telling you the eggs are ready.' This sort of knowledge is accurate. If we know that crocodiles lay their eggs toward the end of the dry season, the calendar can tell us that they will probably start sometime in September or October. March flies tell us exactly.

In addition, this information is not limited spatially. Jessie and I often went to the river to fish; when the march flies started biting us, we turned in a different direction and went to the billabong to hunt for eggs as well as to fish. Likewise, when the green march flies first appear it means that the bush plums are ripe. It is not necessary to check the bush plum trees and follow their progress. It is only necessary to note the appearance of green flies (and one is hard pressed to ignore them) to know that it is time to go and collect bush plums.

There is no master code, and there is no centralised co-ordinator. No one tells the march flies to bite because the crocodiles are laying eggs. Rather, in the big river country where Yarralin is located, march flies know when it is time to hatch and forage. Their time is also crocodile time. Neither causes the other, nor is caused by an external other. In following their own Laws they communicate themselves; those who know the interconnections find information in their actions.

This system of information is based on messages sent out by different agents within the system 'telling' about themselves. Knowledge is localised, and one of the reasons why Yarralin people feel uncomfortable in a strange environment is that they do not know what is being said; without knowing they cannot respond appropriately. Yarralin people want to know how to manage their subsistence activities. There is an immediately discernable pragmatism here: if human beings are to forage with greatest success and minimal outlay of energy, they must know what is happening in the world around them.

Beyond pragmatics, however, there is the question of the political economy of knowledge. In order to act responsibly humans and others must be constantly alert to the state of the sytems of which they are a part. Awareness is achieved by learning a huge body of facts concerning types and behaviour of living things, ways of interpreting behaviour, basic sets of messages, geography, Dreaming Law and places, and by continually observing and assessing what is happening. We have here a category of information that Yarralin people identify as parts talking about the state of their portions of the system. Information is dispersed; specifics emerge from a background of broader categories. From this perspective the cosmos cannot be human-centred. The march flies do not tell anybody to do anything, but those who understand them know that the crocodiles are laying their eggs.

An example of the knowing involved in being is a little piece of advice that was offered to my daughter because her head lice were so prolific. Old Tim told her that if she would put some of her lice onto a classificatory son-in-law then her lice would leave her. The implication is that once having partaken of the son-in-law, feeding on his blood, the lice would know that they must then avoid the mother-in-law. This advice strikes me as profoundly expressive of a whole way of being and knowing, implying the consciousness which different entities have of themselves and of systems.

Individuals of all species know what is going on in the world. They know because they are alive and conscious, capable of knowing, and because they have learned to understand. They know because they pay attention: they take notice of the things which happen or do not happen. This may seem a truism, but it is not. Without information, either positive or negative, there is no knowing. From Yarralin people's perspective, failure to pay attention is either the height of arrogance or gross stupidity.

If beings are to act wisely they must know what is happening, and they can only understand after things have happened. Knowing is not instantaneous, as Hobbles led me to understand when we went chasing turkeys. Knowing develops over time and, in more important issues, depends on information which is dispersed through time and space. I have defined information by reference to Bateson (1979:242) as 'a difference that makes a difference'. Differences that do not make a difference are noise. Many thing happen that are only noise, but one does not know this instantly. One has to wait and find out.

An event happens, but to understand it fully one must wait to see what flows from it. The process of knowing is built up over time. People discuss events, try out different meanings, suggest alternative contexts and interpretations and, with time, sometimes arrive at a decision about what a particular event means. Autonomy includes this also: that no person or group has the right to impose context and meaning on another person or group. It is always possible, even probable, that one person's truth will be another's nonsense.

In 1981 I went with a small group of Lingara people to camp near the Wickham River. Most of the mob left the truck quickly to find a good place to camp and fish; I stayed behind to help the old people. When the first group reached the river bank they saw a large snake. Jimija, ever handy with the rifle, shot at it. He missed, and the snake disappeared into the river. There was some concern that it might have been a rainbow, and by the next morning this group had decided that it most probably had been. About a week later we had unseasonable rains. By then the story of the rainbow had been told all around Yarralin and Lingara. The description of the snake was changing, becoming less ordinary and more rainbow-like with the telling. I was abused by one and all for not having been on hand with my camera before Jimija shot at the snake.

Two weeks later I made a trip to Daguragu and Pigeon Hole with many of the same people. The story was told in both of these places and it became clear that regional opinion was in favour of the snake having been a rainbow. A very old and knowledgeable woman at Pigeon Hole pronounced what became the final verdict: the snake had been a rainbow; the unseasonable rains had come as a direct result of its being 'humbugged'. She asserted that it had been a mistake to have shot at it, and everyone was profoundly relieved that the shot had missed.

When one interferes, one's motives are not a question. It is not a matter of guilt or innocence; it is simply a matter of doing. Interfering can be hazardous because nobody has full knowledge. With any event, it might be years before people come to a conclusion, but once they have understood the meaning, they are then able to say what that event actually was. Jimija's shot at a rainbow was not that complex; it only took several weeks to arrive at an agreement. The case had been discussed in communities separated by about 150 kms, and was probably talked about by over two hundred people; the final decision was expressed by a person who is regionally recognised to be very wise. She knew the regional opinion on the question and she took responsibility for stating it. People's wish for a photograph may have indicated a desire to short cut this process, but I have no doubt that if the photo had not conformed to the final decision it would have been taken as further proof of how cunning a rainbow can be.

Events come into being in the dynamic interplay of communication and interpretation. An isolated event does not seem to be a meaningful unit. We could say that until there is a context to give it meaning, it is simply noise. During the early part of my time at Yarralin I persistently and frequently asked: 'What really happened?' Responses were baffling or disorienting. Yarralin people do not answer such a question by referring to external time frames or to a concept of 'objective' (external) facts. In a total system, nothing can be external. The process of defining meaning requires knowledge and care. People have rarely been hesitant to tell me what they thought 'must have' happened, but the responsibility of asserting what 'really' happened is one which people frequently avoid.

Many events about which I am curious, current events mainly, have not yet been placed into a final context. The process of determining meaning is one of testing meanings; until an agreement is reached events appear to be free-floating, up for grabs for any meaning at all. The process of testing often seems to be an intellectual free-for-all in which personality, political objectives, group loyalty, and sheer imagination all play a part. Once a meaning is settled on, the 'facts' are then defined to fit the meaning. The rainbow that Jimija shot at initially was said to have looked like an ordinary snake. Later it was described as much more rainbow-like. When it was certain that it had been a rainbow, then it was clear that it 'must have' looked something like a rainbow. Similarly, when Hobbles' turkeys would not be shot it became clear that they 'must have been' clever.

As with parts such as species, and parts such as individuals, so with the whole cosmos. There is no centralised source of information, no singular controlling instance, no hierarchy of privilege. There is, as I have said, redundancy. There is also reciprocity. Human actions, too, are being interpreted and made meaningful by other parts of the cosmos. Just as other beings' actions elicit a response from human beings, so also human actions elicit responses from other beings. People say this most explicitly: country and other species are watching us, reacting and responding.

In defining meaning, humans and others rely on a range of messages from different parts of the world. It may take a very long time for the meaning of an event to be definitively known. The one hundred year present (give or take a bit) is the final limit; within this period, meanings can be negotiated. Beyond this, they are either determined of forgotten. Until a meaning is agreed to, events exist as incomplete phenomena. Once understood, the action becomes complete. At this point Yarralin people say '*Marntaj*' meaning 'it is finished'.

And it is finished, unless more information, or a new context, require that it be re-opened, re-discussed, and possibly re-defined. Various forms of closure are available to finish events, and many of them involve a formal exchange of goods which are publicly displayed. Frequently, too, closure is indicated by marking the body, temporarily or permanently. When a woman's husband dies she observes taboos, and when they are lifted she is rubbed with red ochre and hit very lightly on the head. She and others all say and know that it is finished.

The woman who was so badly beaten after the death of her husband was fortunate in this one sense: for her the matter was finished. At any time new information might become available which would allow a more detailed understanding of her husband's death, but it would have no bearing on her for she had accepted her involvement with her husband, and had accepted his mothers' and sisters' right to inflict hurt because they grieved. That experience, the beating, was a closure; she bore the marks to prove it.

The earth bears marks of Dreaming action. Things happen that matter; the signs endure as witness. This is Dreaming: the past that matters. Human beings are microcosms, and body marks show the things that matter, that have gone into the public record as facts and are not open to re-negotiation. Scarification, circumcision, and subincision mark the person as a participant in events which have finished. The scars and broken bones acquired through legitimate violence are the same; they show that whatever the matter was, it is finished.

Nothing lasts forever in ordinary time, but body marks stay with the person until death renders them irrelevant.

Events may be information; then again, they may not. Human beings take notice and remember. And because we remember, we must also forget. We must forget that which it is good to forget; we must finish those things which can be closed, and we must accept that much will be washed away lest the earth be overwhelmed by a tidal wave of noise.

As Stanley Diamond has said, 'history is a thread of contingencies, woven by decisions into cultural forms' (1974:350). Big Mick and others laugh at Europeans because they perceive that Europeans flounder terribly in trying to understand the past. It is funny when people or cockatoos mis-apprehend context and being; context play is a source of humour in most, if not all, human cultures. But it can also be dangerous. Not knowing what to remember and what to forget, Europeans, according to Yarralin people, follow dead laws, fail to recognise living ones, and in their power and denial promote death.

Big Mick possessed the quality of detachment to a remarkable degree. His sense of humour undoubtedly helped him to live through nine decades of European domination, but when he joked about white people failing to recognise their own Dreamings he was also making a serious point. Like others, he indicated a state of epistemological chaos which, for most Yarralin people, is profoundly disturbing.

When Hobbles said that Victoria River people remember Captain Cook, he was asserting that lies cannot be allowed to engulf the present. When he reminded Europeans that Captain Cook is dead now, he was saying that that law has no future and must be put aside. This order of closure can only be achieved through changing the present in order to change the future. As long as those who need to change cling to the dead past, those who are hurt must remember.

Till the end of time

In our mother's body are many wombs. Beneath the tracks and sites, beneath the ordinary life that moves around on top living and dying, is the Earth. Daly once showed me a billabong which the white 'boss' had ordered his Aboriginal workers to enlarge. When they dug into it, he said, the earth bled: 'You know that. The Earth got a culture inside.' Localised and specific, the Earth is also universally alive and universally the source of life.

Ever since Europeans 'discovered' Aboriginal Australians some of them have debated the question: did they recognise the existence of a High God? The issue was as much theoretial as ethnographic; perhaps more so. For some, the existence of belief in a High God would substantiate the view that Aborigines were human beings–worthy of the efforts to convert them to Christianity and otherwise to 'civilise' them. For others, the existence of such beliefs would seriously disrupt their ideas about the evolution of humanity, for in such schemes Aborigines were placed very near the bottom of the ladder and therefore had no business with High Gods (see Swain 1985; Hiatt 1988 for analyses of this issue). The question remains unresolved. Probably it is unresolvable, first because our knowledge is incomplete, second because Aboriginal societies vary, and third because, like most dichotomous questions, it poses the issue falsely.

Controversy is founded on an underlying supposition: something either happened or did not happen. This is precisely what we do not and cannot know. We have no way of knowing how often people thought of and rejected a High God. Yarralin people's beliefs are, I believe, expressive of similar beliefs among many Aboriginal peoples. Taking a Dreaming story as evidence, it appears that the moon certainly had it in mind to dominate. As we have seen, one only 'wins' by disabling; the cost is incalculable loss.

The difference between a High God and a multi-centred earth is profound. We can begin to perceive the difference by thinking about the idea of a High God as an 'asocial intrusion' to be rejected before it could dominate. In a system such as this, a High God is the ultimate conquistador, destroying and devouring all the delicate relationships through which living things sustain each other (for further analysis linking monism with conquest see Rose 1988; Swain 1988). A High God can be understood as that which brooks no opposition, as the victor before whom all lose. As Swain (1990:16) suggests in his insightful analysis of religious adaptation in New South Wales:

> What remained at the end of the century, and what all of the ethnographers for this area maintained existed, was an imbalanced and unequal dualism. The most conspicuous features of this cosmology. . . [can] be summarised in four points.
>
> 1) All existence and all power derives from a single source.
>
> 2) From that singularity a duality emerged between earth and heaven. Ultimate significance and Law reside in the latter non-locative or utopian domain.
>
> 3) The earth is consequently depreciated in comparison with the sky realm, and its maintenance as a closed system is undermined by a dependency upon the potency of the heavens.
>
> 4) Morally the earth again loses its capacity for self-regulation, and the future of a homeostatic process of regeneration becomes problematic as parts of the world are intrinsically Lawless or evil.

Yarralin people's responses to the High God of Christianity, while hardly uniform, tell us about their perceptions of ultimate Otherness. News of Christianity appears to have arrived in the Victoria River District decades ago, and many Yarralin people have either rejected the news or accommodated it within their own moral space. Old Tim, for example, in defining God and Jesus as the descendants of dogs, allocated them a place in the beginning. There is a site where God is said to have walked along the Wickham River, and there is another one where God built a boat and sailed up the Victoria River to the desert. Big Mick seems to conflate Jesus with Ned Kelly, taking Ned as the key figure. This form of accommodation sustains the multi-centred understanding of moral space, giving God and Jesus places as ones among many (see also Swain 1988).

Pentecostal missionaries have only been in direct contact with Yarralin people for the last decade. Primarily representatives of the Assemblies of God, their teachings are marked by strong dichotomies: between earth ('just rubbish' in one sermon) and heaven ('the golden city of God' in another sermon); between good (salvation in Christ) and evil (adherence to traditional beliefs and actions); between body (dirt and dust) and soul (eternal life); between the 'Holy Land' and the wicked periphery.

This form of Christianity, like many other religious movements, asserts an imminent destruction. While millenial movements are not confined to Christianity, Yarralin people encounter these ideas in a particular Christian form: 'the visible Second Coming of Christ and the establishment of Christ's rule or the "Kingdom of God" (usually on this earth), which entail the general Resurrection of the Dead, the Last Judgement, and foreshadow an entirely "new Heaven and new Earth"' (Trompf nd:11; cf Burridge 1969). Asserting that there is now a rupture between this world and the ultimate Other, such movements postulate future total transformation. Time as we know it will be brought to an end through the intervention of the powerful Other who will win the last battle. The message seems to be, as Augustine argued, that free will is impotent; we must give our will over to the Other and await that critical moment in which we shall be changed.

Missionary teachings pose new questions about the nature of God. Is he lawful, or is he wild and lawless? The archetype of lawlessness is, of course, Captain Cook who stole, killed, lied, mocked, refused to understand, and conquered. Many Yarralin people treated me as an informant on Christianity in an attempt to discern the character of God. On one occasion the missionary preached a sermon in which he stated that 'Jesus will lift up the whole world'. The next day I was asked whether I thought this meant that the whole globe would be physically lifted up and put somewhere else, or whether it might be that Jesus would only take the outer, productive portion of the world. In the latter case, people suggested, there might be something left over for Aboriginal people, indicating that Jesus might be willing to come to some accommodation. In the former case, the evidence would be conclusive that Jesus was an invader, even more wild and wilful than Captain Cook.

In a radical inversion of what Yarralin peple take to be a basic moral fact of life, missionaries preach, like the old gospel hymn, that this world is not our home. But for most, if not all, Yarralin people, this world is our home–before birth, during life, and after death. Moreover, she is not home in a generalised or unlocated sense. Aboriginal people have bounded the earth, as Turner (1988:479) says, into a plurality of promised lands, each with its own chosen people. Differentiation and redundancy are the keys to responsibility and autonomy.

Religions of transcendence postulate a dualism such that an external locus of Otherness is the ultimate source of meaning and value. Mysticism, in this tradition, lies in the attempt to overcome 'all the usual barriers between the individual and the Absolute' (James 1902:410). In contrast, religions of immanence are based in a fundamental wholeness of which each singular entity is a manifestation. There is no Other; there are no 'usual barriers' to be transcended. I understand Yarralin people to be saying that there is only Us: this world, these manifestations of life. Spirit moves through us all; to be at One is to be powerfully at Home. Mysticism in this tradition is an apprehension of the world in an intensely heightened awareness of intersubjectivity. Self is not incorporated into Other, but is totally engaged with others.

When ultimate value is attributed to an external Other, the result seems to be closure to intersubjectivity on earth. Conquest was predicated on the idea that there would be winners and losers, and the conquerors were determined to be the winners. What it actually means to 'win' when so much has been and is still being lost is a matter European Australians are now trying to assess. Whether one's world view is religious or secular, as long as one seeks to dominate, recognising only one ultimate principle, one is out of balance and destroying. Moon tried the proposition: 'I, and maybe you, but only as part of me.' He is Dreaming, and so he endures, but the result is perpetual closure. Missionaries also try it: 'Come in on the winning side.' Here too, is closure. Some politicians, bureaucrats and social commentators also try the proposition, asserting, in spite of a policy of self-determination for Aboriginal people, that the only possible future is one of incorporation.

The idea of victory is one for which Yarralin people are still trying to find the sense. The Europeans who first came to the Victoria River valley extolled its beauty, and set about to 'develop' it. The continuing effort to wrest profit from the country is turning it into a wasteland. More recently portions of this same country have been set aside as a National Park where tourists can experience the last of the 'natural beauty' of the 'wilderness'.

In 1986 I made a video of some of the worst badlands in the area, and I asked Daly what he called that country. He looked at it sombrely and finally said: 'It's the wild. Just the wild.' The Aboriginal people for whom these parks, cattle stations, and encroaching badlands are home see wastage: loss of permanent waters, soils, plants, and animals; radical changes in the 'behaviour' of different parts of the ecosystem. They do not see a beautiful wilderness. Where they see beauty they see all the care and attention that generations of their ancestors put into the country. Within their own system, responsible actions combine self-interest with consideration of the interests of others. All parts are interconnected: to destroy a part is to set up a chain of responses which will eventually destroy one's self.

The intense fragility of 'now' lies in this: that there is no higher authority which can coerce responsible behaviour; all parts are dependent upon each other for survival. To deny this is to turn one's back on one's self as well as on others. Most Yarralin adults end up asking a simple question: Why don't you think about it? The question goes beyond the Australian experience; all over the world people are demanding this. Riley Young said it loud and clear:

> You know why? I'm sick of it. Too much! If I get out of the place, what's going to happen? What's going to happen to the place? They gonna damage the place. They going to damage the ground. They going to damage some tree, or they gonna smash all the rocks. What, only rocks? It's the Dreaming! Dreaming been walk [here]. The rock might be standing up. What been happen, just standing up. Grader might push that lot. What been happen [is] standing up there. That [rock is] somebody, been stand up. That kind, we know. We been look. Everybody been tell you this Law. That kind. This one. This one. That Law is that thing come up. Because we know. Why don't you government think?

This is not a matter of dichotomies: of white or black, rich or poor, the West or the rest. It is a matter of life. Social analysts such as Bateson (1973; 1979) and Wilden (1980) urge people to a more encompassing and equitable understanding of self and other, action and system. Gregory Bateson wasted neither words nor sympathy when he wrote:

> If you put God outside and set him vis-a-vis his creation and if you have the idea that you are created in his image, you will logically and naturally see yourself as outside and against the things around you. And as you arrogate all mind to yourself, you will see the world around you as mindless and therefore not entitled to moral or ethical consideration. The environment will seem to be yours to exploit . . . If this is your estimate of your relation to nature *and you have an advanced technology*, your likelihood of survival will be that of a snowball in hell. (1973:436–7, italics in original)

Discourses of resistance tell truths which blow open European ideologies of conquest, attempting to display the emptiness of a 'triumph' achieved through unrestrained will. The Australian tragedy, played out in people's lives and deaths, in the lives of plants and animals, and in the earth, is that there is so much to be taken care of, and so much that has already been destroyed. If this tragedy were unique it would be terrible enough. But as every one must know by now, it is happening everywhere. Rather than many promised lands, each with its own chosen people, the earth is becoming a series of graveyards, each with its own irreplaceable losses.

Visions of the holistic Earth, combined with the rapidly increasing understanding of how badly she is being damaged, force us to confront difficult questions. How do we, as individuals, assert our right to take responsible care of the systems with which we interact and on which we are dependent? What wisdom have we inherited; what systems and knowledge do we bequeath to the future?

Yarralin people do not offer answers. They tell stories which open up possibilities. Old Jimmy spoke of how things ought to have been, and in so doing spoke of how things can be. Hobbles extended offers of friendship and alliance. Big Mick told us that we already have the knowledge, if only we would recognise it. Jessie taught by example, taking exquisite notice and care. They speak as a matter of self-interest, and from a generosity of spirit which is founded in Law: there is only one Earth. Law is replicated across the earth, our species is one among many, and all life has access to sustenance as well as to destruction, to will responsibly directed as well as to domination.

They speak from a sense of this critical moment: Now. Time is a quality of life, and life is dying. When Daly took me to see the trees that were killed by bulldozers in 1986 he spoke with hurt and anger. 'We'll run out of history,' he said, 'because *kartiya* [Europeans] fuck the Law up and [they're] knocking all the power out of this country.' As life is lost so time is running out; the creation which gave birth to the possibility of continuity is being eroded.

Our canine ancestor opens us both to time and to life. This is a heritage which requires that we assent to our responsibilities. As we become predators who know no bounds, we kill not only life but also time. In diminishing life-sustaining relationships we kill the gifts which have been bestowed upon us. We kill ourselves.

Yarralin people direct their words toward others, asking them to take notice and to respond. Speaking from the experience of damage as well as an understanding of how things ought to be, they hope that their words will communicate with other peoples' experience and understanding. In contrast to Western scientific discourse, for which 'human time is turned outwards towards what it can demand of the future without any care for what it has made of the past' (O'Neill 1976:2), Yarralin people tell the stories which situate time and persons dialogically.

These are strong stories; they 'intervene' to 'change the conventions for understanding things' (Benterrak, Muecke and Roe 1984: 173). They are open to the world. Strong stories show how to reclaim the past in order to liberate the present; they offer us all a different future. Social justice includes ecological justice; it is not to be achieved through denying the past, but rather through acknowledging and understanding it. There is no ultimate Other to take charge of us. Nor is there is a new time, 'new age', 'new humanity', or 'new Earth'. There is us–and every other living thing in the cosmos including the Earth–as we are and as we can be. We have only to listen, to learn, to remember our own strong stories, and to act.

Yarralin people tell stories through which they hope to encounter others: not to draw others into their own Law, but to exchange equitably. Founded in the belief that Law is everywhere, people hope that their words will connect with those of others, that others will recognise the key events and find their own strong stories which, as they implement them in their own lives and places, will answer back in affirmation.

Why don't we all listen?

Postscript

Anthropology is, or so one hopes, a thorn: a discomfort to those who like their worlds and ideas neatly packaged. I am particularly grateful to Gregory Bateson's (1973; 1979) challenging work in many fields, and to Stanley Diamond's (1974) critical and humane analyses of civilisation and the 'primitive'. In recent years there has been a surge of critical literature devoted to the process of writing ethnography. All such studies are valuable in stirring us to think beyond the given. I have found particular stimulus in the work of Tedlock (1979; 1982), Rabinow (1982), Fabian (1983), Clifford and Marcus (1986), Marcus and Fischer (1986), and Geertz (1988). Members of the departments of anthropology at Bryn Mawr College and the University of Delaware gave me ample scope and guidance to pursue an education that was intense and varied. The Humanities Research Centre of the Australian National University offered me a Visiting Fellowship which provided the material means for writing this book, along with wide-ranging intellectual discussion. Keith Mitchell of the Australian National University transformed my sketches into elegant maps and diagrams. I salute his skill and patience. The photographs, unless otherwise acknowledged, are my own. Personnel at the Northern Land Council Katherine office graciously allowed me to use space and equipment during the final stages of the book's production.

Jane Goodale has been enormously generous with me. Life, as we all know, is painful at times. I do not think that I have ever seen Jane flinch. Stan Davey and Jan Richardson of Darwin have devoted their lives to changing the written and unwritten rules of oppression. They have been exceedingly kind as well as inspiring. Chantal and Blunt Jackson have tolerated a great deal. It is not always easy having a mother who wants to live in places where the spiders are large and furry and camp in your bed, and where the venomous centipedes are six inches long; where the water gives you intestinal parasites and where people give you headlice as a gesture of affection. In spite of difficulties, they have been patient and adaptable. Darrell Lewis and I have shared many of the day-to-day pleasures and irritations of life, as well as many of the profound moments at Yarralin and elsewhere. Our discussions of our shared work, and his careful editing of mine, are integral to this book. His general knowledge and superb bush skills are gifts to all who rely on him, as is his unfailing sense of humour.

Friendships, chance encounters, and shared objectives are the flesh of lived experience, of which the written word only captures a small portion. Without such experience there would be no words; without written words the experiences do not go beyond the immediacy of the participants. I have shared segments of life with many more people at Yarralin, Lingara, Pigeon Hole, Daguragu, and other Aboriginal communities in the Northern Territory and Western Australia than I have named in this work. I am grateful to all of those people, Aboriginal and European, with whom this sharing produced understanding.

Stories are open to the world, attracting meaning rather than effecting closure. As long as there are people talking, listening, and acting, there can be no final conclusion. This book is the first of three. The second will present Yarralin and Lingara people's narratives concerning the one hundred years of conquest. The third will be a more thorough analysis of Dreaming ecology and Aboriginal and European constructs of 'nature' and 'productivity'.

References

Aboriginal Land Rights (Northern Territory) Act 1976.

ADB. 1966. *Australian Dictionary of Biography, Volume 1: 1788–1850.* Melbourne University Press, Carlton.

– 1983. *Australian Dictionary of Biography, Volume 9: 1891–1913.* Melbourne University Press, Carlton.

Akerman, K. and P. Bindon 1986. Love magic and style changes within one class of love magic objects. *Oceania,* 57, 1: 22–32.

Altman, D. 1987. The Myth of Mateship. *Meanjin,* 2: 163–172.

Arndt, W. 1965. The Dreaming of Kunukban. *Oceania,* 35(4): 241–258.

Bateson, G. 1973 (1972). *Steps to an Ecology of Mind.* Granada Publishing (Paladin Books), London.

– 1979. *Mind and Nature. A necessary unity.* Fontana/Collins, Glasgow.

Bauman, T., K. Akerman, and K. Palmer. 1984. *The Timber Creek Land Claim.* Northern Land Council. Darwin.

Beck, E. 1985. *The Enigma of Aboriginal Health.* Australian Institute of Aboriginal Studies, Canberra.

Bell, D. 1983. *Daughters of the Dreaming.* McPhee Gribble/George Allen and Unwin, Sydney.

Benterrak, K., S. Muecke and P. Roe 1984. *Reading the Country.* Fremantle Arts Centre Press, Fremantle, WA.

Bern, J. 1979. Ideology and Domination: Toward a Reconstruction of Australian Aboriginal Social Formation. *Oceania,* 50, 2: 118–132.

Berndt, C. 1950. Women's Changing Ceremonies in Northern Australia. *L'Homme,* 1: 1–87.

Berndt, R. 1970. Traditional Morality as Expressed Through the Medium of an Australian Aboriginal Religion. In *Australian Aboriginal Anthropology,* R.M. Berndt ed. pp. 216–247. Australian Institute of Aboriginal Studies, Canberra.

– 1979. A profile of good and bad in Australian Aboriginal religion. Charles Strong Memorial Lecture, Colloquium, *The Australian and New Zealand Theological Review,* 12.

Berndt, R. and C. Berndt. 1987. *End of an Era; Aboriginal labour in the Northern Territory.* Australian Institute of Aboriginal Studies, Canberra.

Birdsell, J. 1953. Some Environmental and Cultural Factors Influencing the Structuring of Australian Aboriginal Populations. *The American Naturalist,* Vol. LXXXVII, Supplement 834 (May/June) 171–207.

Bishop, P. 1986. The Shadows of the Holistic Earth. *Spring*: 59–71.

Brady, M. and K. Palmer 1984. *Alcohol in the Outback. Two studies of drinking.* Australian National University North Australian Research Unit, Darwin.

– 1988. Dependency and Assertiveness: Three Waves of Christianity among Pijantjatjara People at Ooldea and Yalata. In *Aboriginal Australians and Christian Missions.* T. Swain and D. Rose, eds. pp. 236–249. Australian Association for the Study of Religions, Bedford Park, SA.

Breckwoldt, R. 1988. *A Very Elegant Animal The Dingo.* Angus & Robertson Publishers, Sydney.

Briscoe, G. 1986. Aborigines and Class in Australian History. Unpublished BA (hons) thesis, Australian National University, Canberra.

Broughton, G. 1965. *Turn Again Home.* Jacaranda Press, Brisbane.

Bruno, J. and B. Alpher, 1988. Elegy. In *Aboriginal Australians and Christian Missions. Ethnographic and Historical Studies*, T. Swain and D. Rose, eds. pp. 11–17. Australian Association for the Study of Religions, Bedford Park, SA.

Burbank, V. 1988. *Aboriginal Adolescence: maidenhood in an Australian community.* Rutgers University Press, New Brunswick.

Burridge, K. 1960. *Mambu: a study of melanesian cargo movements and their ideological background.* Harper & Row, New York.

– 1969. *New Heaven, New Earth: a study of milenarian activities.* Basil Blackwell, Oxford.

– 1973. *Encountering Aborigines: a case study: anthropology and the Australian Aboriginal.* Pergamon Press, Elmsford, NY.

Butlin, N. 1983. *Our Original Aggression: Aboriginal populations of Southeastern Australia 1788–1850.* Sydney.

Clifford, J. and G. Marcus. 1986. *Writing Culture. The Poetics and Poltics of Ethnography.* University of California Press, Berkeley, Cal.

CPP (*Commonwealth Parliamentary Papers*), Vol. II, 1914–17.

Crawford, L. 1895. Victoria River Downs Station, Northern Territory, South Australia. In *Journal of the Royal Anthropological Institute.* XXIV, pp. 180–182.

Dashwood, C. 1899. Select Committee of the Legislative Council of Aborigines Bill, 1899: Minutes of Evidence and Appendices. *Australian Parliamentary Papers*, vol. 2, paper no. 77.

Davidson, D. 1935. Archaeological Problems of Northern Australia. *Journal of the Royal Anthropological Institute of Great Britain and Ireland*, 65: 145–184.

Deleuze G. and F. Guattari. 1981. Rhizome. *I & C*, 8: 49–71.

Diamond, S. 1974. *In Search of the Primitive: a critique of Civilization.* Transaction Books, New Brunswick, NJ.

Doolan, J. 1977. Walk-off (and later return) of various Aboriginal groups from cattle stations: Victoria River District, Northern Territory. In *Aborigines and change: Australia in the 70s*, R. Berndt, ed. pp.106–113. Australian Institute of Aboriginal Studies, Canberra.

Dortch, C.E. 1977. Early and late stone industrial phases in Western Australia. In *Stone tools as cultural markers: change, evolution, and complexity.* Prehistory and Material Culture Series, No. 12, R. Wright, ed. pp: 104–132. Australian Institute of Aboriginal Studies, Canberra.

Eliade, M. 1959 [1957] *The Sacred and The Profane: The nature of religion.* Harvest/Harcourt Brace Jovanovich, San Diego.

Evans-Pritchard, E.E. 1937. *Witchcraft, Oracles, and Magic among the Azande.* Oxford University Press, Oxford.

Fabian, J. 1983. *Time and the Other: how anthropology makes its object.* Columbia University Press, New York.

Fox, J. 1971. Sister's Child as plant: metaphors in an idiom of consanguinity. In *Rethinking Kinship and Marriage*, R. Needham, ed. pp. 219–252. Tavistock Publications, London.

Franklin, M. 1976. *Black and White Australians: an inter-racial history 1788–1975.* Heinemann Educational Australia, Melbourne.

Gale, F. ed. 1970. *Woman's role in Aboriginal society*. Australian Institute of Aboriginal Studies, Canberra.
– 1983. *We Are Bosses Ourselves: the status and role of Aboriginal women today*. Australian Institute of Aboriginal Studies, Canberra.
Geertz, C. 1973. *The Interpretation of Cultures*. Basic Books, New York.
– 1988. *Works and Lives: the anthropologist as author*. Stanford University Press, Stanford.
Gell, A. 1975. *Metamorphosis of the Cassowaries: Umeda society, language and ritual*. Athlone Press, London.
Glowczewski, B. 1983. Le "juluru", culte du "cargo". *L'Homme*, 23, 2: 7–35.
– 1988a. 'Australian Aborigines, Topology and Cross-Cultural Analysis.' Paper presented to the Fifth International Conference on Hunting and Gathering Societies, Darwin 1988 (unpublished).
– 1988b. 'Australian Aborigines: A Paradigm of Modernity?' Paper presented to the Fifth International Conference on Hunting and Gathering Societies, Darwin 1988 (unpublished).
Glowczewski, B. and C. Pradelles de Latour. 1987. La Diagonale de la belle-mère. *L'Homme* 104: 27–53.
Goodale, J. 1971. *Tiwi Wives: A Study of the Women of Melville Island, North Australia*. University of Washington Press, Seattle.
Goodwin, D. 1988. *Is Alcoholism Hereditary?* Ballantine Books, New York.
Gordon Creek Police Journals, in *Timber Creek Police Journals*, Australian Archives, Northern Territory Branch, CRS F302, Item: Timber Creek.
Gould League of Victoria, nd. *The Edge of Extinction. Australian Wildlife at Risk*. Gould League, Melbourne.
Gould, R. 1969. Subsistence behaviour among the Western Desert Aborigines of Australia. *Oceania*, 39: 254–80.
Gregory, A. 1884(facsimile edition 1981). *Journals of Australian Explorations 1846–1858*. Hesperian Press, Victorian Park, WA.
Gumbert, M. 1984. *Neither Justice Nor Reason: a legal and anthropological analysis of Aboriginal land rights*. Queensland University Press, Brisbane.
Hamilton, A. 1972. Aboriginal Man's Best Friend? *Mankind*, 7: 256–271.
– 1981. A complex strategical situation: gender and power in Aboriginal Australia. In *Australian Women. Feminist Perspectives*, N. Brieve and P. Grimshaw, eds. pp. 69–85. Oxford University Press, Melbourne.
Hardy, F. 1968. *The Unlucky Australians*. Nelson, Melbourne.
Harris, J. 1986. Creoles–New languages and an old debate. *Journal of Christian Education*, paper 85, April: 9–21.
Hassall Associates. 1986. *A Reconnaissance Erosion Survey of part of the Victoria River District, N.T.* Report prepared for Land Conservation Unit, Conservation Commission of the NT, Canberra.
Hiatt, L. 1965. *Kinship and Conflict*. Australian National University Press, Canberra.
– 1988. The High-God Controversy. Paper presented to the Fifth International Conference on Hunting and Gathering Societies, Darwin 1988. (unpublished).
Hill, E. 1970 [1951]. *The Territory*. Walkabout Pocketbooks, Ure Smith, Sydney.
– 1940. *The Great Australian Loneliness*. Angus & Robertson, Sydney.
James, W. 1952 (1902). *The Varieties of Religious Experience*. Longman's, Green, London.

Jones, R. 1969. Fire-stick farming. *Australian Natural History*, 16: 224–228 (unpublished).

Kaberry, P. 1939. *Aboriginal Woman: sacred and profane*. George Routledge and Sons, London.

Keen, I. 1980. 'The Alligator Rivers Aborigines: Retrospect and Prospect,' in *Northern Australia: Options and Implications*, R. Jones, ed. pp. 171–186. Research School of Pacific Studies, Australian National University, Canberra.

– 1988. Twenty-five years of Aboriginal Kinship Studies. In *Social Anthropology and Australian Aboriginal Studies, a contemporary overview*, R. Berndt and R. Tonkinson eds. pp.77–124. Australian Institute of Aboriginal Studies, Canberra.

Keesing, R. 1975. *Kin Groups and Social Structure*. Holt, Rinehart & Winston, New York.

Kennedy, M. 1985. *Born a half-caste*. Australian Institute of Aboriginal Studies, Canberra.

Kolig, E. 1980. Captain Cook in the Western Kimberleys. In *Aborigines of the West: their past and their present*, R. and C. Berndt, eds. pp. 274–282. University of Western Australia Press, Perth.

– 1981. *The Silent Revolution*. ISHI Publications, Philadelphia.

Langton, M. 1985. Looking at Aboriginal Women and Power–Fundamental Misunderstandings in the Literature and New Insights' (paper) presented at the August 1985 ANZAAS Conference (unpublished).

Lévi-Strauss, C. 1969. *Elementary Structures of Kinship*, revised edn. (trans. J.H. Bell, J.R. von Sturmer and R. Needham, ed.). Eyre and Spottiswood, London.

Lewis, D. 1988. Hawk hunting hides in the Victoria River District. *Australian Aboriginal Studies*, 2: 74–78.

Lewis, D. and D. Rose 1987. *The Shape of the Dreaming: the cultural significance of Victoria River rock art*. Australian Institute of Aboriginal Studies, Canberra.

Lewis, H. 1982. Fire Technology and Resource Management in Aboriginal North America and Australia. In *Resource Managers: North American and Australian hunter-gatherers*, N. Williams and E. Hunn eds. pp. 45–68. Australian Institute of Aboriginal Studies, Canberra.

Loveday, P. ed. 1982. *Service Delivery to Remote Communities*. Australian National University North Australian Research Unit, Darwin.

Lovelock, J. 1979. *Gaia. A New Look at Life on Earth*. Oxford University Press, Oxford.

Macintyre, S. 1985. *Winners and Losers: the pursuit of social justice in Australian history*. Allen & Unwin, Sydney.

Mackinolty, C. and P. Wainburranga. 1988. Too Many Captain Cooks. In *Aboriginal Australians and Christian Missions*, T. Swain and D. Rose, eds. pp. 355–360. Australian Association for the Study of Religions, Bedford Park, SA.

Maddock, K. 1988. Myth, history and a sense of oneself. In *Past and Present: the construction of Aboriginality*. J. Beckett, ed. pp. 11–30. Aboriginal Studies Press, Canberra.

Makin, J. 1983. *The Big Run; the story of Victoria River Downs*. (2nd edn.) Rigby Publishers, Adelaide.

Marcus, G. and M. Fischer. 1986. *Anthropology as Cultural Critique: an experimental moment in the human sciences*. University of Chicago Press, Chicago.

Mathews, J. 1986. 'Social and Biological Factors of Relevance in Setting Research Priorities to Improve Aboriginal Health.' Background paper for NH & MRC sponsored workshop 'Research Priorities to Improve Aboriginal Health', Alice Springs 26–28 November.

Maze, W. 1945. Settlement in the Eastern Kimberleys, Western Australia. *The Australian Geographer*, Science House, Sydney.

McConvell, P. 1982. Neutralisation and Degrees of Respect in Gurindji. In *The Languages of Kinship in Aboriginal Australia*. Oceania Linguistic Monograph No. 24, University of Sydney.

McConvell, P. and R. Hagen. 1981. *A Traditional Land Claim by the Gurindji to Daguragu Station*. Central Land Council, Alice Springs, Northern Territory.

McConvell, P. and A. Palmer. 1979. *A Claim to an Area of Traditional Land by the Mudbura Traditional Owners*. Northern Land Council, Darwin, Northern Territory.

McGrath, A. 1987. *Born in the Cattle*. Allen & Unwin, Sydney.

Meggitt, M. 1962. *Desert People*. University of Chicago Press, Chicago.

– 1965. The Association between Australian Aborigines and Dingos. In *Man, Culture, and Animals: the role of animals in human ecological adjustments*. Publication No. 78 of the American Association for the Advancement of Science, Washington, DC.

Melville, I. 1981. *A Guide to Porperty Planning and Improved Pastures for the Control of Erosion in the Top End of the Northern Territory*. Land Conservation Unit, Conservation Commission of the Northern Territory, Darwin.

Merchant, C. 1980. *The Death of Nature: women, ecology, and the scientific revolution*. Wildwood House, London.

Merlan, F. 1982. A Mangarrayi representational system: environment and cultural symbolization in northern Australia. *American Ethnologist*, 9, 1: 145–166.

– 1988. Gender in Aboriginal Social Life. A Review. In *Social Anthropology and Australian Aboriginal Studies, a contemporary overview*, R. Berndt and R. Tonkinson eds. pp. 15–76. Australian Institute of Aboriginal Studies, Canberra.

Michaels, E. 1986. *The Aboriginal Invention of Television in Central Australia 1982–1986*. Australian Institute of Aboriginal Studies,Canberra.

– 1988. Hollywood Iconography, A Warlpiri Reading. In *Television and its Audience: interpretational research perspectives*, P. Drummond and R. Paterson, eds. pp. 109–124. British Film Institute, London.

Middleton, H. 1977. *But Now We Want the Land Back*. New Age Publishers, Sydney.

Molony, J. 1980. *I am Ned Kelly*. Penguin Books, Melbourne.

Montague, A. 1974 [1937]. *Coming into Being Among the Australian Aborigines*. Routledge and Kegan Paul, London.

Morphy, H. and F. Morphy 1984. The "myths" of Ngalakan history: ideology and images of the past in northern Australia. *Man*, 19, 3: 459–478.

Mulvaney, D.J. 1975. *The Prehistory of Australia*. Penguin Books, Melbourne.

– 1989. *Encounters in Place: Outsiders and Aboriginal Australians* 1606–1985. University of Queensland Press, Brisbane.

Myers, F. 1982a. Always Ask: resource use and land ownership among Pintupi Aborigines of the Australian Western Desert. In *Resource Managers: North American and Australian Hunter-Gatherers*, N. Williams and E. Hunn, eds. pp. 173–195. Australian Institute of Aboriginal Studies, Canberra.

– 1982b. Ideology and Experience: the cultural basis of politics in Pintupi life.

In *Aboriginal Power in Australian Society*, M. Howard, ed. pp. 79–114. University of Hawaii Press, Honolulu.

– 1986. *Pintupi Country, Pintupi Self: sentiment, place, and politics among Western Desert Aborigines*. Smithsonian Institute Press, Washington, DC.

O'Neill, J. 1976. *On Critical Theory*. Seabury Press, New York.

Pagels, E. 1988. *Adam, Eve, and the Serpent*. Random House, New York.

Perry, R. 1970. Vegetation of the Ord-Victoria Area. In *Lands of the Ord-Victoria Area, WA and NT*. Land Research Series No. 28, Commonwealth Scientific and Industrial Research Organization, Melbourne.

Petri, H. and G. Petri-Odermann, 1988. A Nativistic and Millenarian Movement in North West Australia. In *Aboriginal Australians and Christian Missions: ethnographic and historical studies*, T. Swain and D. Rose, eds. pp. 391–396. Australian Association for the Study of Religions, Bedford Park, SA.

Potts, E. and A. Potts 1985. *Yanks Down Under 1941–45: the American impact on Australia*. Oxford University Press, Oxford.

Rabinow, P. 1982. Masked I Go Forward: reflections on the modern subject. In *A Crack in the Mirror: reflexive perspectives in anthropology*, J. Ruby, ed. pp. 173–185. University of Pennsylvania Press, Philadelphia.

Read, P. and Engineer Jack Japaljarri. 1978. The Price of Tobacco: the journey of the Warlmala to Wave Hill, 1928. *Aboriginal History*, 2, 2: 140–149.

Reid, J. 1983. *Sorcerers and Healing Spirits*. Australian National University Press, Canberra.

Reynolds, H. 1974. Progress, Morality, and the Disposession of the Aborigines. *Meanjin Quarterly*, Spring: 306–312.

Ricoeur, P. 1985. The History of religions and the phenomenology of time consciousness. In *The History of Religions; retrospect and prospect*, J. Kitagawa, ed. pp. 13- 30. Macmillan, New York.

Ronan, T. 1962. *Deep of the Sky*. Cassell, Melbourne.

Rose. D. 1984. The Saga of Captain Cook; morality in Aboriginal and European Law. *Australian Aboriginal Studies*, 2: 24–39.

– 1985. Christian identity versus Aboriginal Identity in the Victoria River District. *Australian Aboriginal Studies*, 2: 58–61.

– 1988. Jesus and the Dingo. In *Aboriginal Australians and Christian Missions*. T. Swain and D. Rose, eds. pp. 361–375. Australian Association for the Study of Religions, Bedford Park, SA.

Rose, D. and D. Lewis. 1986. *Kidman Springs-Jasper Gorge Land Claim*. Northern Land Council, Darwin.

– 1989. *The Bilinara (Coolibah-Wave Hill Stock Route) Land Claim*. Northern Land Council, Darwin.

Rose, D. and T. Swain. 1988. Introduction. In *Aboriginal Australians and Christian Missions: ethnographic and historical studies*, T. Swain and D. Rose, eds. pp. 1–8. Australian Association for the Study of Religions, Bedford Park, SA.

Rose, F. 1965. *The Wind of Change in Central Australia*. Akademie Verlag, Berlin.

– 1968. Australian Marriage, Land-Owning Groups, and Initiations. In *Man the Hunter*, R. Lee and I. DeVore, eds. pp. 200–209. Aldine Atherton, Chicago.

– 1987. *The Traditional Mode of Production of the Australian Aborigines*. Angus & Robertson, Sydney.

Rowley, C. 1972 (1970). *The Remote Aborigines*. Penguin Books, Harmondsworth.

– 1974 (1970). *The Destruction of Aboriginal Society*. Penguin Books, Melbourne.

– 1981 (1978). *A Matter of Justice.* Australian National University Press, Canberra.

Rowse, T. 1987. 'Were You Ever Savages?' Aboriginal Insiders and Pastoralists' Patronage. *Oceania*, 58, 2: 81–99.

Sahlins, M. 1974 (1972). *Stone Age Economics.* Tavistock, London.

Said, E. 1979. The Text, the World, and the Critic. In *Textual Strategies: perspectives in post-structualist criticism*, J. Harari, ed. pp. 161–188. Methuen, London.

Sandefur, J. 1986. *Kriol of North Australia. A Language Coming of Age.* Work Papers of SIL-AAB, Series A, Volume 10. Summer Institute of Linguistics. Australian Aborigines Branch, Darwin.

SAPP (South Australian Parliamentary Papers), No. 64, 1910.

Schebeck, B. 1978. Names of Body-Parts in North-East Arnhem Land. In *Australian Aboriginal Concepts*, L. Hiatt ed. pp. 168–177. Australian Institute of Aboriginal Studies, Canberra.

Schneider, D. 1972 'What is Kinship All About?' In *Kinship Studies in the Morgan Centennial Year*, P. Reining, ed. pp. 32–63. The Anthropological Society of Washington, Washington, D.C.

– 1984. *A Critique of the Study of Kinship.* University of Michigan Press, Ann Arbor, Michigan.

Slayter, R. 1970. Climate of the Ord-Victoria Area. In *Lands of the Ord-Victoria Area, WA and NT.* Land Research Series No. 28, Commonwealth Scientific and Industrial Research Organization, Melbourne.

Spencer, B. 1914. *Native Tribes of the Northern Territory of Australia.* Macmillan, London.

Stanner, W. 1979a. *Report on field work in North Central and North Australia 1934–5.* AIAS Microfiche no. 1. Australian Insititute of Aboriginal Studies, Canberra.

– 1979b. *White Man Got No Dreaming.* Australian National University Press, Canberra .

Steffensen, M. 1977. A Description of Bamyili Creole, unpublished MS. Department of Education, Darwin, Northern Territory.

Stokes, L. 1846. *Discoveries in Australia.* T. and W. Boone, London.

Swain, T. 1985. *Interpreting Aboriginal Religion: an historical account.* Australian Association for the Study of Religions, Bedford Park, SA.

– 1988. The Ghost of Space. In *Aboriginal Australians and Christian Missions. Ethnographic and Historical Studies*, T. Swain and D. Rose, eds. pp. 452–469. Australian Association for the Study of Religions, Bedford Park, SA.

– 1990. A New Sky Hero from a Conquered Land. *History of Religions*, 29 (3), 195–232.

Tedlock, D. 1979. The Analogical Tradition and the Emergence of a Dialogical Anthropology. *Journal of Anthropological Research*, 35, 4: 387–400.

– 1982. Anthropological Hermeneutics and the Problem of Alphabetic Literacy. In *A Crack in the Mirror: reflexive perspectives in anthropology*, J. Ruby, ed. pp. 149–161. University of Pennsylvania Press, Philadelphia.

Thomson, N. 1986. Current Status and Priorities in Aboriginal Health. In *Looking Forward to Better Health.* Better Health Commission, Australian Government Publishing Service, Canberra.

Thomson, N. and L. Smith. 1985. An analysis of Aboriginal mortality in New South Wales country regions 1980–1981. In *The Medical Journal of Australia*, 143, 9: 49–54.

Tindale, N. 1974. *Aboriginal Tribes of Australia.* Australian National University Press, Canberra.
Tonkinson, R. 1977. Semen versus Spirit-Child in a Western Desert Culture. In *Australian Aboriginal Concepts*, L. Hiatt ed. pp. 81–92. Australian Institute of Aboriginal Studies, Canberra.
– 1978. *The Mardudjara Aborigines: living the dream in Australia's desert.* Holt, Rinehart and Winston, New York.
Transcript of Proceedings, Re the Kidman Springs-Jasper Gorge Land Claim. 1988 Commonwealth Reporting Service, Adelaide.
Trompf, G. nd. Introduction in *The Cargo and the Millennium. Trans-oceanic comparisons and connections in the study of new religious movements.* H. DeGruyter, Mouton (in press).
Turner, D. 1987. *Life Before Genesis: a conclusion.* Peter Lang, New York.
– 1988. The Incarnation of Nambirrirrma. In *Aboriginal Australians and Christian Missions. Ethnographic and Historical Studies*, T. Swain and D. Rose, eds. pp. 470–484. Australian Association for the Study of Religions, Bedford Park, SA.
Ward, R. 1966 (1958). *The Australian Legend.* Oxford University Press, Melbourne.
Warner, L. 1969 (1937). *A Black Civilization: a social study of an Australian tribe.* Peter Smith, Gloucester, Mass.
White, I. 1972. Hunting Dogs at Yalata. *Mankind*, 8: 201–5.
White, I., D. Barwick and B. Meehan, eds. 1985. *Fighters and Singers: the lives of some Aboriginal women.* George Allen and Unwin, Sydney.
White, JP and DJ Mulvaney, 1987. How Many People? In DJ Mulvaney and JP White, eds. *Australians to 1788.* Fairfax, Syme and Weldon, Sydney.
Wilden, A. 1980 (1972). *System and Structure: essays in communication and exchange* (2nd edn.). Tavistock, London.
Wilkes, G. 1978. *A Dictionary of Australian Colloquialisms.* Routledge and Kegan Paul, London.
Willey, K. 1971. *Boss Drover.* Rigby, Adelaide.
Williams, N. 1987. *Two Laws: managing disputes in a contemporary Aboriginal community.* Australian Institute of Aboriginal Studies, Canberra.
Willshire, W. 1896. *The Land of the Dawning, being facts gleaned from cannibals in the Australian stone age.* W.K. Thomas Co., Adelaide.

Index